INTEGRITY, HONESTY, AND TR

THE VIRTUES: MULTIDISCIPLINARY
PERSPECTIVES

Series Editor
Nancy E. Snow

*Professor of Philosophy and Director of the Institute for the Study of
Human Flourishing, University of Oklahoma*

Justice edited by Mark LeBar

Humility edited by Jennifer Cole Wright

Integrity, Honesty, and Truth Seeking
edited by Christian B. Miller and Ryan West

INTEGRITY, HONESTY, AND TRUTH SEEKING

Edited by Christian B. Miller

AND

Ryan West

OXFORD
UNIVERSITY PRESS

OXFORD
UNIVERSITY PRESS

Oxford University Press is a department of the University of Oxford. It furthers
the University's objective of excellence in research, scholarship, and education
by publishing worldwide. Oxford is a registered trade mark of Oxford University
Press in the UK and certain other countries.

Published in the United States of America by Oxford University Press
198 Madison Avenue, New York, NY 10016, United States of America.

© Oxford University Press 2020

Library of Congress Cataloging-in-Publication Data
Names: Miller, Christian B., editor. | West, Ryan, editor.
Title: Integrity, honesty, and truth seeking /
edited by Christian B. Miller and Ryan West.
Description: New York, NY, United States of America : Oxford University Press, 2020. |
Series: The virtues | Includes bibliographical references and index.
Identifiers: LCCN 2019041113 (print) | LCCN 2019041114 (ebook) |
ISBN 9780190666026 (hardback) | ISBN 9780190666033 (paperback) |
ISBN 9780190666057 (epub) | ISBN 9780190666064 (updf)
Subjects: LCSH: Virtues | Honesty | Integrity | Truthfulness and falsehood
Classification: LCC BJ1521 .H76 2019 (print) |
LCC BJ1521 (ebook) | DDC 179/.9—dc23
LC record available at https://lccn.loc.gov/2019041113
LC ebook record available at https://lccn.loc.gov/2019041114

1 3 5 7 9 8 6 4 2

Paperback printed by Marquis, Canada
Hardback printed by Bridgeport National Bindery, Inc., United States of America

Christian would like to dedicate this volume to the
Wake Forest University Philosophy Department,
which has been such a supportive and rewarding
place to teach these past fifteen years.

Ryan would like to dedicate this volume to
Karla, Ella, Greyson, and Maxwell, with love.

CONTENTS

CONTENTS

SERIES EDITOR'S FOREWORD

Typically, having a virtue means being disposed to having certain kinds of perceptions, thoughts, motives, emotions, and ways one is inclined to act. The end of the twentieth and the beginning of the twenty-first centuries have seen an upsurge of interest in the topic of virtue. This is true not only in philosophy but also in a variety of other disciplines, such as theology, law, economics, psychology, and anthropology, to name a few. The study of virtue within disciplines is vitally important, yet the premise of this series is that the study of virtue in general, as well as of specific virtues, can be enhanced if scholars take into account work being done in disciplines other than their own.

Cross-disciplinary work can be challenging. Scholars trained in one field with its unique vocabulary and methods do not always move seamlessly into another discipline and often feel unqualified to undertake the task of serious cross-disciplinary engagement. The upshot can be that practitioners of disciplines can become "siloed"—trapped within their own disciplines and hesitant to engage seriously with others, even on important topics of mutual interest.

This series seeks to break the silos, with fifteen volumes on specific virtues or clusters of virtues. For each book, an introduction by the editor highlights the unity of writings by identifying common themes, threads, and ideas. In each volume, the editor seeks to include a chapter from a "wild card" discipline, a field one would not expect to see included in a collection of essays on a particular virtue. We do this both to highlight the diversity of fields in the study of specific virtues and to surprise and challenge readers to broaden their horizons in thinking about virtue.

The audience for this series is practitioners of different disciplines who seek to expand their thinking about virtue. Each volume contains chapters that are accessible and of interest to scholars from many disciplines. Though the volumes are not comprehensive overviews of the work on virtue that is occurring in any given field, they provide a useful introduction meant to pique the curiosity of readers and spur further engagement with other disciplines.

Nancy E. Snow,
Professor of Philosophy and Director of the Institute for
the Study of Human Flourishing, University of Oklahoma

ACKNOWLEDGMENTS

This volume was made possible through the support of a grant from the Templeton Religion Trust for the Beacon Project at Wake Forest University, and also a grant from the John Templeton Foundation for the Honesty Project at Wake Forest University. The opinions expressed in this volume are those of the authors and do not necessarily reflect the views of the Beacon Project, Honesty Project, Wake Forest University, John Templeton Foundation, or Templeton Religion Trust. We would in particular like to thank Christ Stewart at the Templeton Religion Trust for all of his support.

We were invited to edit this volume as part of the Virtues series for Oxford University Press. Thanks especially to Nancy Snow, the editor of the series, for her constant support and advice throughout the publication process, as well as to Lucy Randall at Oxford University Press for guiding us along the way. Thanks also to an external reviewer for helpful comments on the entire manuscript.

We are also grateful to Nancy for hosting a conference in the fall of 2017 which allowed the contributors and editors to gather at the University of Oklahoma and workshop the chapters together. This was extremely helpful in refining the papers, but it also made for a large organizational undertaking. Thanks so much to Nancy and her team, especially Max Parish, for all their hard work.

Many thanks as well to our amazing contributors. We greatly appreciate both their hard work and their receptiveness to our detailed feedback. Thanks as well to Meridith Murray for doing a wonderful job preparing the index.

Christian would also like to thank the Wake Forest philosophy department, and especially his chair, Win-Chiat Lee, for so much support over the years. It is truly a wonderful place to work. And for tremendous support on the home front, thanks to Bill and Joyous Miller, and especially Jessie Lee Miller, during the many years it took to see this project to completion. Finally, I am very grateful to Ryan for coming onboard as a co-editor. His attention to detail, dedication, and editorial prowess are amazing, not to mention his knowledge of these topics. It was a delight to work with him on this project.

Ryan would also like to thank his family: for their consistent encouragement, I thank my father and stepmother, Harold and Annette West, and my father- and mother-in-law, Joe and Trudy Defries; for being my first, finest, and funniest editor, I thank my late mother, Kay West (I miss you, Mom); and for their seemingly boundless love and patience throughout the editing process (not to mention all other times), I especially thank my dearest ones, Karla, Ella, Greyson, and Maxwell. Thanks also to Grove City College for offering such a supportive environment in which to teach and do research. And finally, thanks to Christian for including me in this project. I learned much from him along the way, philosophically, professionally, and otherwise, and am very grateful to count him both a colleague and friend.

CONTRIBUTORS

Jason Baehr is Professor of Philosophy at Loyola Marymount University.

Philip E. Dow is Superintendent of Rosslyn Academy in Nairobi, Kenya.

Janie Harden Fritz is Professor of Communication and Rhetorical Studies at Duquesne University.

Stuart P. Green is Distinguished Professor of Law at Rutgers University.

Jennifer A. Herdt is Gilbert L. Stark Professor of Christian Ethics at Yale Divinity School.

Martin Jay is Ehrman Professor Emeritus of European History at the University of California Berkeley.

Margarita Leib is a Ph. D. candidate at the Center for Research in Experimental Economics and Political Decision Making at the University of Amsterdam.

Christian B. Miller is A. C. Reid Professor of Philosophy at Wake Forest University.

Steven L. Porter is Professor of Philosophy and Theology at Biola University.

Robert C. Roberts is Distinguished Professor of Ethics Emeritus at Baylor University.

Greg Scherkoske is Associate Professor of Philosophy at Dalhousie University.

Shaul Shalvi is Associate Professor in Experimental Economics and Psychology at the University of Amsterdam.

Ryan West is Assistant Professor of Philosophy at Grove City College.

W. Jay Wood is Professor of Philosophy at Wheaton College.

INTRODUCTION

CHRISTIAN B. MILLER AND RYAN WEST

It is well known that in philosophy there has been a dramatic resurgence of interest in virtue and virtue ethics in the past forty years. Virtues are typically understood in the literature as character traits that dispose one to think, feel, and act with excellence. Take compassion, for example. When in compassion-relevant circumstances, the deeply compassionate person reliably notices the suffering of others, feels compassion for them, reasons wisely about how to alleviate their suffering, and seeks to help, all from altruistic motives.

During this resurgence, some virtues have received extensive scholarly attention. For instance, since 2012 multi-million-dollar grants have been awarded for research projects on faith (Baylor University), intellectual humility (Fuller Seminary/Saint Louis University), hope and optimism (University of Notre Dame), and understanding (Fordham University).

Surprisingly, two of the virtues discussed in this volume have received almost no attention by comparison. Consider integrity. In philosophy there is a small literature on integrity stemming from

Christian B. Miller and Ryan West, *Introduction* In: *Integrity, Honesty, and Truth Seeking.* Edited by: Christian B. Miller and Ryan West. Oxford University Press (2020). © Oxford University Press. DOI: 10.1093/oso/9780190920487.002.0010

Bernard Williams's integrity objection to utilitarianism. But little has been said about the virtue of integrity in its own right.[1] Indeed, our first contributor, Greg Scherkoske, authored one of only three monographs that we know of on the topic.[2]

With respect to honesty, the situation is even bleaker. Some philosophers have worked on lying and deception.[3] But during the past forty years, almost no articles in leading peer-reviewed philosophy journals have focused on the virtue of honesty. Very little has been said in monographs or edited volumes either. This is a stunning omission.[4]

When it comes to truth seeking, things are a bit different. For one aspect of the recent virtue renaissance has been an increased interest in the virtues among epistemologists. Indeed, several recent epistemologists have focused attention on a number of intellectual virtues—character traits like open-mindedness, firmness, autonomy, and the intellectual variants of courage, humility, and generosity—that together make for excellence in seeking the truth.[5] Inasmuch as virtuous motivation for the truth (and related epistemic goods) is taken to be an aspect of many, or even all, intellectual virtues,[6] virtuous truth seeking has been a hot topic of late.

At the same time, though, philosophical analyses of virtues tend to focus more on the dispositions that differentiate one virtue from another, and less on the features they have in common. As a result, "truth seeking"—understood narrowly as the virtuous inquirer's motivational stance toward the truth and related epistemic

---

1. For exceptions, see Taylor 1981, McFall 1987, Calhoun 1995, and Ashford 2000.
2. See also Halfon 1989 and Cox et al. 2003.
3. See Fallis 2010 and Carson 2010.
4. For existing work that we are aware of, see Baier 1990, Smith 2003, Carson 2010: chapter 14, Miller 2017, and Wilson 2018.
5. See, e.g., Roberts and Wood 2007 and Baehr 2011.
6. See, e.g., Zagzebski 1996: chapter 4.

goods—has not been singled out for much sustained philosophical reflection.[7]

For these reasons, we saw a real need for a volume that significantly advances discussion of this cluster of truth-related virtues. Importantly, we did not want the contributors and audience to be limited to academic philosophers. Rather, we wanted to incorporate the insights and perspectives of experts working in a variety of disciplines. Hence, while several leading philosophers serve as contributors, they are joined by prominent scholars in law, communication and rhetorical studies, theology, psychology, history, and education. We are confident that the interdisciplinary nature of the volume will greatly enrich existing discussions in the literature and help to attract even more work on these virtues going forward.

We have organized the volume in three sections, with one section per virtue. For each virtue, there is:

A *conceptual chapter*, where the author explores what integrity, honesty, or truth seeking involves.

An *application chapter*, where the author explores how one of the virtues plays a central role in some important area of life. These areas are law (for integrity), communication (for honesty), and history (for truth seeking).

A *developmental chapter*, where the author explores some of the ways that people can foster or cultivate the virtue in question.

The one exception to this pattern is chapter six by Margarita Leib and Shaul Shalvi, which focuses on recent research in psychology on honest and dishonest behavior. Thanks to the work of Dan Ariely, Francesca Gino, Lisa Shu, Nina Mazar, and Shaul Shalvi, among others, the study of honest and dishonest behavior is one of the fastest

---

7. For exceptions, see Zagzebski 2007, Roberts and Wood 2007: chapter 6, and Griffiths 2009.

growing and most influential areas of research in moral psychology today.[8] We thought that it would be a major omission in the volume not to have at least one chapter engage with this work. At the same time, there has been very little done in psychology on either integrity or truth seeking, so there was no parallel rationale for chapters on psychological research in those areas.

The remainder of this introduction has two goals. In sections one through three, we provide some brief conceptual background on each of the three virtues. Then in section four, we turn to summarizing the volume's ten chapters.

1. CONCEPTUAL BACKGROUND ON INTEGRITY

Philosophers have had a difficult time arriving at consensus about what the virtue of integrity consists in. Some claim that it is a purely formal relation of consistency, others that it has to do primarily with one's identity, and still others that it involves subjective or objective moral requirements. Here we offer a brief guide to the leading proposals in the contemporary philosophical literature.[9]

1.1 Integrity as Coherence

On this view, integrity is a formal relation of coherence between various components of a person, so that the person with integrity is said to be harmonious, undivided, or intact, and to desire and

8. For some examples of this work, see Mazar et al. 2008, Shalvi et al. 2011, and Gino et al. 2013.
9. The material in this section is drawn from Miller 2013, and is reprinted with permission of Blackwell Publishing. See Scherkoske 2013 and Cox et al. 2008 for related taxonomies. Each of the three chapters on integrity in this volume discusses various accounts of integrity as well.

act wholeheartedly in various ways. Such agents are not "wantons," simply expressing their strongest desires, but rather agents whose actions exhibit that with which they identify or align themselves.[10] As a strictly formal matter, then, integrity as coherence does not involve any normative constraints on what the components themselves may consist in.[11]

An advocate of integrity as coherence can postulate a number of different coherence relations as being centrally relevant.[12] One is coherence among the agent's own principles, commitments, or values. If a person is deeply conflicted about whether or not to keep a promise in a given situation, that person is not exhibiting integrity at that moment. A second is coherence between the agent's values and behavior, especially in the face of temptation or societal pressure. A person with integrity would not value a political cause but then act contrary to it when facing mild opposition from others. And a third is the coherence relation between the agent's values and behavior such that the behavior is *based on* the values. A person might value a given charity, and in fact make a sizeable donation to it, but if she donated primarily because of peer pressure or feelings of guilt, then the act would not count as a genuine display of integrity with respect to that value.

John Bigelow and Robert Pargetter offer a simple model of integrity as coherence. We can distinguish between first-order desires (such as a desire to eat candy or to read a book) and second-order desires (such as a desire to stop desiring to eat candy). Strength of will, on their view, is a matter of one's lower-order desires conforming to the higher-order ones. So if I desire to stop desiring to eat candy, and that desire is effective in precluding my first-order desire for

10. See Frankfurt 1971 and Dworkin 1988.
11. For more, see Halfon 1989: chapters 3 and 4, and Calhoun 1995: 236–8.
12. McFall 1987: 7–8.

candy from leading to action, then I am exhibiting strength of will. Integrity, then, is the character trait of having the capacity to exercise strength of will in a wide range of relevant situations.[13]

1.2 Integrity as Practical Identity

Some people worry that the foregoing view trivializes integrity. Here's the concern: advocates of integrity as coherence make no distinction between coherence relations involving commitments that are central to an agent's identity and those involving peripheral commitments. So the view seems to imply that we exhibit integrity even in the most mundane of activities, from eating to brushing our teeth to turning out the lights.[14] To avoid this problem, the integrity as practical identity view focuses on what are variously called "identity-conferring commitments" or "ground projects." These are an agent's fundamental commitments that provide a sense of purpose and meaning to her life, and could include her family, her job, or her most deeply valued activities or principles.[15] Integrity, then, is a matter of having a character constituted by such ground projects, and being true to that character when the time comes. It is easy to see how integrity on this approach is anything but trivial, for it is something about which people care deeply, and are even willing to die to preserve.[16]

1.3 Integrity as Social Virtue

Where the previous two approaches go wrong, according to Cheshire Calhoun, is in understanding integrity as a personal virtue concerned primarily with maintaining a proper relation to oneself, rather than

---

13. Bigelow and Pargetter 2007: 44.
14. See McFall 1987: 12–13 and Calhoun 1995: 242.
15. See Williams 1973: 116; 1981: 12–13.
16. For more, see Taylor 1981, McFall 1987: 13, Halfon 1989: chapter 1, Calhoun 1995: 241–6, Korsgaard 1996: 102–103, and Schauber 1996.

as a social virtue that is concerned primarily with having a proper relation to others.[17] For Calhoun, we should begin by noting that we are trying to answer the question "What is worth doing?" as one among many deliberators. To exhibit integrity centrally involves the concept of *standing for* something in front of one's fellow deliberators, "because doing so matters to deliberators' common interest in determining what is worth doing."[18] A person of integrity cares about what other members of that community have to say, but also stands up for her own best judgment. In doing so, she acts not just for herself but also for all deliberators trying to answer the question of what is worth doing.[19] Thus, the person who fails to stand for certain principles is not in the first instance violating his or her own internal norms or commitments, but rather those of the community of people pursuing the good life.[20]

1.4 Integrity as Reasonability

The first three approaches to integrity are purely formal in that they deny any substantive normative constraints on the agent's relevant commitments. This leads to worries about moral monsters of various kinds serving as counterexamples to the sufficiency of their accounts. So a natural next step would be to add such normative constraints to a larger account of integrity. One way to do so is to employ normative criteria about what is reasonable for an agent to value. Here is Lynne McFall:

> When we grant integrity to a person, we need not *approve* of his or her principles or commitments, but we must at least recognize them as ones a reasonable person might take to be of great

17. Calhoun 1995: 252.
18. 1995: 259.
19. 1995: 257.
20. 1995: 254.

importance and ones that a reasonable person might be tempted to sacrifice to some lesser yet still recognizable goods.[21]

So on this approach, a person of integrity does not need to have objectively correct values, but only reasonable ones.[22]

The integrity as reasonability view can be developed in at least two different ways. One is to maintain that there are objective standards as to what counts as reasonable for a person to value. Thus, a deeply committed Nazi or a serial murderer could not have integrity, but someone could who had objectively reasonable views opposing ours on, say, the moral permissibility of the death penalty or stem cell use. Such an approach allows for a diversity of normative outlooks to count as reasonable, while also appropriately excluding extreme cases. As it turns out, this approach seems to be the leading way of developing the integrity as reasonability view in the literature. But one could instead index what is reasonable to an agent's subjective opinions. On this way of thinking, there would not be integrity as such, but rather integrity relative to what a given observer or group of observers deems to be reasonable. Thus, this subjective reasonability approach would allow for the deeply committed Nazi to have integrity, at least from certain Nazi perspectives, although not from our own perspective. Perhaps unsurprisingly, such an alternative approach has found few supporters.

1.5 Integrity as Objective Accuracy

The integrity as reasonability view provides some normative constraints on the content of the commitments of agents with integrity.

---

21. McFall 1987: 11, emphasis original.
22. For more, see Taylor 1981: 148, McFall 1987: 11, Halfon 1989: chapter 2, and Graham 2001; for a recent, extensively developed version of integrity as reasonability, see Scherkoske 2013 and chapter 1 of this volume.

But it still allows for a diverse range of such commitments, many of which could be false. The integrity as objective accuracy approach goes one step further, requiring that the commitments be objectively correct, both in their moral claims and in their empirical presuppositions. As Elizabeth Ashford writes:

> [The agent's] self-conception must be grounded in reality: it must not be based on her being seriously deceived either about empirical facts or about the moral obligations she actually has. In particular, her self-conception as being morally decent must be grounded in her leading a genuinely morally decent life.[23]

To conclude, our aim here is not to try to adjudicate between these different approaches, but simply to outline the leading options in the literature as helpful background to the three chapters on integrity in this volume.

2. CONCEPTUAL BACKGROUND ON HONESTY

Unlike the case of integrity, there is little background to provide from the contemporary philosophical literature on different accounts of honesty. This is because no such literature exists, outside the chapters in this volume and a small handful of other essays.[24] Hence in this section our focus is on clarifying the scope of honesty. In doing so, we can see better the task that is set before anyone who aims to give an account of this virtue.

23. Ashford 2000: 424.
24. See footnote 4 for references.

At least five kinds of behavior intuitively seem to be incompatible with the virtue of honesty:

Lying
Stealing
Cheating
Promise Breaking
Misleading

Someone who repeatedly steals for insufficiently good moral reasons is not someone we would tend to describe as honest. The same goes for someone who consistently withholds key information in order to mislead her audience into false beliefs.

On the flip side, an honest person is disposed to act with excellence in each of these five areas of the moral life. Note that the "excellence" here goes beyond mere external behavior to include virtuous motivation and other internal factors. In other words, the honest person's character is disposed in at least the following ways:

Truthfulness: The reliable disposition to tell the truth when appropriate for good moral reasons.
Being Respectful of Property: The reliable disposition to respect the property of others for good moral reasons.
Proper Compliance: The reliable disposition to follow fair and appropriate rules in situations of voluntary participation for good moral reasons.
Fidelity to Promises: The reliable disposition to keep reasonable promises when appropriate for good moral reasons.
Forthrightness: The reliable disposition to avoid misleading by giving a sufficient presentation of the relevant facts when appropriate for good moral reasons.

Serious failure in any one of these areas, say by being a habitual liar or cheater, is sufficient for failing to be an honest person. In other words, success in all five is necessary for honesty.

This list is not intended to be exhaustive, but it does purport to capture much of the scope of the virtue of honesty. It also gives rise to a challenge, which Christian Miller has elsewhere stated as follows:[25]

> *The Unification Challenge*: What is it, exactly, that these various dispositions have in common such that they all pertain to the virtue of honesty?

Telling the truth to someone seems rather different from not stealing other people's property, which in turn seems rather different from not cheating at a sports game or on one's taxes. Yet they all are said to be related in some way to honesty. In virtue of what? What property or set of properties do they all have in common such that they all pertain to honesty?

There are different ways to proceed in considering this question. The most straightforward is to offer an account of honesty that identifies that virtue's unifying property or properties. Miller offers one such account elsewhere.[26]

Alternatively, one could suggest that the various aspects of honesty are bound together by a kind of family resemblance that resists articulation in a set of necessary and sufficient conditions. In this volume, Robert C. Roberts and Ryan West present a version of this approach, arguing that honesty's facets are unified "not by a single shared property, but by their high degree of relevance to one another."[27]

---

25. See Miller 2017, in progress. The next several paragraphs draw from Miller in progress, chapter 1.
26. See Miller 2017, in progress.
27. Roberts and West, chapter 4 in this volume.

A third option would be to argue that there is nothing that unifies *all* these dispositions under the heading of honesty, but only *some* of them. Perhaps one or two of them, upon deeper reflection, are not members of the honesty family after all, and deserve to be treated as separate virtues in their own right. Note that this strategy would require an error theory to explain the mistaken thought that all of these dispositions are linked to honesty, even though, strictly speaking, some are not.

Finally, one could say that there is nothing that unifies *any* of these dispositions with each other. In other words, they really don't share enough in common to pertain to honesty. Rachana Kamtekar has raised this possibility:

> Although we use a single word, 'honest,' to describe the behaviors of not lying, not cheating, and not stealing, it does not seem obvious that not lying, not cheating, and not stealing are the same sort of thing, or even that they are deeply connected. It may be that underlying this single word are three distinct and unrelated dispositions . . . .[28]

On this view, talk of "honesty" at best functions as a convenient shorthand for referring to one of the more specific virtues. Here, too, an error theory is needed to explain why honesty has so often been thought to be a distinct virtue in its own right, and why the various other virtues so often have been linked to it.

We will not pursue the unification challenge further here. But this discussion of the broad scope and rich complexity of the virtue of honesty should be helpful background for chapters 4 through 7 in this volume.

---

28. Kamtekar 2004: 468–469. For similar claims, see Adams 2006: 128–129.

3. CONCEPTUAL BACKGROUND ON TRUTH SEEKING

[handwritten marginalia: the uncertainty of what Distinguishes justified belief from opinion]

While the conceptual terrain of both integrity and honesty has been underexplored of late, recent epistemologists have exerted a great deal of energy mapping the intellectual character of the excellent truth seeker. Among these "virtue epistemologists," as they are often called, the consensus is that virtuous motivation for the truth and related epistemic goods is essential to virtuous truth seeking.[29] But how should we understand such a motivational disposition? Is it a virtue in its own right? Or is it an aspect of several intellectual virtues—or perhaps of *every* intellectual virtue?

Linda Zagzebski defends the latter view, arguing that all of the intellectual virtues share "the same foundational motivation," namely, "the motivation to have cognitive contact with reality."[30] It's true that the intellectual virtues differ from one another in their particular aims: open-mindedness aims at receptivity to new ideas and arguments, intellectual thoroughness aims at exhaustive investigation, courage aims at fearlessly defending one's beliefs and answering objections, and so on.[31] But according to Zagzebski, these virtue-specific aims each arise from the same virtue-generic motivation, whose object includes not only truth, but also understanding (including non-propositional understanding), certainty, knowledge, and other epistemic goods.[32]

---

29. It is common to differentiate two camps of virtue epistemologists: "virtue reliabilists" conceive of intellectual virtues, roughly, as reliable cognitive faculties, such as vision and memory (see, e.g., Sosa 2007, Greco 2010), while "virtue responsibilists" think of intellectual virtues as excellences of character. We focus on the latter.
30. Zagzebski 1996: 166, 167.
31. Ibid., 269. A reviewer noted that Zagzebski's conception of open-mindedness may be too narrow, for it seems to ignore the virtue's characteristic receptivity to *familiar* ideas and arguments stemming from those who disagree with us. We agree that this is a good point to raise about Zagzebski's view, but our goal here is simply to present Zagzebski's view as it was originally stated.
32. Ibid., 167. For more discussion, see pp. 166–176.

Jason Baehr offers a similarly "two-tiered" analysis of the psychological structure of the intellectual virtues:

> At a basic or fundamental level, all intellectual virtues involve ... a positive orientation toward epistemic goods. . . . However, each intellectual virtue also has its own characteristic psychology. That is, each virtue involves certain attitudes, feelings, motives, beliefs, actions, and other psychological qualities that make it the virtue it is and on the basis of which it can be distinguished from other intellectual virtues. . . . The characteristic psychology of each individual virtue is 'rooted in' or 'flows from' the more fundamental positive orientation toward epistemic goods.[33]

By contrast, other virtue epistemologists, such as James Montmarquet, claim that the desire for truth (Montmarquet's "epistemic conscientiousness") is an aspect of and/or gives rise to some, but not all, intellectual virtues.[34] Despite this difference, though, each agrees that virtuous intellectual motivation is essential to being an excellent truth seeker.

Among the thinkers just described, analyses of individual intellectual virtues like fair-mindedness and intellectual humility have tended to highlight the distinguishing marks of each virtue, without providing in-depth treatments of the motivational disposition toward the truth and related epistemic goods that they take to be shared across several virtues.[35] A handful of other thinkers, however,

---

33. Baehr 2011: 103.

34. Montmarquet 1993: 27–8; for discussion, see Zagzebski 1996: 174–176.

35. One exception—or perhaps better, *near* exception—is Zagzebski 2007, in which the author offers an analysis of the relationship between intellectual motivation and the good of truth. While Zagzebski very helpfully distinguishes the motivational value of the love of true belief from several other kinds of epistemic value, and persuasively argues that the love of true belief "has a kind of value that is capable of conferring additional value on the acts it motivates" (Zagzebski 2007: 147), she does not offer anything like a map of the virtuous form of that love.

take this motivational disposition to be a distinct virtue of its own, and have said much more about its psychological contours. Here we chart two such analyses: one from philosophy, and the other from theology.

3.1 Roberts and Wood on "Love of Knowledge"

Robert C. Roberts and W. Jay Wood do not dispute the idea that virtuous epistemic motivation is "a component of intellectual character as a whole" and may be "*associated* with other virtues and skills."[36] But they treat it as more than a mere aspect of other virtues, offering a chapter-length analysis of a virtue they call "the love of knowledge," where the term "knowledge" is meant to include a wide array of epistemic goods, including true belief, warrant, propositional knowledge, understanding, acquaintance, and more.[37] Even if "all humans by nature desire to know," to have the *virtue* of the love of knowledge, one's epistemic desires must be *discriminating*. After all, some propositions are simply more important than others. (On this point, Roberts and Wood invite us to compare "(1) a charge of capital crime against [one's] mother and (2) the proposition that the third letter in the 41,365th listing in the 1977 Wichita telephone directory is a 'd.'")[38] So it would be foolish to have an equal and undifferentiated interest in the truth-values of each and every proposition. Roberts and Wood suggest that the discrimination we need relates to three issues: "significance, relevance, and worthiness."[39] Let's consider each briefly.

Some propositions are more *significant* than others in terms of their respective "epistemic loads."[40] That is, beliefs may receive more

36. Roberts and Wood 2007: 73; italics original.
37. Ibid., 153–182.
38. Ibid., 156.
39. Ibid., 155.
40. Ibid., 156–157.

or less support from other propositions, and may provide more or less support to other propositions, and both of these properties contribute to a belief's load-bearing significance. But load bearing on its own does not matter much if the load in question does not matter much. Thus, a virtuous lover of knowledge also attends to *worthiness*. "Propositional knowledge, understanding, and insight are important, not taken in abstraction, but in connection with their bearing on human flourishing and the intrinsic importance of their objects."[41] So the discriminating inquirer will care about and seek truths that are more worthy of her attention, either because of their eudaimonic or intrinsic value. She'll also discriminate on the basis of the *relevance* of the propositions to her own station, calling, and circumstances. After all, "no human being can know all important knowledge," and some epistemic goods, even worthy and significant ones, simply do not bear on the concerns of some individuals or groups. These three kinds of considerations, balanced against each other by practical wisdom rather than by some formulaic method, provide the bearings for a virtuous truth seeker (and truth purveyor).[42]

Since humans learn by contrast, Roberts and Wood fill out their account of the excellent epistemic will with an analysis of its faulty counterparts. Faultiness comes in two broad forms, immaturity and vice:

> Roughly, immaturity relative to the love of knowledge will be a shortfall of proper love for the epistemic goods or of proper aversion to epistemic harm, while vice will be a perverse love for

41. Ibid., 157–158.

42. Though our focus is on truth seeking, Roberts and Wood point out that "the love of knowledge would not be in the fullest sense an intellectual virtue in a person who loved it only for himself" (Roberts and Wood 2007: 164). Here we see a connection between truth seeking and the truthfulness side of honesty. For more on this connection, see Ibid., 164–8, as well as Roberts and West, chapter 4 in this volume.

or aversion to the epistemic goods and/or perverse attraction to other things that affect epistemic performance.[43]

This division admits a fourfold subdivision: "(1) failures of concern to know, (2) unvirtuous concerns to know, (3) failures of concern not to know, and (4) unvirtuous concerns not to know."[44] Of course, these immature or vicious concerns and failures of concern are deeply interrelated, and are often found together. Wood discusses several of them in his essay in this volume.

3.2 Griffiths on "Intellectual Appetite"

We are aware of only one monograph that treats excellence in epistemic motivation as a virtue in its own right. Interestingly, it comes not from philosophy, but from theology. In *Intellectual Appetite: A Theological Grammar*, Paul Griffiths offers a distinctively Christian analysis of the desire for truth and related epistemic goods.[45] His starting point is a distinction invoked by both Augustine and Aquinas—as well as Jay Wood in this volume—between *curiositas* and *studiositas*, or "curiosity" and "studiousness," as they are "inevitably but misleadingly" rendered in English.[46] In contrast with contemporary usage, where "curious" is a label for delightfully inquisitive children (and monkeys!) and the "studious" among us are simply bookish, Griffiths treats the two as terms of art, denoting distinctive intellectual character traits resulting from rigorous, if not always intentional, training.[47]

---

43. Roberts and Wood 2007: 169.
44. Ibid., 169. The four varieties of faulty epistemic will are discussed, respectively, on pages 169–172, 172–177, 177–179, and 179–180.
45. Griffiths 2009. Roberts and Wood (2007: 155) note that their account "is not an exposition of the Christian tradition, but it is inspired by it."
46. Griffiths 2009: 9.
47. In Griffiths words, they are "highly catechized forms of intellectual appetite" (Ibid., 22).

In his technical vocabulary, curiosity is a vice, and studiousness a virtue. What makes the difference?

To begin, the curious and the studious differ from one another in three respects: (1) their purposes in seeking knowledge, (2) the kinds of knowledge they seek, and (3) their methods for seeking knowledge. Griffiths is worth quoting at length:

> Curiosity is a particular appetite, which is to say a particular ordering of the affections, or, more succinctly, a particular intentional love. Its object, what it wants, is new knowledge, a previously unexperienced reflexive intimacy with some creature. And what it seeks to do with that knowledge is control, dominate, or make a private possession of it. Curiosity is, then, in brief, *appetite for the ownership of new knowledge,* and its principal method is enclosure by sequestration of particular creatures or ensembles of such. . . . Studiousness, like curiosity, is a particular love, a specific ordering of the affections. And like curiosity it has knowledge as its object, which it seeks. But the studious do not seek to sequester, own, possess, or dominate what they hope to know; they want, instead, to participate lovingly in it, to respond to it knowingly as gift rather than as potential possession, to treat it as icon rather than as spectacle. A preliminary definition of studiousness, then, is: *appetite for closer reflexive intimacy with the gift.*[48]

But deeper than any of these differences, says Griffiths, is another:

> The deepest contrast between curiosity and studiousness has to do with the kind of world that the seeker for and professor of each inhabits. The curious inhabit a world of objects, which can be sequestered and possessed; the studious inhabit a world

48. Ibid., 20–21; italics original.

of gifts, given things, which can be known by participation, but which, because of their very natures can never be possessed.[49]

Thus, both curiosity and studiousness are not simply patterns of desire; they are also sensibilities, complex and ordered ways of construing epistemic goods against a background understanding of the rest of reality and the place of knowledge within human life.

Griffiths goes on to provide analyses of each of the key ideas mentioned above (world, appetite, participation, gift, knowledge as intimacy, etc.), and compares and contrasts curiosity and studiousness on several fronts (attitudes of ownership vs. stewardship, attitudes toward novelty, attitudes toward communicating knowledge, etc.). Though his analysis is worthy of close attention, the foregoing will suffice for our purpose of providing conceptual background for this volume's treatment of virtuous truth seeking in chapters 8 through 10.

4. CHAPTER OVERVIEWS

In the first section's conceptual chapter, Greg Scherkoske notes that most accounts of integrity in the philosophical literature see the virtue as having little to do with truth. At most, typically, one sort of integrity—intellectual integrity—is supposed to exhibit a close connection with truth seeking; a concern for truth is (nearly) absent from other sorts of integrity (e.g., personal integrity, professional integrity, artistic integrity, etc.). This is puzzling, according to Scherkoske, not least because of longstanding connections between integrity, honesty, and sincerity. Against these accounts, he argues that integrity is best understood as a complex character trait that concerns a person's relation to her own judgment.

49. Ibid., 22.

Understood this way, the proper concern for one's judgment that is characteristic of the person of integrity essentially involves responsiveness to facts and evidence and a concern for truth. Scherkoske ends his chapter by considering advantages of this account.

Shifting to application, Stuart Green observes that talk of "integrity" is ubiquitous in law and legal discourse. Protecting the integrity of our political system is cited as a basis for anti-corruption laws; preserving the integrity of the legal profession appears as a principle underlying the rules of lawyer ethics; ensuring integrity in policing and in the wider criminal justice system is given as a justification for excluding evidence obtained in violation of the Constitution; and protecting bodily integrity is offered as a potential goal for the law of rape and sexual assault. His chapter examines what integrity means in each of these contexts, what these uses have in common, and whether thinking about these various rules and doctrines in terms of integrity rather than other moral concepts leads to any practical difference in outcome. It also asks what the examination of integrity in the law can tell us about the concept of integrity in other contexts.

But how might we develop integrity? According to Jennifer Herdt, becoming a person of integrity—that is, someone who stands virtuously for her commitments—is in many ways like other developmental processes. We receive some direct moral instruction, but the process gets underway in earnest when we glimpse, however dimly, the special goodness of this particular virtue, and desire to instantiate it. Exemplars are studied and emulated. One's own successes and failures in emulation are scrutinized. The role of trusting relationships and supportive communities is essential, even as insulation from critique short-circuits the development of integrity. The account Herdt develops clarifies how it can be the case that admiration and emulation play such a key role in the acquisition of a virtue like integrity, despite the fact that integrity has to do with a willingness to stand for one's own commitments and therefore for one's own best judgments.

Turning to the virtue of honesty in section two, Robert C. Roberts and Ryan West claim that honesty is two-handed: it encompasses both truthfulness and parts of justice, not as a haphazard assemblage, but more like two hands mutually coordinated—different, but essential to each other's function. Honesty as truthfulness is more than a disposition to tell the truth; it is also a disposition to face and seek the truth, and essentially involves a circumspect concern for and sensitivity to the values of truth in the context of human life. Honesty as justice, too, is a propensity to both actions and emotions, consisting in an intelligent concern that justice be done (i.e., that people get what's coming to them) in the areas of justice having to do with keeping agreements, complying with rules, and respecting others' property. Given the many available motives for dishonesty, they argue that honesty is reliable only when it partners with other virtues like compassion, humility, self-control, and conscientiousness.

Writing from the field of communication and rhetorical studies, Janie Harden Fritz notes that honesty is a central concept in interpersonal communication ethics, typically studied through the lens of self-disclosure in close relationships. Across relational contexts, at least two aspects of human communication are relevant to honesty: (1) the content dimension, which concerns what factual information is carried by a message, and (2) the relationship dimension, which concerns the implied stance or attitude toward the other and/ or the relationship. This dimension provides interpretive nuance for the content dimension, and its implications for honesty are shaped by culture and context. In her chapter, Fritz consider five themes relevant to communication research—self-disclosure and restraint, Grice's theory of conversational implicature, message design logic, communication competence, and civility, authority, and love—and explores the implications of each for honesty in human relationships.

In their guide to the latest honesty research in psychology, Margarita Leib and Shaul Shalvi survey a variety of justification processes that tend to free people to seek profit in dishonest ways when tempted. They distinguish two main categories: (1) self-serving justifications, in which one justifies one's actions by processing information in a self-benefiting way, and (2) socially motivated justifications, in which one justifies unethical acts by reference to an additional, socially beneficial factor. They end with a discussion of the ethical hazard of corrupt collaboration (i.e., joint unethical acts). Corrupt collaboration is a major challenge to institutions and societies as it places individuals in a dilemma: collaborate with peers or follow ethical rules of conduct. Recent work suggests that in such situations, people prefer collaboration over honesty. Leib and Shalvi discuss the dynamics of corrupt collaboration, the ways in which these toxic relationships emerge and spread, and how we can curb such behavior and encourage honest, ethical conduct.

In the final, developmental chapter on honesty, Steven L. Porter and Jason Baehr note that while there is more to being honest than not lying, becoming the sort of person who does not lie unjustifiably is essential to becoming an honest person. They provide an account of the underlying psychology of a certain kind of lie: namely, morally unjustified lies we tell due to a perceived benefit to ourselves. Their proposal is that such lies naturally spring from a personal orientation to the world that centers on self-protection, self-preservation, and self-enhancement. This analysis suggests that a way to refrain from lying is to engage in a relationally connected way of life that brings about an alternative orientation to the world in which one's protection, preservation, and reputation are secure apart from lying. An aspect of this new orientation, they claim, will be the emerging willingness to relinquish control over the perceived disadvantages of honesty. So, on this view, lying (and other forms of dishonesty) is largely unnecessary when the perceived disadvantages are no longer viewed as a threat to one's secure standing in the world.

The third and final section of the volume is dedicated to truth seeking. In his conceptual chapter, Jay Wood begins by noting that from antiquity temperance has been viewed as the virtue that moderates our appetites for food, drink, and sex. Yet the notion of *intellectual* temperance—a virtue governing our appetites for truth, knowledge, and related epistemic goods—may sound somewhat counterintuitive to contemporary ears. Wood offers his own analysis of this overlooked virtue, drawing inspiration chiefly from Augustine's and Aquinas's work on *studiositas* and *curiositas*, which reveals how our pursuit of knowledge can be virtuous or vicious insofar as it conforms to or deviates from right reason and wise concerns. According to Wood, their distinctively Christian accounts of temperance differ from Aristotle's in denying that one can ever be perfected in temperance. Temptation, and our susceptibility thereto, remains an inescapable feature of this life. Wood surveys a number of ways Augustine and Aquinas thought the intellectual life goes awry for lack of intellectual temperance, with an eye toward the relevance their warnings may have for our contemporary context. The defective forms of intellectual appetite he discusses include the inordinate desire for knowledge that is forbidden or utterly mundane, knowledge that is harmful to oneself or others, knowledge that is vain or fruitless, knowledge sought and applied wrongly, as well as knowledge that can frustrate various intellectual goals.

Martin Jay's application chapter explores the relevance of truth seeking to the discipline of history. Most working historians have focused on epistemological questions concerning the relationship between history as what actually happened and history as its present representation. Jay argues that two extreme positions on these issues—naïve positivism and radical constructivism—have proven equally untenable. He then examines three alternatives: falsificationism, the new experientialism, and institutional justificationism. Jay defends the last of these, which posits a self-reflective community of competence, morally obliged to be truthful and engaged in a search for plausible narratives and compelling explanations of past occurrences, as the most persuasive answer to skepticism about historical truth.

In the final chapter, Philip Dow argues that because truth is both innately valuable and directly connected to human flourishing, the development of truth seekers within the context of formal K–12 education should be a principal aim of a healthy society. He further argues that while the fruits of truth are profoundly rewarding, virtuous truth seeking is neither easy, nor natural, nor widespread. To develop the sort of truth seeking needed to support both individual growth and human progress, we need a truth-centered vision for education—a vision that aims to develop in students the deeply rooted and virtuous traits of intellectual character that flow from a love for truth and produce the kind of intellectual and moral goods that result in human flourishing. Dow highlights several practical ideas related to the development of intellectual virtue that have come out of schools like Rosslyn Academy and the Intellectual Virtue Academy—institutions founded on the express goal of developing intellectual character in their students. He closes by reflecting on several ways a truth-centered classroom might revitalize education.

BIBLIOGRAPHY

Adams, Robert. *A Theory of Virtue: Excellence in Being for the Good.* Oxford: Clarendon Press, 2006.

Ashford, Elizabeth. "Utilitarianism, Integrity and Partiality." *Journal of Philosophy* 97 (2000): 421–439.

Baehr, Jason. *The Inquiring Mind: On Intellectual Virtues and Virtue Epistemology.* Oxford: Oxford University Press, 2011.

Baier, Annette. "Why Honesty is a Hard Virtue." In *Identity, Character, and Morality: Essays in Moral Psychology*, edited by O. Flanagan and A. Rorty, 259–282. Cambridge, MA: MIT Press, 1990.

Bigelow, John, and Robert Pargetter. "Integrity and Autonomy." *American Philosophical Quarterly* 44 (2007): 39–49.

Calhoun, Cheshire. "Standing for Something." *Journal of Philosophy* 92 (1995): 235–260.

Carson, Thomas. *Lying and Deception: Theory and Practice*. Oxford: Oxford University Press, 2010.

Cox, Damian, Marguerite La Caze, and Michael Levine. "Integrity." In *Stanford Encyclopedia of Philosophy*. Edited by Edward N. Zalta. Stanford, CA: Stanford University Press, 2008. http://plato.stanford.edu/entries/integrity/.

Dworkin, Gerald. *The Theory and Practice of Autonomy*. Cambridge, UK: Cambridge University Press, 1988.

Fallis, Don. "Lying and Deception." *Philosophers' Imprint* 10 (2010): 1–22.

Frankfurt, Harry. "Freedom of the Will and the Concept of a Person." *Journal of Philosophy* 68 (1971): 5–20.

Gino, F., E. Krupka, and R. Weber. "License to Cheat: Voluntary Regulation and Ethical Behavior." *Management Science* 59 (2013): 2187–2203.

Graham, Jody L. "Does Integrity Require Moral Goodness?" *Ratio* 14 (2001): 234–251.

Greco, John. *Achieving Knowledge: A Virtue-Theoretic Account of Epistemic Normativity*. Cambridge, UK: Cambridge University Press, 2010.

Griffiths, Paul J. *Intellectual Appetite: A Theological Grammar*. Washington, DC: Catholic University of America Press, 2009.

Halfon, Mark. *Integrity: A Philosophical Inquiry*. Philadelphia: Temple University Press, 1989.

Kamtekar, Rachana. "Situationism and Virtue Ethics on the Content of Our Character." *Ethics* 114 (2004): 458–491.

Korsgaard, Christine. *The Sources of Normativity*. Cambridge, UK: Cambridge University Press, 1996.

Mazar, N., O. Amir, and D. Ariely. "The Dishonesty of Honest People: A Theory of Self-Concept Maintenance." *Journal of Marketing Research* 45 (2008): 633–644.

McFall, Lynne. "Integrity." *Ethics* 98 (1987): 5–20.

Miller, Christian B. "Integrity." In *The Blackwell International Encyclopedia of Ethics*, edited by Hugh LaFollette, 2640–2650. Oxford: Blackwell Publishing, 2013.

Miller, Christian B. "Honesty." In *Moral Psychology, Volume V: Virtue and Character*, edited by Walter Sinnott-Armstrong and Christian B. Miller, 237–273. Cambridge: MIT Press, 2017.

Miller, Christian B. *Honesty: The Philosophy and Psychology of a Neglected Virtue*. Book manuscript.

Montmarquet, James. *Epistemic Virtue and Doxastic Responsibility*. Lanham, MD: Rowman and Littlefield, 1993.

Roberts, Robert C., and W. Jay Wood. *Intellectual Virtues: An Essay in Regulative Epistemology*. Oxford: Oxford University Press, 2007.

Schauber, Nancy. "Integrity, Commitment and the Concept of a Person." *American Philosophical Quarterly* 33 (1996): 119–129.

Scherkoske, Greg. *Integrity and the Virtues of Reason: Leading a Convincing Life*. Cambridge, UK: Cambridge University Press, 2013.

Shalvi, S., J. Dana, M. Handgraaf, and C. De Dreu. "Justified Ethicality: Observing Desired Counterfactuals Modifies Ethical Perceptions and Behavior." *Organizational Behavior and Human Decision Processes* 115 (2011): 181–190.

Smith, Tara. "The Metaphysical Case for Honesty." *The Journal of Value Inquiry* 37 (2003): 517–531.

Sosa, Ernest. *A Virtue Epistemology: Apt Belief and Reflective Knowledge, Volume 1*. Oxford: Oxford University Press, 2007.

Taylor, Gabriele. "Integrity." *Proceedings of the Aristotelian Society* 55 (1981): 143–159.

Williams, Bernard. "A Critique of Utilitarianism." In *Utilitarianism: For and Against*, edited by J. J. C. Smart and Bernard Williams, 77–150. New York: Cambridge University Press, 1973.

Williams, Bernard. "Persons, Character and Morality." In *Moral Luck: Philosophical Papers 1973–1980*, 1–19. Cambridge, UK: Cambridge University Press, 1981.

Wilson, Alan. "Honesty as a Virtue." *Metaphilosophy* 49 (2018): 262–280.

Zagzebski, Linda. *Virtues of the Mind: An Inquiry into the Nature of Virtue and the Ethical Foundations of Knowledge*. Cambridge, UK: Cambridge University Press, 1996.

Zagzebski, Linda. "Intellectual Motivation and the Good of Truth." In *Intellectual Virtue: Perspectives from Ethics and Epistemology*, edited by Michael DePaul and Linda Zagzebski, 135–154. Oxford: Clarendon Press, 2007.

INTEGRITY, HONESTY, AND TRUTH SEEKING

PART I

INTEGRITY

Chapter 1

To Thine Own Self Be True?
Integrity and Concern for Truth

GREG SCHERKOSKE

Perhaps the least controversial thing to say about integrity is that it is something both admired and sought, its absence lamentably common and its loss costly. Integrity matters to us, and it seems to matter in a way that is neither merely instrumental nor conditional upon valuing other things. Even if having integrity is good for business, and lacking integrity would cost us the good opinion of others, this seems incidental to the value of integrity itself. Perhaps the second least controversial thing to say about integrity is that it is a moral virtue: it is an excellence of character, specifically as it relates to good conduct.[1] Persons of integrity, it seems, are not morally corrupt, are committed to and act from sound moral principles, and so on.[2]

---

1. The *Oxford English Dictionary*: 'Integrity . . . 3. In moral sense. A. Unimpaired moral state, freedom from moral corruption; innocence, sinlessness. *Obs.*

2. For a fulsome gloss on "and so on," Cox, La Caze, and Levine 2003: 41: "It [integrity] stands as a mean to various excesses: on the one side, conformity, arrogance, dogmatism, fanaticism, monomania, preciousness, sanctimoniousness, rigidity; on the other side, capriciousness, wantonness, triviality, disintegration, weakness of will, self-deception, self-ignorance, mendacity, hypocrisy, indifference."

Greg Scherkoske, *To Thine Own Self Be True? Integrity and Concern for Truth* In: *Integrity, Honesty, and Truth Seeking*. Edited by: Christian B. Miller and Ryan West. Oxford University Press (2020). © Oxford University Press.
DOI: 10.1093/oso/9780190920487.003.0001

This apparent lack of controversy conceals, or at least ignores, further important questions. Why, exactly, does integrity matter? What, precisely, is it that we admire and seek? Even the common sense view that integrity is a moral virtue is complicated, if not challenged, by long-standing links between integrity and truth, honesty, and sincerity. Persons of integrity are characteristically concerned with the truth.[3] A disregard for the truth—being insincere, duplicitous, or shifty—seems incompatible with having integrity. Given this last observation, it is surprising that most views of integrity offered in the philosophical literature seem largely unconcerned with truth.[4] Of the five (more or less) mainstream views of integrity that claim currency—call them the Integrated Self, Identity, Clean Hands, Strength of Will, and Moral Purpose views—none features any obvious or direct link between integrity and a concern for truth.

Against these accounts—and in a way that sounds the themes of this volume: integrity, honesty, and truth seeking—I argue for an alternative, outlier view. On the view I explore and recommend here, integrity is more promisingly understood as a complex character trait that concerns a person's relation to her own capacity for judgment.[5] I call this a *judgment-centered* account: specifically, persons of integrity exhibit characteristically proper concern for their judgment, where this proper concern essentially involves responsiveness to facts and evidence and thus, a fundamental concern for truth.

---

3. To return to the *OED*: "Integrity . . . 3B. Soundness of moral principle; the character of uncorrupted virtue, esp. in relation to truth and fair dealing; uprightness, honesty, sincerity." To take a recent and more prosaic example: "Integrity *means* telling the truth, even if the truth is ugly." Tracy 2016: 1 (italics in original).

4. For most accounts of integrity, if there is a direct connection to be found between integrity and a concern for truth, it is only one variety of integrity—intellectual integrity—that exhibits such a connection.

5. I say "promisingly" both to signal the advantages of this outlier view, and to acknowledge that the present defense is incomplete. For a fuller defense, see Scherkoske 2013.

My case proceeds as follows. Section 1 introduces some of the "data points" or intuitions that philosophical accounts of integrity have tried to accommodate. These are, loosely speaking, the 'appearances" that extant accounts of integrity have tried to "save." Section 2 briefly canvasses five more or less widely held views of integrity. In order to motivate the acceptance of the alternative, judgment-centered account of integrity I prefer, I attempt to show that these mainstream views struggle, and perhaps fail, to persuasively accommodate all the data points. As I briefly suggest, these views also come to grief in their explanations of why integrity matters, and what it is, precisely, about integrity that we admire and seek. Section 3 sketches the general outlines of a judgment-centered approach to integrity and then distinguishes the version I defend from that of Cheshire Calhoun. I then offer reasons to prefer my version of the judgment-centred view over the five mainstream views. Section 4 further explores the links between a judgment-centered view of integrity and a concern for truth, and closes by considering a few wider consequences of accepting the view I defend.

1. SOME DATA POINTS

Philosophical treatments of various virtues often start from exemplars or paradigm cases. With respect to integrity, this approach is complicated by two challenges: the existence of non-human exemplars of integrity and the use of conflicting paradigm cases. First, unlike canonical virtues such as wisdom, courage, temperance, and others that are ascribed only to agents and their acts, integrity is quite commonly ascribed to a wide variety of things. There are strong etymological links between integrity and wholeness or soundness, so we intelligibly speak of the integrity of bridges, databases, buildings, ecosystems, and even law, among many other things.[6] When applied to individuals, integrity is often used to describe an aspect of someone's character, though the term *integrity* can also be applied to aspects of a person's life, or even the entirety of that life.[7] When philosophers try their hand at understanding integrity, there is a natural temptation to model our understanding of the integrity of persons on the comparatively more tractable idea of the wholeness or soundness of things. There naturally follows from this a search for the aspect or aspects of persons that could support this extension in usage.[8]

A cursory glance at the philosophical literature on integrity illustrates the second challenge to getting clearer on the nature of integrity. Put simply, different philosophers select conflicting cases as paradigm instances of integrity. For some, both Abraham Lincoln and General Robert E. Lee are given as obvious examples of persons of integrity.[9] Some allege that Mozart's Don Giovanni shows integrity.[10] Others deny this.[11] For some it is obvious that persons of integrity have arrived at a sort of "true self" that is largely free of "conflict and compartmentalization."[12] Others disagree, arguing that ambivalence and even conflict can be marks of integrity.[13]

Given both of these challenges, and the diversity of conceptions of integrity in the literature, it might help to set out some data points in order to get a better grasp on the range of features that successful

6. See Miller 2013. On integrity of law, see Dworkin 1986, and Green (chapter 2 in this volume).

7. A point nicely stressed by Cox, LeCaze, and Levine 2017.

8. This is particularly salient with Integrated Self, Identity, and Clean Hands views of integrity, as we will see. See also Scherkoske 2013: chapter 1.

9. "Whatever integrity is, Abraham Lincoln had it .... Lincoln was not the only one with integrity in the Civil War. Some of his opponents in the Confederacy had it too, as, for instance, General Robert E. Lee .... So to display integrity is *not* just 'to do what is right.'" Bigelow and Pargetter 2007: 39–40 (italics in original).

10. Taylor 1985: 127.

11. Graham 2001: 249.

12. Cottingham 2010: 6–9.

13. Calhoun 1995: 238–241.

analyses of integrity have attempted to capture and systematize, with variable success.

1) <u>Stick-to-itiveness</u>: Integrity requires sticking to one's convictions,[14] particularly in the face of disagreement, challenge, or temptation. Integrity is most obviously exhibited in a person's resistance to sacrificing, betraying, or otherwise compromising her convictions.[15]

2) <u>Integrity-within-reason</u>: A person of integrity's disposition to stand by her convictions must be responsive to reasons. Integrity cannot plausibly consist in a stance of "my convictions right or wrong, no matter how culpably stupid and ill-formed." This data point captures the idea that integrity is importantly distinct from (and incompatible with) fanaticism, dogmatism, or lack of appetite for self-scrutiny.[16]

3) <u>Range</u>: People can exhibit integrity in many domains of activity. The sorts of convictions with regard to which people exhibit integrity is not limited to moral convictions; integrity is also expressed in intellectual, aesthetic, and artistic matters, as well as those relating to one's role or profession.[17]

---

14. Since I defend a "judgment centered" view of integrity, to avoid confusion I will speak of "convictions" rather than "judgments" in what follows. I mean "convictions" to pick out those things to which one assents or would endorse upon reflection, as distinct from merely occurrent beliefs.

15. See Williams 1973, 1981; Calhoun 1995.

16. I adopt this term to avoid having to distinguish, out of the gate, this named-though-undefined property and the properties of reasonableness or rationality. In one or another form this data point is emphasized by McFall 1987, Halfon 1989, Graham 2001, and McLeod 2004. See Miller 2013 for a useful treatment of this point.

17. I set aside for the moment several important issues: whether this range requires positing different *kinds* of integrity (moral, personal, intellectual, aesthetic, professional, etc.); in what ways (if any, apart from content) these varieties of integrity differ from each other; what it is that these varieties share, in virtue of which each constitutes a species of the genus *integrity*; etc.

4) Coherence: Integrity involves a certain sort of consistency and integration among a person's varied convictions. For persons of integrity, as Susan Mendus point out, "Their lives form a coherent whole and their lives are led for their own reasons."[18] Call this elusive property—of a person's convictions 'hanging together'—*Coherence*.

5) Resoluteness: Integrity is expressed in behavior. Persons of integrity have a characteristic kind of volitional strength in acting on their convictions. Integrity is incompatible with being weak willed, prone to untimely instability of judgment, or otherwise lacking resolve.[19]

6) Moral Sanity: Having integrity is incompatible with gross moral turpitude. No matter how principled or resolute Hitler or Stalin (or some other single-mindedly bad person) might have been, they cannot be said to have integrity.[20]

7) Judgment: When we seek advice, guidance, or mentoring in matters of importance, and in contexts of leadership, we are especially keen that those whose assistance we seek and leadership we follow possess integrity. This concern suggests not merely that we seek and expect probity from such persons; it suggests persons of integrity are valued in part for

18. Mendus 2009: 16. As McFall 1987: 7–8 rightly points out, there are likely several different kinds of coherence relations: consistency among one's commitments, values or principles, as well as coherence between one's principles and conduct that requires doing what one thinks is right because it is believed to be right. See Miller 2013: 1–2. For some, this coherence data point might also encompass the sort of coherence between one's principles and conduct that is incompatible with weakness of will. For expository purposes, I consider this variety of coherence separately in Section 2.

19. Resoluteness is distinct, if not always easily distinguishable, from Stick-to-itiveness in that the latter is fundamentally about the stability of one's judgments, and the former is fundamentally volitional. As this brief characterization only hints, talk of "weakness of will" and "resoluteness" conceals a great deal of detail and nuance. For useful discussions, see Rorty 1980, Holton 1999.

20. See McFall 1987, Halfon 1989, Ashford 2000, Graham 2001, and Miller 2013 for discussion.

their understanding and judgment as interlocutors, advisors, mentors, and leaders.[21]

These data points are deliberately left vague in an ecumenical spirit. Not all of them will figure in everyone's intuitions about integrity. Some may seem intuitive in their vague form, but less so when specified in certain ways.[22]

2. INTEGRITY: FIVE OPTIONS

While not explicitly oriented around the need to accommodate the data points as I have described them, the five mainstream views of integrity attempt to accommodate these intuitively plausible features of integrity. These data points serve as more or less core "appearances" that the accounts attempt to save—that is, explain and systematize.[23]

21. While less prevalent in the philosophical literature on integrity, this data point is prominent in literature from business (especially leadership, see Tracy 2016) and mentoring (in coaching and in health professions, e.g., see Canadian National Coaching Certification Code of Ethics 2016, Levison et al. 2014, and Johnson 2015).

22. Some of these data points may be interpreted more or less widely, as in the case of *Range* (e.g., some might lack the intuition that integrity can be properly ascribed to a person on the basis of her aesthetic convictions). Others admit of more or less stringent interpretations. Graham 2001, for example, would argue mere *Moral Sanity* is too permissive a condition on integrity; rather, to possess integrity requires being morally good. To take a final example, some would interpret *Integrity-within-reason* to require that persons of integrity merely have some (not necessarily good) reason for their convictions (see McLeod 2004); others explain this data point in terms of reasonableness (see Miller 2013 for a useful summary); still others take sensitivity to a particular sort of reason—moral reasons or correct moral principles—to be the relevant marker (see Ashford 2000, Graham 2001). Note that if one were to accept Ashford or Graham's view, *Moral Sanity* would be secured by *Integrity-within-reason.*

23. More precisely, one mark of a satisfactory conception of integrity is *descriptive adequacy*: An account of integrity is descriptively adequate just in case and to the extent that it fits with our more or less agreed upon experience, linguistic practice, and judgments of integrity. Descriptive adequacy clearly admits of a more and a less. One account is more descriptively adequate than another to the extent that the first accommodates more of the data points, or does so more plausibly than the second. Put simply, descriptive adequacy—or what I here

It will be helpful to canvass the strengths and limitations of these mainstream theories, pausing briefly to examine the extent to which these options successfully accommodate the data points.[24] While this quick overview cannot claim to be dispositive, the highlighted shortcomings of these options are instructive, and help motivate an alternative, more promising view of integrity: the judgment-centered approach.

2.1 Integrated Self, Identity, and Clean Hands Views of Integrity

Philosophical accounts of integrity often focus, as noted, on some aspect(s) of the conventional usage of the word—for example, ideas of wholeness, completeness, unity, or being uncorrupted.[25] What aspect of persons could support this extension of usage? Three promising candidates have seemed to be a person's self, or practical identity, or some subset of commitments thought to constitute the self or identity. In this spirit, we have the first three analytically distinct conceptions of integrity: the Integrated Self, Identity, and Clean Hands views.

2.1.1 INTEGRITY AS INTEGRATED SELF

Leaning on etymological links between "integrity," "integer," and "integration," the first conception seeks to extend these protean idea to persons. To have integrity is to have decided who one is, what one desires or values, and, additionally, to stand by these, even if (and

---

loosely call "saving the appearances"—is an indication that we really do have an account of the thing that most people take themselves and others to be talking about, rather than some other thing. See Scherkoske 2013: 17–18.

24. We can for present purposes set aside the issue of whether any of the following options can plausibly be taken to provide either necessary or sufficient conditions for an adequate conception of integrity. See Miller 2013 for a helpful overview.

25. Here I draw from Scherkoske 2013.

paradigmatically *when*) this stand proves unpopular.[26] On Integrated Self views, to have integrity is first and foremost to have settled the question of what one wants; it is to have rid oneself of ambivalence in one's preferences or values. As Calhoun nicely puts the core idea, "people of integrity decide what they stand for and have their own settled reasons for taking the stands they do. They are not . . . crowd followers . . . nor are they so weak-willed or self-deceived that they cannot act on what they stand for."[27] On this conception, integrity finds expression in a person's conduct, precisely because such conduct is the expression of an integrated self. This explains our intuitive sense that people of integrity do not pander for approval, nor are they susceptible to backsliding or the sort of ambivalence that reflects a failure to achieve such a unified or integrated self.

This conception of integrity nicely captures some key data points: *Stick-to-it-iveness, Resoluteness,* and *Coherence.* Since, in its pure form, the integrated self view is very ecumenical as to what commitments may happen to be central to a person's identity, it also accommodates *Range.* However, since a person's self is understood expansively to include everything he values, utterly trivial or base commitments—having the perfect tan or "six-pack abs"—are potential integrity-sustaining commitments on this view. Thus, the Integrated Self conception of integrity might exhibit an undesirable, indiscriminate sort of range.

Unfortunately this conception does not accommodate the remaining data points. There is nothing in this conception to secure

26. Defenders of this view include Taylor 1981, McFall 1987, Blustein 1991, McLeod 2004, and Cottingham 2010. Shelly Kagan writes: a person "who acts in keeping with her moral views can be at one with herself. Such unity, I think, is part of what we mean when we say that an individual's life has integrity" (1988: 390). Whether, and to what extent, a person needs to have self-consciously or reflectively decided these matters is a further question. I will set this interesting issue aside in what follows.

27. Calhoun 1995: 237; see also Mendus 2009: 16–18.

Moral Sanity, since an integrated self may be one that has morally repugnant commitments. Nor is there anything to require that an integrated self be responsive to reasons, so it is compatible with dogmatism and fanaticism; this leaves out *Integrity-within-reason*. Given these worries, finally, *Judgment* looks manifestly insecure as well on this view. To the extent that an integrated self is compatible with having morally repugnant, dogmatic, and base or trivial commitments, it is unclear why such a person's judgment would be worthy of seeking out in matters of importance.

2.1.2 INTEGRITY AS IDENTITY

On this second conception, integrity is a relation of fidelity to one's practical identity. Bernard Williams gave early and influential expression to this view. Persons, he writes, have a more or less unique set of "projects," which are fundamentally a "set of desires, concerns . . . which help to constitute a *character*."[28] The most important of these concerns are what Williams terms "ground projects," which provide the person with "the motive force which propels him into the future, and gives him a reason for living."[29] Integrity involves fidelity to these ground projects with which a person identifies; it involves "sticking to what one finds ethically necessary and worthwhile."[30] When a person compromises her integrity, she suffers a kind of loss of her identity: she is no longer the same person, since she has given up part of what defines her identity.[31] Since this view (unlike the previous one) does not see one's integrity implicated in everything one desires, but rather in just those concerns that define one's identity, it offers an advance over the Integrated Self view. The Identity view

28. Williams 1981b: 5. Italics in the original.
29. Ibid., 13.
30. Williams 1995: 211.
31. The sense of identity at issue is much looser than that invoked in, for example, the metaphysics literature concerning personal identity.

helps make sense of the idea that compromising one's integrity is a considerable loss—because, intuitively, it is a great harm—without it being true that every loss, frustration, or setback to the things we care about is a threat to integrity.

This conception of integrity, like the previous view, intuitively captures *Stick-to-itiveness, Resoluteness,* and quite possibly *Coherence.*[32] Problems arise, however, in cases where people's sense of identity is predicated on morally repugnant commitments, or they are fanatically or dogmatically resistant to changing or scrutinizing their commitments. To the extent that the Identity view is neutral with respect to these identity-conferring commitments, it too appears unable to secure *Moral Sanity* and *Integrity-within-reason.*[33] And since this view, like the Integrated Self conception, does not obviously establish that the person is well suited to offer advice, guidance, mentoring, or leadership, it leaves *Judgment* insecure.

2.1.3 INTEGRITY AS CLEAN HANDS

On the Clean Hands view, integrity requires that a person have some "bottom line" principles or convictions, and that her allegiance to these be such that she would never betray or violate them.[34] As Lynne McFall puts this:

> Unless corrupted by philosophy, we all have things we think we
> would never do, under any imaginable circumstances, whatever

32. For arguments that the identity view of integrity does not capture a desirable sort of coherence, see Calhoun 1995, Scherkoske 2013: chapter 2, and Miller 2013. As Nancy Schauber observes: "Because we can reasonably abandon serious commitments, we can also reasonably abandon, or oversee . . . the demise of our selves . . . . This being so, there is no need to cultivate integrity to keep the real self intact" (Schauber 1996: 124).

33. See Scherkoske 2013: chapters 2 and 3.

34. Williams 1973: 98–99 sets out this distinct aspect of his view in the discussions of George the chemist and Jim and the "Indians." (While difficult to separate, Williams's view of integrity seems to incorporate elements of both Identity and Clean Hands views.) McFall also endorses this conception of integrity (in tandem with the Integrated Self view).

we may give to survival or pleasure. . . . [There is] some part of ourselves beyond which we will not retreat. . . . And if we do that thing, betray that weakness there is nothing left that we may even in spite refer to as *I*.[35]

Setting aside her contentious singling-out of philosophy as a corrupting influence, this view, even more clearly than the Identity conception, links integrity with adherence to personal and fundamental principles or values that one not merely endorses but takes to be inviolable. Unlike the two previous views—which allow for the possibility that a well-integrated self may contain few, if any, such bottom line principles, and also for the possibility that a person's identity may not be anchored by such principles—the Clean Hands view makes fidelity to such principles essential to having integrity. Put simply, if there is no proverbial hill upon which a person is prepared to die, the person cannot possess integrity. This view comports well with some paradigmatic cases of integrity: it accounts for not only those people who publicly refuse to cooperate with corrupt or evil regimes, or who speak truth to power and suffer for it, but also those people who undertake private, smaller, or even symbolic acts of resistance.[36]

The Clean Hands conception of integrity vindicates *Stick-to-itiveness* and *Resoluteness*. But while defenders of this view might disagree with me, there is nothing in the logic of the Clean Hands view to rule out any number of dubious principles.[37] The principles *Never give a sucker a fair break* or *Avenge every slight tenfold* are principles that a person might never betray, but the refusal to compromise such

---

35. McFall 1987: 12. Italics in original.
36. As illustrated by Williams's example of George the chemist. Williams 1973: 96.
37. Or so I argue in Scherkoske 2013. In a sense, the Clean Hands view secures *Range*, but surprisingly at the expense of *Moral Sanity*. Williams 1981: 45 notes this possibility. In keeping one's hands clean from what he memorably called "ultimately unreal dirt," one may soil them with what proves to be very real dirt.

principles is not obviously grounds for ascribing integrity to them. Indeed, as made vivid by countless fictional and nonfictional characters, the possibility that people will sometimes treat dubious principles as inviolable suggests that the Clean Hands view of integrity is unable to secure *Moral Sanity*. Without some further argument, or ad hoc manoeuver, the Clean Hands view would not secure *Integrity-within-reason* or *Judgment*, either.[38]

As I noted above, these passing criticisms are not intended to be dispositive. Rather than dwell upon this point, it is helpful to note a further worry. As Cheshire Calhoun has persuasively argued, these three conceptions of integrity worryingly reduce the virtue to something else: "to the conditions of unified agency, to the conditions for continuing as the same self . . . [or] the conditions for having a reason to refuse cooperating with some evils."[39] While people do in fact display integrity in the ways these three conceptions describe, not all intuitively plausible or important cases are captured.[40] What makes this worrying is not that these accounts are reductive per se. It is rather that on all three views, the things to which integrity ultimately reduces, while in many cases beneficial or desirable, are neither obvious excellences of character nor do they invariably betoken integrity.[41] Other things equal, it is desirable that persons exhibit an integrated, rather than disintegrated, self. But while an integrated self is an obvious benefit to welfare, it seems to be neither an obvious virtue (since it is not clearly an excellence of character), nor admirable as such (since it notably fails to secure *Moral Sanity* and

38. Scherkoske 2012; McLeod 2005 offers further argument.
39. Calhoun 1995: 252.
40. Recall Schauber's point (supra note 32). As Calhoun notes, "Although persons with integrity will sometimes stand for what they wholeheartedly endorse, or for what is central to their identity, or for deontological principles, integrity is not equivalent to doing these things. Continuing to be of two minds, conscientiousness about small matters and dirtying one's hands can also be matters of integrity." See Calhoun 1995: 252.
41. Calhoun 1995: 252.

Integrity-within-reason). Or to take another example, it seems to matter whether a person keeps her hands clean only if (and to the extent that) the bottom line principles that she considers inviolable are morally or otherwise worthy of treating as such. On these three views, the explanation of why integrity matters to us does not allow us to retain the idea that integrity matters to us in a way that is neither instrumental nor conditional upon our valuing other things.

To some this might be a price worth paying—or a price that must be paid.[42] There is good reason to resist this suggestion, however. On any of the three views considered thus far, integrity is understood to involve a fundamentally partial—that is, self-concerned and perhaps egoistic—stance toward oneself and one's commitments. This courts two risks. First, there is the worry that integrity is vulnerable to a charge of moral self-indulgence—a dubious and deformed concern for oneself, one's identity, or the cleanliness of one's moral ledger. Second, there is the problem of moral danger: acting to preserve one's integrity, on these views, will not obviously, much less reliably (and still less, necessarily), lead one to act rightly or well.[43] Thus, we are not merely left without a plausible account of why integrity matters; we are left with the worry that a person's concern to act with integrity might serve as a misplaced bulwark *against* self-scrutiny and improvement.

Summing up, somewhat discouragingly: on these conceptions, whether integrity is valuable is contingent upon the desires, commitments, values, or principles a person happens to have. And to the extent this is so, it becomes unclear what exactly it is that we seek and admire. Finally, it is worth noting that these accounts are silent regarding the link between integrity, truth, and truthfulness.

42. I offer reasons to believe that it is a price that must be paid, before offering an alternative that is not so costly. See Scherkoske 2010, 2013: chapter 1.
43. These are serious worries; see Scherkoske 2010, 2013. The first point was noted by Williams, who worried that integrity might easily tip into a fetishized concern with one's self and its principled purity. See Williams 1981: 47–49.

2.2 Strength of Will and Moral Purpose Views of Integrity

There remain two further, and decidedly different, conceptions of integrity to consider before turning to the judgment-centered view of integrity I recommend in Section 3.

2.2.1 INTEGRITY AS STRENGTH OF WILL

Several times we've noted the intuition that weakness of will—very roughly, not acting on one's judgment about what is best to do—seems inconsistent with having integrity. John Bigelow and Robert Pargetter have made this intuition the focal case of integrity: for them, nothing compromises integrity more clearly than weakness of will; conversely, nothing constitutes integrity more clearly than strength of will. Invoking the distinction between higher and lower-order desires,[44] Bigelow and Pargetter understand strength of will to be that desirable property of higher-order desires that consists in their being motivationally decisive over conflicting lower-order desires:

> Integrity is a character trait. It comes in degrees. A person with integrity is one who can display strength of will not only when the temptations are slight but also when they are acute, not only on freak occasions but over a wide range of likely situations, and not only over short term but long term projects.[45]

To put it simply, integrity on this view is exhibited in a person's effective power to do what she values (or desires that she desires) doing in a way that is not only cross-contextually robust but temporally stable.

This view is quite clearly elegant. It also makes strength of will central to integrity in a way that accommodates *Resoluteness*. And

44. Frankfurt 1988; Watson 1975, 1987.
45. Bigelow and Pargetter 2007: 39.

there are (arguably, at least) resources within the Strength of Will view to accommodate *Stick-to-itiveness* and perhaps one variety of *Coherence*.[46] But from what we have seen in the previous discussion, the drawbacks should be readily apparent: there is nothing in the Strength of Will view of integrity that would accommodate *Integrity-within-reason, Moral Sanity,* or *Judgment*.[47] This trait or capacity is surely necessary for virtue—perhaps many virtues; but it is not obviously itself a virtue. Thus, it seems unlikely that integrity is simply strength of will.

2.2.2 INTEGRITY AS MORAL PURPOSE

The last conception of integrity to consider takes seriously the sense of integrity as soundness of moral principle, uncorrupted virtue, and uprightness common in ordinary use. Where other conceptions of integrity allow at most a contingent connection between having integrity and standing for moral principles, the Moral Purpose conception makes the unswerving commitment to moral values and principles to be essential to integrity. There are several different variants of this view, and they feature varying degrees of moral demandingness. Elizabeth Ashford, for example, defends the view that what she terms "objective integrity" requires a commitment to *correct* moral principles, and this would presumably rule out the possibility that a person of integrity would find herself in moral failure.[48] Less demanding moral purpose views require that persons of integrity

---

46. See supra 16.

47. Jeffrey Blustein recognizes this and adds some useful nuance: "Not every instance of weakness of will, of acting contrary to one's better judgment, and not even repeated akratic failure, necessarily indicates a lack of integrity. There must be a deficiency of self-control with respect to commitments or principles that has some bearing on the agent's broad conception of his or her life direction or sense of self-identity" (1991: 100). This added nuance seems to add elements from other views.

48. Graham 2001 defends a view that is at least as morally demanding as Ashford's. See Scherkoske 2010 for discussion and criticisms.

occupy a moral point of view that others find intelligible, and that clear and rational thought informs their understanding of their moral obligations, even if their overall moral outlook is itself limited or in some respects faulty.[49] Moral Purpose views have the advantage of explaining common and long-standing associations between integrity and morality. It further explains why integrity is thought to matter (since it is inseparable from the moral worth of persons) and why its absence or loss is so serious (since it reliably occasions moral failure and blameworthiness).

Moral Purpose conceptions of integrity quite neatly—indeed, focally—capture *Moral Sanity*, and can also elegantly accommodate *Resoluteness*, since the commitment to moral values and principles is constitutive of the virtue, and an irresolute failure to act on one's moral demands is an all-too-common failing of integrity. Nevertheless, there are significant limitations to such views of integrity. Most obviously, these views forego *Range*, since they deny that non-moral principles and values are constitutive of integrity. To the extent that moral principles and values come into conflict with other important values, Moral Purpose views also sacrifice *Coherence*. After all, fidelity to moral values and principles might occasion not just practical conflicts but (potentially) tragic dilemmas that would deeply, and perhaps irremediably, compromise the unity or coherence of a person's practical and moral agency.[50] As for *Judgment*, Moral Purpose views of integrity would seem to secure the moral dimensions of leadership, mentoring, and guidance, and this is not insignificant. Yet part of the intuitive appeal of *Judgment* extends beyond probity. We seek out persons of

49. Halfon 1989 and McFall 1987 defend view of integrity with at least a component of a moral purpose view. Their views feature less epistemically and morally demanding requirements on the principles and values for which a person of integrity might stand.

50. As Williams argued (1973, 1981). For a recent defense, see Tessman 2015. Scherkoske 2010 and 2013 argue that the grounds for moralizing integrity in ways required for Moral Purpose views of integrity are unconvincing.

integrity for their understanding and judgment in many matters: strategic, technical, athletic, and managerial, to name but a few.

Because Moral Purpose conceptions of integrity accommodate *Moral Sanity* and *Resoluteness*, and because these views give an intuitively plausible explanation of why integrity matters, such views enjoy wide appeal. Given this, it is worth taking a slightly longer look at their drawbacks. In response to the worry that Moral Purpose views cannot accommodate several data points, a defender has two ready responses. Regarding *Coherence,* she could concede the point about conflicts between moral and non-moral values, yet insist that *Coherence* is, after all, but one data point. This admission is far from fatal, she might add. The first point is correct, of course: it isn't obvious that a persuasive account of integrity must accommodate every intuitive data point. Some revision to our common sense understanding of integrity is perhaps inevitable, and in any case may be a price worth paying.

Alternatively, she could insist that the variety of coherence worth wanting—a bit of nuance concealed by the vagueness of *Coherence,* as I sketched it—is *moral* coherence, understood not merely as the coherence between a person's moral values and her action, but (further, and at least as importantly) the more narrow coherence among a person's varied moral values and principles. While this is certainly a possible response, this second suggestion reveals a deeper problem with Moral Purpose views of integrity. Such views risk being committed to the idea that integrity itself lacks any distinctive content. On these more robust Moral Purpose views, integrity seems to amount to the virtue of being morally virtuous, a kind of second-order virtue of being moral in the right ways on the right occasions, and so on. But clearly, this would leave little distinctive work for integrity to do.[51]

---

51. Thus, Moral Purpose views risk becoming *normatively redundant.* To put the point in purely virtue-theoretic terms, the risk here is that integrity is exhibited in all moral conduct: being

To be sure, we are right to admire people who steadfastly adhere to their moral values and principles. But on this proposal, it appears that integrity has become the confluence of all morally good traits, dispositions, and conduct. As it does so, integrity's distinctive nature and value slip from our grasp.

3. INTEGRITY AS AN EPISTEMIC VIRTUE: A JUDGMENT-CENTERED APPROACH

A more promising direction involves reorienting our view of integrity toward the sort of judgment that is worth sticking to, refusing to compromise, and resolutely acting upon. Perhaps having integrity consists in having the proper regard for —rather than an uncritical, unswerving, or pathological commitment to—one's judgment as it is manifested both in the convictions one has, and the degree of confidence one has in them.

In her influential paper, "Standing for Something," Cheshire Calhoun advances what I take to be the first judgment-centered view of integrity in the philosophical literature.[52] She persuasively argues that what is distinctive to (and distinctively valuable about) integrity is not merely having and maintaining a certain relation to oneself. The full expression of a person's commitment to what she believes and values is shown in her willingness to *stand for* her convictions before others. This, among other things, involves a readiness to accept reasoned challenges to those beliefs and perhaps to modify or suspend her judgment in response to reflection on those challenges.

---

honest when honesty is called for, courageous when courage is called for, etc. There seems no distinctive success or failing left to integrity; there is no failure of integrity that is not at the same time, a failure to exhibit one or another specific first-order virtue. See Scherkoske 2013: 80–83.

52. Calhoun 1995.

> To lack integrity . . . is to underrate both formulating and exem-
> plifying one's own views. People without integrity trade action
> upon their views too cheaply for gain, status, reward, approval
> or for escape from penalties, loss of status, disapproval . . . . [O]r
> they trade their own views too readily for the views of others
> who are more authoritative [or] less demanding of themselves,
> and so on.[53]

For Calhoun, the distinctive vice of those who lack integrity is the failure to have a proper regard for their own best judgment on the fundamental matters of how to live justly and well. Integrity, on this view, is expressed in our ability to resist the temptations, incentives, and sanctions that would have us defer to, uncritically comply with, or unthinkingly act on someone else's judgment on these fundamental matters. This is an important part of what having a proper regard for one's judgment involves.

But having a proper regard for one's judgment involves more than this, as Calhoun notes: while it is possible to "underrate both formulating and exemplifying one's own views," it is also possible to *overrate* one's views:

> [W]hen what is worth doing is under dispute, a concern to act
> with integrity must pull us both ways. Integrity calls us simulta-
> neously to stand behind our convictions and to take seriously
> others' doubts about them. Thus neither ambivalence nor com-
> promise seems inevitably to betoken a lack of integrity.[54]

This is an intuitive and attractive idea: integrity, it might be thought, hits the virtuous mean between the vices of deficiency

53. Calhoun 1995: 250.
54. Calhoun 1995: 255.

("underrating") and excess ("overrating") with respect to stand-ing for one's judgments. In a loose and intuitive way, this seems to capture the idea that when one's convictions are well grounded, the proper response to disagreement and the challenge of others is to resist compromise or deference; when one's convictions are not so well-grounded, by contrast, taking others' doubts seriously might appropriately occasion the loss of, or diminution in, confidence in one's specific judgment. In a way that signals an important difference with the view I will sketch, we should note that for Calhoun the range of convictions through which people come to express their integrity is limited to questions of what is worth doing; thus, the proper regard through which persons of integrity express proper regard for their judgment is limited to moral and evaluative judgments.[55]

I have elsewhere defended a different judgment-centered view of integrity.[56] My view differs from Calhoun's in numerous ways, but two respects are salient. First, a judgment-centered view need not restrict itself—in the manner of Calhoun's view—to matters of what to do and how to live. While judgments about such matters are of obvious and central importance to our lives, as *Range* suggests, it is not *exclusively* moral, political, and perfectionist values that persons of integrity are concerned to stand for. Second, rather than leave the important notion of *proper regard* intuitive and loose, I think it use-ful to understand this notion in terms of epistemic responsibility and truth. The more precision we can bring to the idea of having a proper regard for one's own judgment, the better we can limn the shape of the virtuous response characteristic of a person of integrity.

What is it to show proper regard for one's judgment? As I see it, the sort of proper regard characteristic of integrity on a

---

55. This interpretation is supported by Walker 2003 and McLeod 2004, who endorse aspects of Calhoun's view and seem to agree that integrity for Calhoun is focally concerned with questions of what is worth doing.
56. Here I draw from Scherkoske 2012, 2013.

judgment-centered approach consists in at least three overlapping sets of dispositions:[57]

    a. The complex disposition to maintain and revise one's convictions in epistemically responsible ways. The person of integrity is committed to holding and revising her convictions on the basis of facts, evidence, good reasons, and sound reasoning.

    b. An awareness (not necessarily explicit or reflective) of the quality of one's judgment or competence to judge on a matter in a specific domain. Seeking to exhibit good judgment in her convictions—indeed, being focally concerned to have and act from a set of defensible and correct convictions—the person of integrity is disposed to *hedge* her confidence in her convictions to the extent that they fail by her lights to enjoy the support of good reasons. [58] Conversely, in paradigmatic cases of standing for her convictions, the person of integrity will strongly adhere to those commitments to the extent that (and because) they enjoy the support of good reasons.

    c. The ability and, indeed, willingness to give to others what she takes to be good reasons for both her convictions and the conduct that issues from her convictions. The reasons that support a person's convictions are, at the same time, the reasons for acting on those convictions.[59] These reasons are well suited to offer others when

---

57. See Scherkoske 2013: 88–90.

58. Ryan West has helpfully pressed me on this point. Will a person have integrity if "her lights" are not objectively correct? One could argue that the success conditions of possessing integrity rule out the possibility of error. On the specific view I defend in Scherkoske 2013, I do not. I argue that it is possible for the person of integrity to nevertheless be mistaken.

59. To be clear, this does not require that the reasons that actually motivate a person to act are necessarily identical to the normative reasons she has for acting that way. It is possible that

challenged or asked for advice and guidance, as well as
in other contexts, such as conversation aimed at settling
questions of what to believe.

Having integrity, on the judgment-centered view I recommend, is
a matter of having one's regard for one's judgment be epistemically
responsible in general. Integrity also requires a sort of "meta-cognitive"
sensitivity to specific variations in contexts in which one's competence
to judge responsibly is prone to be reliable and those contexts in which
it is not. Finally, integrity on this judgment-centered view requires the
willingness to accept the discursive responsibilities that attend holding
the convictions one has. That is, a willingness to respond to requests or
demands to offer reasons for one's convictions, and if need be hedge
(or even, in some cases, withdraw) one's confidence in them. Central to
integrity as I conceive of the virtue is the idea that integrity consists in
being responsible to ourselves and others for the judgments we make
and the lives we lead on the basis of those judgments.[60]

More would obviously need to be said to make this proposal compelling. Here I am concerned only to motivate a general judgment-
centered view of integrity. But even at this stage, there are important
advantages over the previous options we canvassed.

---

the reasons that support one's convictions are not present to one's consciousness at the
time of acting. Indeed, as I argue in Scherkoske 2013: chapter 4, this is quite often the case.
Thanks to Ryan West for pressing me here.

60. Here I am indebted to Alice MacLachlan. My aim in this paper is to motivate the general
judgment-centered approach rather than to defend a particular variant of it. Nevertheless,
the judgment-centered view of integrity I defend in Scherkoske 2013 is oriented around the
idea that persons of integrity lead convincing lives. Having proper regard for one's judgment
involves not just well placed self-trust in one's judgment (which is grounded in domain-
sensitive epistemic trustworthiness) but also a willingness to accept discursive responsibility for the judgments we make and the reasons we give others to believe and act on what we
tell them. More specifically, leading a convincing life will, on the view of integrity I defend,
require both the fidelity to the aim of having only defensible convictions that are worthy
of acting on and affirming to others, and the disposition to stick to those defensible and
epistemically trustworthy convictions.

Returning to the data points with which we began, understanding integrity along these lines gives a natural explanation of *Stick-to-itiveness* and *Integrity- within-reason*. If integrity is (among other things) expressed in complex dispositions to maintain and revise one's convictions in epistemically responsible ways, then it would naturally find expression as a desirable and intelligent disposition to stick to one's convictions in the face of disagreement, challenge, and temptation.[61] But crucially—and in a way that explains *Integrity-within-reason*—this resistance to change varies with the degree to which one's judgment in the relevant domain enjoys the support of good reasons. The complex set of dispositions picked out in *a*, taken alongside the "meta-cognitive" sensitivity to one's competence and reliability to judge matters in a certain domain, picked out in *b*, afford a plausible and attractive explanation of both *Coherence* and *Resoluteness*. The convictions that are maintained and revised in ongoing processes of epistemically responsible belief regulation will naturally tend toward coherence.[62] To the extent that a person's beliefs and judgments are regulated responsibly—in the light of available evidence and guided by a concern for truth—there will be rational pressure toward *Coherence*.[63] Furthermore, this pressure will also underpin the kind of desirable stability of judgment and intention that is the hallmark of *Resoluteness*. (This is of course compatible with the possibility of reasoned revision of those intentions.) Thus, a judgment-centered account of integrity captures the sense that integrity is importantly distinct from an unwillingness to revise

---

61. Ryan West suggested that such a view would need supplementation along the lines of the Strength of Will views. I respond to this suggestion in Scherkoske 2013: 141–143.

62. Though (some) incoherence in a person's convictions could nevertheless be epistemically responsible, as Christian Miller has reminded me. As Calhoun noted above, ambivalence may not betoken a lack of integrity.

63. As Stephen Galoob rightly pointed out to me in conversation, this diachronic aspect of belief and intention regulation allows for integrity-preserving changes and evolution in our convictions.

one's judgments and intentions "come what may": this epistemically irresponsible, overweening regard for one's judgment is incompatible with integrity, as *Integrity-within-reason* requires.

Concerning *Range*, it is a decisive advantage of judgment-centered accounts of integrity that they can accommodate our sense that people manifest integrity in many domains of their lives. It is not merely with respect to moral convictions that people of integrity are admired, praised, and emulated. Persons of integrity (or perhaps, persons of exceptional integrity) display the virtue across many aspects of their lives. Happily, the judgment-centered account does not merely accommodate this intuition but actually helps explain it. To the extent that having a set of convictions that is defensible, reasoned, and grounded in relevant and available facts and evidence is important to the person's proper regard for her judgment, *Range* looks to be secured. The aspect of integrity picked out in *a*, above, isolates an extensive but cross-contextual set of dispositions that will likely be expressed in many domains of judgment and conduct.[64]

With respect to *Moral Sanity*, there is no need for ad hoc stipulations or epicycles to explain how to handle the "Nazi with integrity" worry. A judgment-centered view of integrity, as we have seen, takes the virtue to involve not just a complex first-order set of dispositions and traits of epistemic responsibility, but also a more or less reflective "meta-cognitive" grasp of one's reliability of judgment in particular domains. But as Calhoun's influential notion of "standing for" suggests, there is an important social, epistemic dimension to integrity: having the virtue requires willingness to give reasons to others,

---

64. Moreover, on this view there is no need to posit distinct types of integrity (personal, moral, intellectual, professional, artistic, political, etc.). Thus, we are not burdened with having to explain why there are not innumerable types of integrity (would there be different subtypes of artistic or professional integrity depending on whether one is a visual or performing artist, a professional in the public or private sector?). And it no longer becomes puzzling what is common to all (apparently) different types of integrity in virtue of which they are all species of the same genus. See Scherkoske 2013: 98–101.

reasons that are putatively justifying when challenged or criticized. If we accept this, integrity is plausibly seen to be a virtue that is not separable from the sorts of complex reason-responsiveness that is implicated in holding one another responsible for our *moral* convictions and the conduct that springs from them.[65] This is plausibly seen to be a core component of *Moral Sanity*. The mere possibility of someone beyond the moral pale possessing integrity is not ruled out by conceptual fiat, but rather by the fact that it is difficult to imagine how an epistemically responsible person could hold manifestly repugnant moral convictions, and retain these convictions, in the face of reasoned challenge and scrutiny.[66]

Finally, and unsurprisingly, on judgment-centered views *Judgment* is both accommodated and explained. We do not merely admire, praise, and attempt to emulate persons of integrity, we seek out such persons precisely when, in matters of importance, we are in need of advice, guidance, mentoring, and good leadership. Persons of integrity are disposed to offer their judgments to others, but in a way that neither overestimates nor overstates the grounds for which those judgments are held and offered to us. In contexts of advising, leadership, etc., the person of integrity characteristically offers her judgments to others with a lively awareness of her own variable competence and reliability in the relevant domains.

---

65. This highly compressed chain of reasoning is unpacked and defended in Scherkoske 2013: chapter 5.
66. Thus we are not lead to a panicky embrace of a Moral Purpose conception to respond to the "Nazi with integrity" complaint. I say that the "mere possibility" is not ruled out by fiat. This hedge is needed out of respect for the ingenuity of epistemologists in constructing elaborate counterfactual scenarios with which to test our intuitions. Perhaps one could construct a thought experiment in which a person who grows up in an insular, backward, and thoroughly immoral culture might, with the impoverished epistemic and moral resources available to him, hold morally repugnant beliefs in epistemically responsible ways that survive weak challenges from morally like-minded, similarly epistemically impoverished members of the same insular, isolated culture. This is not obviously the case with the "Nazi with integrity," but its mere possibility cannot be ruled out.

4. "TO THINE OWN SELF BE TRUE": INTEGRITY AND TRUTH

On the broadly epistemic, judgment-centered conception of integrity I recommend, the virtue is characteristically expressed in a person's commitment to have, and act from, a set of convictions that is defensible and true. There remains, nevertheless, a kind of essential partiality—of self-preference or self-deference—to the virtue of integrity on this approach. But it is of an entirely different from the type of partiality we see in the mainstream views of integrity. The partiality of judgment-centered views of integrity stems from the fact that a person's best judgment cannot but be authoritative for her thought and action. (This is true even in cases in which one treats the superior expertise or competence of another's judgment as giving one reasons for one's own.[67]) To the extent that truth is regulative in a person's judgment, it is to the deliverances of that judgment—hedged in epistemically responsible ways—that she must be true. It is in this sense that the person of integrity can endorse the sentiment, "to thine own self be true." Integrity is not, as many have claimed, manifest in a kind of brute fidelity to the "self," identity, or what one happens to value.[68] On the epistemic, judgment-centered account of integrity sketched here, the *Resoluteness* and *Stick-to-itiveness* that characterize integrity are fundamentally to the deliverances of a person's judgment, and derivatively to the particular convictions supported by her judgment. Thus an abiding concern for truth is partly constitutive of having

---

67. Even when one defers to the judgment of another, one nevertheless maintains the authority of one's own judgment. One judges that another's judgment is more authoritative *in this or that particular matter.*

68. While the most recognizable expression of integrity may come in the paradigmatic act of maintaining one's commitments at great cost, as Jennifer Herdt persuasively argues in this volume, on the judgment-centered view of integrity I defend, it is no less an expression of integrity for a person to revise (or hedge credence in) his commitments at great cost when these cease to enjoy the support of good reasons.

integrity. [69] There is no worry of self-indulgence or moral danger (as with other conceptions of integrity that see it as essentially involving a partial concern with some aspect of oneself).[70]

It is, I think, a decisive advantage of judgment-centered views of integrity that these give a persuasive explanation of what integrity is and why it matters in the way we ordinarily take it to matter. Integrity matters partly because it matters that we regulate our belief and conduct in epistemically responsible ways, that we have a lively sense of our competence and reliability in particular domains, and that we trim the sails of our confidence appropriately.[71] These three traits are plausibly thought to be excellences of epistemic agency, and as such, are valuable quite apart from their conduciveness to other practical and epistemic goods. So while integrity is, on this view, conducive to a great many other things we value, its value is not merely instrumental. Integrity matters because it matters to us that we are responsible to ourselves and others for the judgments we make and the lives we lead on the basis of those judgments.[72] Nor is its goodness merely conditional: integrity matters (on this view) apart from the desirability of having a volitionally unified or otherwise integrated self, a practical identity, a set of "die-in-a-ditch" bottom-line principles, strength of will, or allegiance to some (perhaps favored set of) moral principles

69. While the most recognizable expression of integrity may come in the paradigmatic act of maintaining one's commitments at great cost, as Jennifer Herdt persuasively argues in this volume, on the judgment-centered view of integrity I defend, it is no less an expression of integrity for a person to revise (or hedge credence in) his commitments at great cost when these cease to enjoy the support of good reasons. While Herdt's view is compatible with this point, it is central to my view that commitments or convictions must enjoy the support of good reasons. One might maintain one's commitments at great cost without this act being expressive of integrity.

70. See Scherkoske 2010, 2013: chapter 3 for further argument.

71. As Nancy Snow rightly pointed out to me, this will often involve the virtue of being open minded.

72. And to gesture at the arguments of Scherkoske 2013: chapter 5, integrity also matters because others hold us responsible and accountable for the judgments we make and the lives we lead.

or values. What is more, on such an account, we are quite right to think that integrity's value is distinctive. While integrity is undoubtedly implicated in having a unified self, some particular identity or other, a commitment to some bottom line principles, being resolute, and having moral purpose, integrity is plainly not identical to these things and its value is distinct from that of these other things.[73]

As I have attempted to show, integrity is usefully seen as a complex epistemic virtue. If we understand integrity along the lines I have sketched, then we are committed to the claim that integrity is constitutively oriented toward truth. This makes the judgment-centered view of integrity I offer an outlier, precisely because it prompts us to doubt that integrity is a distinctively moral virtue.

What then of long-standing associations between integrity and moral virtue? Can a judgment-centered approach explain why people untainted by philosophy—or more precisely, innocent of the view defended here—believe that integrity is a moral virtue? On the approach recommended here, the connection between integrity and moral character and conduct is mediated through epistemic virtue.[74] For now, it may suffice to note, or merely assert, that

---

73. The distinctiveness of integrity on my view might be illustrated in response to an objection. One might object that the dispositions a, b, and c sound like a more or less complex set of intellectual virtues. If this is so, doesn't my proposal come to grief (over the lack of distinctiveness) for structurally similar reasons that Moral Purpose views do? I would resist this for at least two reasons. First, while it is undoubtedly open to the defender of a judgment-centered view of integrity to cash out a–c as intellectual virtues, for the very reason cited in the objection I think this temptation should be resisted. Second, understanding a–c in terms of epistemic responsibility, rather than epistemic virtue, affords a persuasive explanation of the distinctively social dimensions of integrity (as I argue in Scherkoske 2013: chapter 5), an account that is unified with the account of proper regard as well placed self-trust I offer (Scherkoske 2013: chapter 4). Thanks to Christian Miller and Ryan West for pressing me on this point.

74. For my part, I tend to think that moral character is shaped and sustained to a significant degree by practices of reflecting on, defending, revising, and acting on the basis of our convictions. I also tend to think, perhaps too optimistically, that these practices are—or at least, are when well functioning—reason-guided enterprises that are essentially responsive to considerations of truth and evidence. See Scherkoske 2013.

while integrity is, on this view, essentially oriented to truth, this orientation is nevertheless indispensable for our concern with right action and good conduct.

To conclude, I have sought to motivate an approach to integrity that secures not just our pre-theoretic intuitions that integrity matters and that it essentially involves a concern for truth and truthfulness. This judgment-centered approach, I argued, can also give a persuasive account of other data points that have featured in philosophical accounts of integrity—one that can lay some claim to doing better than rival views. For all of that—in philosophical reflection as in life—the judgment-centered view of integrity cannot give us everything we might have hoped for. On such a view, the link between integrity, good character, and right conduct is mediated by epistemic agency. Such an account can vindicate the common sense idea that there is an intimate link between having integrity and having good moral character, but it cannot vindicate the "second least controversial thing to say"—namely, that integrity is itself a moral virtue. Whether this is a price worth paying is left for the reader to decide.[75]

BIBLIOGRAPHY

Ashford, Elizabeth. "Utilitarianism, Integrity and Partiality." *Journal of Philosophy* 92 (2000): 421–439.
Bigelow, John, and Pargetter, Robert. "Integrity and Autonomy." *American Philosophical Quarterly* 44 (2007): 29–49.

75. I am grateful to the audience and fellow contributors at the Institute for the Study of Human Flourishing's "Integrity, Honesty, and Truth Seeking" conference at the University of Oklahoma, September 2017. For comments and suggestions, I am especially grateful to Jennifer Herdt, Stephen Galoob, Stuart Green, Nancy Snow, and Aiden Hayes. Special thanks to Ryan West and Christian Miller for the invitation to the conference and for their saintly patience and generous feedback. And (finally) thanks to the Institute for organizing this conference.

Blustein, Jeffery. *Care and Commitment: Taking the Personal Point of View*. Oxford: Oxford University Press, 1991.

Calhoun, Cheshire. "Standing for Something." *Journal of Philosophy* 92 (1995): 235–260.

Coaching Association of Canada Code of Conduct. At https://www.coach.ca/files/CAC_Code_of_Conduct_EN.pdf. Accessed November 16, 2018.

Cottingham, John. "Integrity and Fragmentation." *Journal of Applied Philosophy* 27 (2010): 2–14.

Cox, Damian, Marguerite La Caze, and Michael Lavine. *Integrity and the Fragile Self*. Aldershot, UK: Ashgate, 2003.

Cox, Damian, Marguerite La Caze, and Michael Lavine. "Integrity." In *Stanford Encyclopedia of Philosophy*. Edited by Edward N. Zalta. Stanford, CA: Stanford University Press, 2017. http://plato.stanford.edu/entries/integrity/. Accessed December 22, 2017.

Dworkin, Ronald. *Law's Empire*. Cambridge, MA: Harvard University Press, 1986.

Frankfurt, Harry. "Freedom of the Will and the Concept of a Person." In *The Importance of What We Care About*, 11–25. New York: Cambridge University Press, 1987.

Graham, Jody. "Does Integrity Require Moral Goodness?" *Ratio* 14 (2001): 234–251.

Halfon, Mark. *Integrity: A Philosophical Inquiry*. Philadelphia: Temple University Press, 1989.

Holton, Richard. "Intention and Weakness of Will." *Journal of Philosophy* 96 (1999): 241–262.

Johnson, W. Brad. *On Being a Mentor: A Guide for Higher Education Faculty*. New York: Psychology Press, 2015.

Kagan, Shelly. *The Limits of Morality*. New York: Oxford University Press, 1988.

Levinson, W., Ginsburg, S., Hafferty, F., and Lucy, C., eds. *Understanding Medical Professionalism*. New York: McGraw-Hill, 2014.

McFall, Lynne. "Integrity." *Ethics* 98 (1987): 5–20.

McLeod, Carolyn. "Integrity and Self-Protection." *Journal of Social Philosophy* 35 (2004): 216–232.

McLeod, Carolyn. "How to Distinguish Autonomy from Integrity." *Canadian Journal of Philosophy* 35 (2005): 107–134.

Mendus, Susan. *Impartiality in Moral and Political Philosophy*. New York: Oxford University Press, 2009.

Miller, Christian. "Integrity." In *International Encyclopedia of Ethics*, edited by Hugh LaFolette, 2640–2650. New York: Blackwell, 2013.

Rorty, Amelie Oksenberg. "Where Does the Akratic Break Take Place?" *Australasian Journal of Philosophy* 58: 4 (1980): 333–346.

Schauber, Nancy. "Integrity, Commitment and the Concept of a Person." *American Philosophical Quarterly* 33 (1996): 119–129.

Scherkoske, Greg. "Integrity and Moral Danger." *Canadian Journal of Philosophy* 40 (2010): 335–358.

Scherkoske, Greg. "Could Integrity be an Epistemic Virtue?" *International Journal of Philosophical Studies* 20 (2012): 185–215.

Scherkoske, Greg. *Leading a Convincing Life: Integrity and the Virtues of Reason.* New York: Cambridge University Press, 2013.

Taylor, Gabriele. "Integrity." In *Proceedings of the Aristotelian Society* 55 (1981): S143–S159.

Taylor, Gabriele. *Pride, Shame and Guilt: Emotions of Self-Assessment.* New York: Oxford University Press, 1985.

Tessman, Lisa. *Moral Failure: On the Impossible Demands of Morality.* New York: Oxford University Press, 2015.

Tracy, Brian. "The Importance of Honesty and Integrity in Business." *Entrepreneur* (December 2016): 12–13

Walker, Margaret Urban. "Moral Luck and the Virtues of Impure Agency." In *Moral Contexts*, 21–34. New York: Rowman and Littlefield, 2003.

Watson, Gary. "Free Agency." *Journal of Philosophy* 72 (1975): 205–220.

Watson, Gary. "Free Action and Free Will." *Mind* 96 (1987): 145–172.

Williams, Bernard. "Integrity." In *Utilitarianism: For and Against*, edited by J. J. C. Smart and Bernard Williams, 93–118. Cambridge, UK: Cambridge University Press, 1973.

Williams, Bernard. "Persons, Character and Morality." In *Moral Luck: Philosophical Papers 1973–1980*, 1–19. New York: Cambridge University Press, 1981a.

Williams, Bernard. "Utilitarianism and Moral Self-Indulgence." In *Moral Luck: Philosophical Papers 1973–1980*, 40–53. New York: Cambridge University Press, 1981b.

Williams, Bernard. "Replies." In *World, Mind, Ethics: Essays on the Ethical Philosophy of Bernard Williams*, edited by J. E. J. Altham and Ross Harrison, 185–224. Cambridge, UK: Cambridge University Press, 1995.

Chapter 2

The Legal Enforcement of Integrity

STUART P. GREEN

Talk of "integrity" is ubiquitous in law and legal discourse. For example, (1) protecting the integrity of our political system has been cited as a basis for anti-corruption laws; (2) preserving the integrity of the legal profession appears as a principle underlying the rules of lawyer ethics; (3) ensuring integrity in policing and in the wider criminal justice system is given as a justification for excluding evidence obtained in violation of the Constitution; and (4) protecting bodily integrity has been offered as a potential goal for the law of rape and sexual assault. This list is not meant to be comprehensive. There are certainly other ways in which the concept of integrity has been invoked in the law.[1] But these four examples are offered as a sampling of the wide range of legal contexts in which integrity plays a key role, and the wide range of meanings attributed to it.[2]

These examples also provide real-world contexts in which to consider several conceptual puzzles that the concept of integrity raises.

---

1. To cite just one example, see Kramer 2014 (discussing integrity in the context of torture).
2. The fact that three of the four examples come from the criminal law mainly reflects my own expertise as a scholar; it is not meant to imply that integrity talk is any more common in criminal law than in other areas of the law.

Stuart P. Green, *The Legal Enforcement of Integrity* In: *Integrity, Honesty, and Truth Seeking.* Edited by: Christian B. Miller and Ryan West. Oxford University Press (2020). © Oxford University Press. DOI:10.1093/oso/9780190920487.003.0002

For example, integrity has frequently been described as a practice of "holding steadfastly true to [one's] commitments."[3] But what if those commitments are themselves immoral? In the philosophical literature, the issue has traditionally been discussed in the context of hypothetical cases positing Nazi officials acting in accordance with their beliefs, but it also arises in everyday circumstances involving practicing lawyers and government officials. Another puzzle arises in ethical theory: would living a life of integrity, understood as a virtue, lead to actions that conflict with those required by consequentialist or deontological principles? This question has particular significance in the context of the Supreme Court's exclusionary rule, which applies with respect to illegally obtained evidence in criminal trials. A final puzzle concerns the practical difference between integrity and partially overlapping ethical values such as honesty, loyalty, and autonomy. This issue arises, among other places, in the literature surrounding the law of rape and sexual assault. In each case, it will be worth asking what the concept of integrity adds to our understanding of these legal rules, and whether thinking about these various rules and doctrines in terms of integrity rather than other moral concepts is likely to lead to any practical difference in outcome.

As we shall see, integrity often serves in the law as an attractive label for an aspirational goal, a positive quality that individuals and institutions ought to promote. The concept applies broadly, but often vaguely and inconsistently, to a wide range of contexts. Indeed, its versatility and adaptability are both its strength and its weakness.[4] In this chapter, I hope to make some progress toward a more theoretically sound understanding of the role that integrity plays in the law and more generally in our moral lives.

---

3. See, e.g., Cox, La Caze, and Levine 2017, as well as the introduction to this volume and the chapters by Scherkoske and Herdt.
4. On the versatility of integrity as a moral concept, see Audi and Murphy 2006: 5.

We begin, in section 1, by considering three overlapping senses of integrity, which I refer to as "steadfastness," "clean hands," and "intactness." In section 2, we consider four contexts in which "integrity talk" appears in law and legal discourse: (1) protecting the integrity of the political system as a rationale for criminalizing corruption; (2) protecting the integrity of the legal profession as a rationale for the lawyer disciplinary system; (3) preserving the integrity of the criminal justice system as a rationale for the rule that excludes evidence that has been obtained in violation of the Constitution; and (4) protecting the sexual or bodily integrity of potential victims as a rationale for the law of rape and sexual assault.

1. THREE SENSES OF INTEGRITY

As an initial matter, we can identify three separate conceptions of integrity that occur in both legal and extra-legal contexts. I shall refer to them as (1) "steadfastness," (2) "clean hands," and (3) "intactness."[5] These conceptions are not meant to be mutually exclusive; there is a good deal of overlap among them. Nor are they meant to exhaust the concept of integrity; there are undoubtedly other senses that could be developed.[6]

The notion of holding "steadfastly to one's commitments" entails both a deliberative and an active component. It is deliberative in the sense that it requires some degree of reflectiveness. A person with this sort of integrity "adopts values [not] only because her group does," but because she has thought them through, has consciously adopted them as her own, and is able to articulate the reasoning that

---

5. In doing so, I draw mainly on Calhoun 1995, Cox, La Caze, and Levine 2017, McFall 1987, and Taylor 1981.
6. See, e.g., Miller 2013, as well as the different accounts discussed in the introduction to this volume and in the chapters by Scherkoske and Herdt.

lies behind such commitments.[7] Integrity in this sense also requires consistency in practice. The actor with integrity acts in accordance with her values over the course of time; she commits herself to some course of action both now and in the future. Integrity-as-steadfastness can be thought of as a matter of "standing up for one's values,"[8] of being "dedicate[ed] to the pursuit of a moral life."[9] Although we often use the "steadfastness" sense of integrity to describe the character or actions of individuals, it can also apply in connection with institutions or processes. For example, we can say that a court, legislative body, corporation, nonprofit organization, or athletic competition has or lacks integrity in this sense of the term.

A second conception of integrity involves the notion of "clean hands," the idea that the moral actor should not be complicit in the wrongful conduct of others. Here again integrity seems to involve a matter of character. The person with integrity is one who does not "sell himself out." He does not, as Cheshire Calhoun puts it, "trade action on [his] own views too cheaply for gain, status, reward, approval, or for escape from penalties, loss of status, [or] disapproval."[10] Integrity, functioning as a form of virtue, can be distinguished from consequentialist-based approaches to morality. Consequentialists often argue that persons are permitted, and even required, to engage in harmful or wrongful acts when doing so would avoid a greater harm or wrong or other negative consequence from occurring.[11] "To have integrity," by contrast, "is to view some actions as morally disagreeable apart from their consequences and to reflect that view in

---

7. Taylor 1981: 116. Cf. Galoob and Hill 2015: 619 (making a similar point about norm following).
8. Cox, La Caze, and Levine 2017: 3
9. Ibid., 4.
10. Calhoun 1995: 250.
11. For an influential discussion of the differences between virtue ethics and utilitarianism, see Williams 1973: 108–118.

one's actions and sentiments."[12] Again, this type of integrity applies most obviously to individuals and their character, but it can also be used to describe the character of institutions and other entities.

A final sense of integrity involves what we can call "intactness." This is the kind of integrity that shares an etymology with other unity words such as *integer, integral*, and *integrate*, all deriving from the Latin *integrare*, "to make whole."[13] Although one can talk about integrity in this sense in connection with a person's character, it seems even more apt as a way of describing a quality we attribute to physical objects, human bodies, works of art, institutions, procedures, and processes of various sorts. As such, it is not limited to matters of morality but embraces the aesthetic as well. For example, one might believe that the process of strip-mining mars the integrity of a physical environment, that the use of microphones spoils the integrity of a musical or operatic performance, or that the application of tattoos mars the integrity of a human body. One might also say that the admission of tainted evidence undermines the integrity of the criminal justice system.

Although there is certainly overlap among the three senses of integrity, they should be understood as conceptually distinct. Consider, for example, a person who refuses to be complicit in the wrongdoing of others even though it is costly for him to do so. Such a person might be said to have integrity in the sense of clean hands even if he was not reliably steadfast in his commitments. Similarly, a person who was consistently steadfast in his commitments could be said to have integrity even if he was rarely in a position to consciously avoid being complicit in others' wrongdoing (imagine that he lived by himself on a mountaintop practicing simplicity and solitude). Moreover, various entities and processes might be said to have

12. Calhoun 1995: 247.
13. See Luban 2003: 280.

integrity in the (aesthetic) sense of intactness apart from any (moral) considerations of clean hands or steadfastness.

2. INTEGRITY IN THE LAW

Having looked in the previous section at various senses of "integrity," we now consider four contexts in which "integrity talk" appears in the law or legal discourse: (1) in the law of corruption, (2) in legal ethics, (3) as a rationale for the exclusionary rule of criminal procedure, and (4) in the discourse surrounding the law of rape and sexual assault. Part of our task will be to consider the extent to which these various meanings of integrity play out or fail to play out in these four contexts.

2.1 Protecting the Integrity of the Political System as a Rationale for Criminalizing Corruption

Anti-corruption laws, such as those that prohibit bribery, have often been described as intended to protect the integrity of some aspect of our governmental system. For example, the offense of Federal Program Bribery (Section 666 of U.S. Code, title 18) prohibiting theft and bribery related to programs receiving federal funds, was, according to its legislative history, expressly designed by Congress to "protect the integrity of the vast sums of money distributed through Federal programs."[14] Similarly, the Criminal Division of the U.S. Department of Justice has a "Department of Public Integrity," whose job it is to investigate allegations of criminal misconduct on the part of federal judges, supervise the nationwide investigation and prosecution of election crimes, and bring other selected cases against

---

14. U. S. Senate Report 1983–1984: 369–370; see also *Salinas v. United States* 1997.

federal, state, and local officials.[15] And the Center for Public Integrity describes itself as a nonprofit investigative news organization whose mission is to "serve democracy by revealing abuses of power, corruption and betrayal of public trust by powerful public and private institutions, using the tools of investigative journalism."[16]

How exactly is the concept of integrity being used in this anticorruption context? Part of the problem is that there is little discussion in the sources themselves. Nevertheless, a number of observations can be made. The first is that offenses like Federal Program Bribery seem to have more to do with ensuring the integrity of institutions and processes than that of individuals. Such laws focus on the integrity of the appropriations process, the administration of federal programs, the courts, election process, and other "public and private institutions." Of course, all of these entities are ultimately managed and administered by individuals, but whatever integrity such individuals are supposed to have is once removed from the integrity of the entities themselves.

Related is the fact that statutes like Section 666 do not make it a crime to "fail to have integrity" as such, or even to "fail to protect the integrity of the political process." Rather, protecting the integrity of the political process is offered as an underlying rationale for criminalizing specific kinds of corrupt acts, such as accepting or giving a bribe or misusing government funds. Thus, to say that Section 666 is intended to "protect the integrity of the political process" is analogous to saying that the point of homicide laws is to "protect the sanctity of life," or that theft laws are intended to "protect the security of property ownership."

Integrity is usually thought of as a positive virtue or character trait that ought to be encouraged in individuals and institutions, rather

---

15. U.S. Department of Justice.
16. Center for Public Integrity.

than a quality that should be enforced by the coercive means of the law, especially the criminal law.[17] Like virtues such as courage, temperance, and prudence, integrity has to do with perfecting the individual, rather than, say, preventing harm to others. Any attempt to legally "enforce" integrity would likely be self-defeating.[18] Like these other virtues, integrity is achieved by the actor through the development of character and motivated by internal, rather than external, reasons.

Perhaps, then, individuals or institutions are to be punished for *not* having integrity. But that does not seem quite right either. Consider a politician who engaged in one or more "everyday" acts of dishonesty, pandering, deception, promise breaking, or hypocrisy. We would no doubt say that such an official lacked integrity and therefore deserved condemnation. But in all likelihood, he would not be subject to prosecution, except in relatively rare cases in which it could be shown that he had committed bribery or theft. Given its stated goal of integrity preservation, existing anti-corruption law therefore seems grossly underinclusive—that is, they fail to cover cases that ought to be covered.

So how does this understanding of integrity relate to the three models described in Part 1? Whether we subscribe to the model of "steadfastness," "clean hands," or "intactness," under-inclusiveness remains a problem. There is little in anti-corruption law that requires an official to deliberate over what principles she subscribes to or be consistent in applying them in practice (i.e., to be steadfast in her commitments). There are also many circumstances in which an official could trade action for cheap gains in status or popularity or be complicit in others' mendacity (i.e., have unclean hands) without violating the law. And though a political system in which officials are

17. See generally Green 2013.
18. Cf. Brien 2013: 73.

taking bribes and stealing money surely would not be "intact," neither would a system in which officials break promises, pander, or act hypocritically—all acts that are not typically illegal.

In the end, I believe that the concept of integrity that appears in anti-corruption law is one that does not directly correspond to any of the three senses of integrity identified previously. Rather, when Congress, the Department of Justice, and others talk about protecting "integrity" in government, they are using that as a shorthand for preventing "corruption" in the narrow sense of abusing the public trust in the interest of private gain.[19] If I am right, this helps explain why we prosecute public officials for taking bribes and stealing, but not for pandering, breaking promises, or hypocrisy.

2.2 Failing to Protect the Integrity of the Legal Profession

Like the anti-corruption laws that apply to government officials, the ethical rules that apply to members of the bar have also been framed in terms of integrity. For example, the American Bar Association's Model Rules of Professional Conduct state that lawyers have "special duties . . . as officers of the court to avoid conduct that undermines the integrity of the adjudicative process."[20] Unlike anti-corruption law, however, in which integrity preservation functions solely as a background rationale for narrower prohibitions on bribery and theft, in the lawyer ethics context, the actor is directly required to help preserve the integrity of the profession. On the other hand, while anti-corruption law subjects offenders to potential criminal sanctions, attorney ethics rules subject offenders, at most, to disciplinary action, such as suspension or disbarment.

19. Cf. Miller 2018.
20. American Bar Association 2013: Rule 3.3.

There are essentially two ways in which integrity is understood in the context of lawyer ethics, which we can refer to as the "traditional" and "reformist" approaches. Under the traditional, or minimalist, approach (which has been endorsed by the American Bar Association in its Model Rules), the lawyer's role is taken to be one of "zealous advocacy." Her function is to be a "neutral advocate," or, more pejoratively, a "hired gun." As such, she does "whatever is possible, within the bounds of the law, to serve her client's interests regardless of what the lawyer herself thinks of the client's ends."[21] Under this approach, it does not matter who the lawyer's clients are or what they stand for. Thus, as Sharon Dolovich puts it, it is of no consequence that

> in the course of zealously representing their clients, lawyers may be called upon to act in ways that considerably compromise the health, safety, or financial well-being of innocent third parties, harm the environment, undermine public institutions including our regulatory system, and/or weaken public trust in the fairness [of the legal system].[22]

The lawyer's only ethical obligation, *qua* lawyer, is to abide by specific ethical rules. For example, she must: affirmatively "correct a false statement of material fact or law previously made to the tribunal by the lawyer"; avoid representing two or more clients whose interests conflict; report to the Bar ethical violations by others; and avoid commingling client funds and property.[23]

Standing in contrast to this traditional view of lawyer ethics is what we might think of as a "reformist" view, espoused mainly by academic commentators. This, more "contextual" approach reflects a

21. Dolovich 2002: 1629
22. Ibid., 1637.
23. American Bar Association 2013: Rules 3.3, 1.7, 8.3, 1.15, respectively.

"thicker," or more "robust," understanding of integrity. Here, lawyers must "reflect critically on the question of what justice requires."[24] It is not enough simply to comply with rules about, say, lying to the court or destroying documents; they must also take account of the larger interests at stake and consider the consequences of their actions, both legal and moral. Only a lawyer who acts in such a manner can, under this view, be said to have acted with integrity (though, as far as I can tell, even the academic reformers view this sort of integrity as an aspirational goal; they do not recommend that lawyers who fail to subscribe to it should be subject to disciplinary action).

How does the debate between the traditionalists and reformers relate to the modes of integrity described previously? I think an argument could be made that the reformist understanding of integrity is similar to that of integrity-as-steadfastness. A person with this sort of integrity is deliberative in the sense of thinking critically about what values she will subscribe to and acting in accordance with those values. She does not merely follow the minimalist rules prescribed, say, by the Bar Association. Rather, she has thought through what it means to be an ethical lawyer, what the consequences of her actions might be, and is consistent in her application of her principles. A person who has integrity in the traditional sense of lawyer ethics is arguably practicing in the less robust sense of integrity-as-clean-hands. Not only must she avoid being complicit in the wrongful acts of others, she must also affirmatively report others' unethical behavior to the Bar.

The debate between the traditionalists and the reformers with respect to lawyer ethics also parallels an important debate that appears in the philosophical literature on integrity. The question has been asked whether a Nazi or agent of ISIS or Boko Haram—someone who is bent on genocide or the killing of innocent people—can be

---

24. Dolovich 2002: 1639.

said to have integrity.[25] Such persons often do act with the singularity of purpose and commitment to principles that are said to characterize integrity. The problem, of course, is that the purposes and principles to which they commit themselves are perverse and immoral.

Philosophers are divided over whether an individual acting in accordance with his commitment to immoral ends can be said to have integrity. For example, Mark Halfon has found "no a priori restrictions concerning the object or content of the commitments of those who have integrity."[26] Gabrielle Taylor has similarly argued that there is no clear incompatibility between integrity and some forms of immorality.[27] Thus, under their view, even a devoted Nazi or member of ISIS could possess integrity.

Others take a contrary view. Dolovich, for example, distinguishes between persons with integrity and those she calls "fanatics." Both kinds of person "act according to strongly held commitments and values despite the risk of social opprobrium or other personal costs."[28] But, she, says, persons of integrity choose their path only after due reflection and are willing to expose their views to criticism and reassess and revise their principles in light of arguments and evidence. A fanatic, by contrast, "cleaves to her principles no matter what. No evidence, no argument, however powerfully it may refute the central tenets of her belief, will dissuade the fanatic from her commitments or lead her to rethink them."[29]

While Dolovich has undoubtedly captured something interesting about the psychology of fanaticism, I do not think her analytical move solves the problem posed. Her definition of "fanatic" is both too broad and too narrow. Not all terrorists are fanatics as she defines

25. See, e.g., Halfon 1989: 134–136.
26. Ibid., 136.
27. Taylor 1981: 152.
28. Dolovich 2002: 1650
29. Ibid.

the term: Some do choose their path after due reflection, and others rethink their views and choose to withdraw from terrorist activities. Moreover, there may well be virtuous non-fanatics with integrity who are past the point in their lives at which any arguments or evidence could dissuade them from their beliefs.

Unfortunately, Halfon and Taylor's approach also leads to an arguably unsatisfactory solution. To view integrity as nothing more than a purely procedural virtue, a mere vessel for even the most pernicious views, is to reduce it to a strictly formalistic, essentially amoral concept.

One possible way out of this dilemma is to acknowledge a basic ambiguity in how we use the term "integrity." We can speak of integrity in either a "procedural" or "substantive" sense.[30] A person who acts in accordance with his principles can be said to have integrity in the procedural sense, no matter how immoral or perverse such principles may be. For him, integrity is merely a character "trait." Under this view, integrity is said to function as something of a "place-holder," concerned less with achieving right outcomes or right decisions than with the "way in which we relate to, think about, schedule, prioritise, and act on and through our other (substantive) values, whatever they happen to be."[31] Only a person who acts in accordance with principles that are themselves moral can be said to have integrity in the substantive sense. For him, integrity is a true "virtue."[32]

So how would this distinction work in the case of Nazis and terrorists, on the one hand, and lawyers and government officials, on the other? I think we should say that, while Nazis and terrorists can have integrity in the procedural sense, they cannot have it in the substantive sense. Admittedly, the concept of terrorism can be contested; one

30. Cf. Miller 2013.
31. A point made by Roberts, Hunter, Young, and Dixon 2016: 11.
32. I have previously offered an analogous argument with respect to loyalty. See Green 2006: 100.

person's extremist can be another's "freedom fighter." But, regardless of the legitimacy or illegitimacy of the terrorist's ultimate goals, it is hard to see how certain of his methods—including the intentional killing of innocent civilians—can ever be justified.

The lawyer and government official differ from the terrorist in this respect. To take what is perhaps the most obvious case, criminal defense lawyers are often called upon to represent clients who have committed very bad acts and who may continue to do so if not incarcerated. Yet our system of law requires that criminal defendants receive effective assistance of counsel, and defense lawyers play an indispensable role in seeing that the state does not imprison its citizens without due process. Moreover, the right to counsel is not merely a requirement of positive constitutional law; it is a right that reflects deep principles of substantive justice—the idea that no person should have to face the power of the state alone; that conviction is proper only if reached in accordance with procedural rules; and that, without a lawyer, it is unlikely that the accused will be able to enjoy the benefits of the other rights to which she is entitled.[33] It thus seems possible that a lawyer could zealously represent a bad person bent on doing bad things while still maintaining her integrity in the substantive sense.

This is not to say, of course, that a lawyer would be acting with integrity if she defended a murderer solely because she would make a lot of money for doing so; or, worse, because she wanted the murderer to be acquitted and go on to commit more murders. Nor is it to suggest that a lawyer who refused to represent a particular client because she was disgusted by his views would thereby lack integrity. To act with integrity, at least in the substantive sense of the term, the lawyer would have to defend her client out of a desire to do what justice requires.

33. For a classic statement, see Kamisar 1962: 7.

A similar dynamic plays out in the case of government officials who adhere to their principles even though doing so causes, or fails to alleviate, harm to others. Consider, for example, a legislator who must decide whether to vote for a law like the Affordable Care Act, including its individual mandate requirement.[34] Without that mandate, the ACA could not function properly, and, absent a meaningful alternative, many citizens would lose health-care coverage. Let us assume, however, that a plausible argument could be made that the mandate requirement exceeded Congress' power under the Constitution's Commerce Clause.[35] A legislator (or judge) who was committed— thoughtfully, sincerely, and consistently—to what she regarded as a "strict" reading of that constitutional provision could decide to vote against the legislation on principled grounds, even while regretting the fact that millions of people would be denied coverage as a result. Like a criminal defense lawyer who defended a dangerous person, such a legislator could nevertheless be said to have acted with integrity. Unlike killing innocent citizens, voting against legislation that one honestly believes violates the Constitution is not an immoral means to an end. Even though millions of people would lose coverage as a result of the legislator's decision, she could still maintain her integrity with respect to her commitment to the Constitution.

Finally, it should be noted that integrity is not unique in having a procedural or "due process" character of this sort. Virtues such as loyalty and courage can also be put to morally inconsistent uses. If it is possible for two individuals to pursue their divergent agendas, yet both with integrity, it is also possible for them to pursue their contradictory agendas with loyalty and courage. By contrast, it may be that purely "substantive" virtues such as kindness, honesty, temperance, and prudence, can only be put to consistently good ends.

34. Patient Protection and Affordable Care Act 2010.
35. For what arguably constitutes such an argument, see the opinion of Chief Justice Roberts in *National Federation of Independent Business v. Sebelius* 2012.

2.3 Preserving the Integrity of the Criminal Justice System Through Exclusion of Evidence

So far, we have considered two contexts in which the desire to preserve integrity (in government or the legal profession, as the case may be) serves as a justification for imposing sanctions on nonconforming subjects: criminal punishment, in the case of bribery; and disciplinary action, in the case of professional ethics violations. In both cases, there was little dispute about whether the promotion of integrity was an appropriate goal; the only debate, if there was one, was about exactly what it meant to act with integrity in a given case. We now turn to a context in which the pursuit of integrity itself is controversial—criminal procedure's exclusionary rule.[36]

A bit of background concerning the workings of criminal procedure will be helpful here. Under the Fourth, Fifth, and Sixth Amendments to the Constitution, respectively, the government is prohibited from obtaining evidence by means of illegal searches and seizures, through illegal interrogations, or when a defendant's right to counsel has been denied. While the Constitution clearly prohibits such conduct, however, it is less explicit about what the remedy should be when it is engaged in.

In the landmark 1961 case of *Mapp v. Ohio*, the Supreme Court held for the first time that when state or local police officers obtain evidence by means that violate an individual's right against illegal search or seizure (or, by extension, other constitutional rights), the proper remedy is to exclude such evidence from trial.[37] Two rationales were offered in support of such a rule. One was deterrence. The other was what the Court called the "imperative of judicial integrity."[38]

---

36. This, it should be noted, is just one of numerous aspects of criminal procedure in which integrity is said to play a role. See, e.g., Ashworth 2003, Duff, Farmer, Marshall, and Tadros 2007: 225–257, Roberts, Hunter, Young, and Dixon 2016.
37. Mapp 1961.
38. Ibid., 659.

The meaning of deterrence is fairly clear. By barring from use in court evidence obtained in violation of a citizen's constitutional rights, the Court reasoned, the police will be deterred from obtaining evidence in ways that violate such rights.[39] The meaning of judicial integrity, however, requires more explanation. In *Mapp* itself, the Court famously explained:

> The criminal goes free, if he must, but it is the law that sets him free. Nothing can destroy a government more quickly than its failure to observe its own laws, or worse, its disregard of the charter of its own existence. As Mr. Justice Brandeis, dissenting, said in *Olmstead v. United States*, 277 U.S. 438, 485 (1928): "Our Government is the potent, the omnipresent teacher. For good or for ill, it teaches the whole people by its example. . . . If the Government becomes a lawbreaker, it breeds contempt for law; it invites every man to become a law unto himself; it invites anarchy."[40]

The sense of integrity the Court is invoking here seems to combine elements of all three senses of integrity described previously. It embodies "clean hands" in the sense that individual judges should refrain from being complicit in the wrongdoing of the police and prosecutors.[41] It reflects "steadfastness" in the sense that judges and the court system more broadly should adhere to the principles embodied in the Fourth, Fifth, and Sixth Amendments. And it represents "intactness" in the sense that the criminal justice system—from investigation through arrest, prosecution, trial, and conviction—is viewed as an integrated manifestation of government power.

39. Ibid., 656.
40. Ibid., 659.
41. Cf. Bloom and Fentin 2010: 75 (making a similar point).

State courts, interpreting their own version of the exclusionary rule under their state constitutions, have also offered insight into the role that integrity should play. For example, the Hawaii Supreme Court explained that "[t]he 'judicial integrity' purpose of the exclusionary rule is essentially that the courts should not place their imprimatur on evidence that was illegally obtained by allowing it to be admitted into evidence in a criminal prosecution."[42] Similarly, the Canadian Supreme Court opined that (1) the Canadian Charter of Rights and Freedoms gives courts discretion to exclude evidence obtained in violation of a Charter right if "admission . . . would bring the administration of justice into disrepute," and (2) the phrase "bring the administration of justice into disrepute" should in turn be "understood in the long-term sense of maintaining the integrity of, and public confidence in, the justice system."[43]

This sense of integrity is different from the "procedural" sense of integrity previously discussed. There is no conceptual puzzle here about Nazis or terrorists holding steadfastly to their (immoral) commitments. Even the conservative, "law and order" justices, who are generally opposed to the exclusionary rule, do not maintain that it's a *good* thing for the police to violate citizens' rights. Rather, they seem to believe that "holding steadfastly" to the requirements of the Fourth, Fifth, and Sixth Amendments, itself, in this context, is

---

42. *State v. Bridges* 1996: 366.

43. *R. v. Grant* 2009 (interpreting Canadian Charter of Rights and Freedoms, Part I of Constitution Act, 1982, being Schedule B to the Canada Act, 1982 c. 11, § 24(2) (UK)). According to the Court, the rule is aimed not at "punishing the police or providing compensation to the accused." Rather, it is focused on "systemic concerns." It "seeks to ensure that evidence obtained through [illegal means] does not do further damage to the repute of the justice system." Ibid. Elsewhere, the Court has characterized the "integrity of . . . judges" in terms of "their fidelity to their oaths of office." *United States v. Grayson* 1978: 54. In yet another case, Justice Marshall, in dissent, wrote that "[p]reservation of judicial integrity demands that unlawful intrusions on privacy should 'find no sanction in the judgments of the courts.'" *United States v. Casere* 1979: 770 (Marshall, J., dissenting). See also *Schneckloth v. Bustamonte* 1973: 242 (equating "the fairness of the trial" with the "integrity of the fact-finding process").

simply too costly: it will lead to the exclusion of otherwise proba-
tive evidence.

Imagine, for example, that the police stop a motorist on the
road, search his car, and find a kilo of heroin. If the stop and search
were done without the reasonable suspicion or probable cause
that the Fourth Amendment requires, the "remedy" would be to
exclude the evidence from trial. The consequence is that the prosecution will be denied use of what could be its strongest evidence;
its case may be so impaired that it will have to drop the charges
altogether; a factually guilty person will go free, perhaps to commit
other crimes; public safety will be threatened; retributive justice
will have been denied.

The debate over the rationale for the exclusionary rule can thus
be interpreted in light of a classic conflict between virtue ethics, on
the one hand, and consequentialism, on the other.[44] For the conservative justices, who view criminal procedure through the latter lens,
the costs imposed by the exclusionary rule are generally too high.
The liberal justices, by contrast, seek to preserve (the virtue of) judicial integrity and act in accordance with the duty to protect citizens'
rights, despite the costs. For the conservatives, judicial integrity is
not entirely irrelevant, but neither is it particularly important (at least
in this particular context). As Chief Justice Rehnquist put it, strik-
ingly, in his dissent in *California v. Minjares* (arguing for the virtual
abandonment of the exclusionary rule), "While it is quite true that
courts are not to be participants in 'dirty business,' neither are they to
be ethereal vestal virgins of another world."[45]

In practice, the conservative justices' rejection of the integrity
approach, in favor of one based almost exclusively on deterrence, has
been quite consequential. The case of *Herring v. United States* offers a

---

44. The duty to exclude tainted evidence could also be described in deontological terms.
45. *California v. Minjares* 1979 (Rehnquist, J., dissenting).

good illustration.[46] Herring was arrested on the basis of an outdated and recalled arrest warrant, apparently owing to an error by a clerk maintaining the police department's database. The arrest led to the discovery of a gun and contraband narcotics, which Herring sought to exclude from evidence on the grounds that they were the fruit of an unlawful search. In upholding the admission of the evidence, and rejecting the application of the exclusionary rule, a majority of the Court reasoned that "[t]o trigger the exclusionary rule, police conduct must be sufficiently deliberate that exclusion can meaningfully deter it, and sufficiently culpable that such deterrence is worth the price paid by the justice system."[47] The error in this case, the Court said, "[did] not rise to that level" of culpability. Such culpability would exist only if officers relied on "systemic" errors in "an unreliable warrant system."[48]

In her dissent, Justice Ginsburg challenged the majority's exclusive adherence to the consequentialist approach. She began by conceding that "a main objective of the rule 'is to deter—to compel respect for the constitutional guaranty in the only effectively available way—by removing the incentive to disregard it.'" But beyond that, she said,

> the rule also serves other important purposes: It "enable[es] the judiciary to avoid the taint of partnership in official lawlessness," and it "assur[es] the people—all potential victims of unlawful government conduct -- that the government would not profit from its lawless behavior, thus minimizing the risk of seriously undermining popular trust in government."[49]

46. *Herring v. United States* 2009.
47. Ibid., 144.
48. Ibid.
49. Ibid., 152 (Ginsburg, J., dissenting) (quoting *United States v. Calandra* 1974: 357).

Although Justice Ginsburg did not use the term "judicial integrity" to describe her rationale for the exclusionary rule, that is clearly what she had in mind, and especially the "clean hands" version.

There are also other circumstances in which the Court has chosen to apply an exclusively deterrence-based rationale for the exclusionary rule, rather than look to judicial integrity. For example, the Court has had to decide whether evidence illegally obtained should be excluded not only from the government's case in a criminal trial, but also from civil trials, deportation hearings, preliminary hearings, bail proceedings, and sentencing proceedings.[50] From an integrity-based perspective, it seems clear that the exclusionary rule should apply: admitting such evidence in any of these contexts would entail a judicial "imprimatur" on constitutional violations. But the consequentialist-based approach leads in a quite different direction. The Court has determined, whether accurately or not, that the deterrent value of excluding evidence in such "ancillary" proceedings is less than that of doing so in "core" criminal proceedings; and that, as a result, the exclusionary rule is not worth applying.[51]

The exclusionary rule thus offers a particularly rich context in which to examine the role integrity can play in informing legal doctrine. The concept of integrity we see here reflects all three of the models described previously—steadfastness, clean hands, and intactness—and characterizes both individuals and institutions. Adherence to the concept of integrity stands in sharp contrast to the competing consequentialist approach, leading to clear differences in legal doctrine.

50. See, e.g., *United States v. Janis* 1976 (tax proceedings); *I.N.S. v. Lopez-Mendoza* 1984 (deportation hearings); *Pennsylvania Bd. of Probation and Parole v. Scott* 1998 (parole revocation hearings); *Giordenello v. United States* 1958 (preliminary hearings); *United States v. McCrory* 1991 (sentencing proceedings).
51. See cases cited in previous footnote.

2.4 Violating Another's (Sexual) Integrity as a Means of Characterizing the Wrong in Rape and Sexual Assault

There is one final integrity-invoking context in law that I would like to consider briefly. Since the feminist revolution in rape law that occurred in Anglo-American jurisdictions beginning in the 1980s, rape has been widely conceptualized as a violation of what is referred to as a victim's right to sexual "autonomy," with that term loosely understood to refer to the capacity to make decisions about one's sexual conduct according to reasons and motives that are one's own, rather than being the product of coercive or deceitful external forces.[52]

But there is an alternative to sexual autonomy theory. Nicola Lacey and other feminist scholars have argued that we ought to reconceptualize rape and sexual assault as involving a violation of what they call bodily "integrity."[53] To understand what they have in mind, we need to take a step back and consider what underlies this claim.

Lacey believes that the contemporary criminal law of rape reflects an "impoverished conception of the value of sexuality."[54] Among other things, she says, it reflects the view that "a woman or man has a right in her or his body much like that in other property, and it is the right freely to dispose of this odd form of property which rape violates."[55] As a result, she says, contemporary rape law has little to do with "those things which contemporary social discourses of sexuality mark as its values and risks—things like "self-expression, connection, intimacy, [and] relationship" (its values) or "violation of trust, infliction of shame and humiliation, objectification and exploitation" (its risks).[56]

---

52. See Christman 2011.
53. Lacey 1998: 50; see also, e.g., Craig 2010.
54. Lacey 1998:50
55. Ibid., 53–54.
56. Ibid., 54.

By focusing on autonomy-infringement and non-consent as the basic wrongs underlying rape, Lacey says, the law privileges the mental over the corporeal, and in so doing "blocks the articulation of the inextricable integration of mental and corporeal experience."[57] To remedy this situation, and give appropriate weight to the corporeal, Lacey argues, we should frame the law of rape around the idea of "personal integrity" and the related idea of "embodied" or "relational" autonomy.[58] This approach, she says, "promises to escape the dangers both of essentialising a particular conception of the body and of propagating a vision of feminine empowerment which is premised, paradoxically, on a victim status which accords access to 'truth.'"[59]

Lacey offers three ways in which a law of rape framed around the concept of sexual integrity and relational autonomy would differ from one focused on what she calls "proprietary autonomy." With respect to the definition of rape, she says, "the most obvious change would be a move away from the emphasis on lack of consent understood in abstract and asymmetrical terms as the central determinant of sexual abuse."[60] This concept of consent would "assume a mutuality of relationship and responsibility between victim and defendant" that current law does not assume.[61] With respect to evidentiary and procedural rules, "the analysis of rape in terms of relational autonomy and integrity would necessitate . . . [allowing] victims more fully to express their own narrative in the court room setting, as well as ensuring that they are able to do so without having the rape trial turned into an at large examination of their sexual history."[62] And it would lead to a "rethinking of the symbolic role of the criminalisation of

---

57. Ibid., 59.
58. Ibid., 64. For a very different take on the difference between autonomy and integrity, see McLeod 2005.
59. Lacey 1998: 65.
60. Ibid.
61. Ibid.
62. Ibid., 66.

rape," including an "unambiguous commitment to the positive integrity as well as the full humanity of both rape victims and men accused of rape."[63]

So how does the idea of integrity invoked by Lacey compare to the conceptions of integrity discussed elsewhere in this chapter? Certainly, integrity in the sexual context *could* mean something like steadfastness—say, in the sense of a person who remains faithful to a spouse or significant other, especially in the face of temptation, or who lives in a manner that is consistent with a deeply held sense of his or her sexual identity, even in response to social disapproval and discrimination. It might also characterize a person who values his or her sexual self, such that he or she refrains from "sleeping around" with people he or she does not love or have true affection for, or from using sex merely as a means of achieving status or professional advancement.

But that is not the sense of integrity Lacey has in mind here. Rather, what she seems to be thinking of is closer to the notion of integrity-as-intactness. The unwanted penetration or other intimate contact that comprise rape and sexual assault are taken to violate the unity or wholeness of the victim's mind and body. Not only that, but they also undermine the unity we hope to achieve through "sustaining and respectful relationships," without which we "cannot realise our personhood."[64]

63. Ibid., 65.
64. Ibid., 64. Reference to integrity in this sense of intactness also arguably bears some resemblance to the notion of integrity that has been invoked in the law of evidence, with respect to the collection and preservation of physical evidence. In general, police and prosecutors are required to maintain a clear chain of custody. They must account for how evidence was gathered at the scene of a crime and how it was treated after collection. See, e.g., Murphy 2014: 633. It must be properly preserved, labeled and stored, kept free of contaminants, and maintained at an appropriate temperature. It must be interpreted and evaluated in accordance with standard practices. When investigators and law enforcement officials fail to maintain evidence in such a manner, it is no longer intact. In such cases, we might say that its integrity has been compromised.

3. CONCLUSION

By focusing on the various roles that the concept of integrity plays in the law, I have sought to shed light on both the workings of several significant legal doctrines and the concept of integrity itself.

In the realm of anti-corruption law, upholding the integrity of our political system is understood quite narrowly—essentially, as an obligation of public officials not to accept bribes or steal public funds. This body of law says nothing about an official's obligation to use his office for the good of society, or to tell the truth, keep promises, and not be hypocritical.

In the case of legal ethics, lawyers are potentially subject to sanctions for failing to behave in a manner that upholds the integrity of the profession. But, as we have seen, the definition of what constitutes integrity, on the traditional view, is also quite narrow—limited to specific rules about matters such as candor to the court, avoiding conflicts of interest, and the proper handling of client assets. Under current rules, and contrary to what some reformers would like to see, upholding the integrity of the legal profession does not mean that a lawyer has an obligation to use her professional skills to advance the larger good of society; it is a purely procedural virtue.

Integrity means something yet again with respect to judges' duty to enforce the rules of criminal procedure. In an earlier era, the rule that evidence obtained in violation of the Constitution should be excluded from use at trial was justified primarily as a means of preserving the integrity of the courts. That way of thinking about the exclusionary rule has fallen out of favor, with the advent of more politically conservative justices on the Court. Under current law, the exclusionary rule is typically justified, if at all, on the consequentialist grounds that it deters police wrongdoing.

Finally, among some feminist scholars, there has been a suggestion that, rather than thinking of rape and sexual assault as violations of (what the liberal views as) "personal" or "proprietary" autonomy, such offenses should instead be thought of as involving a violation of a broader sexual "integrity," or "relational autonomy." If this were embraced by courts and legislatures, they claim, it would result in a broader definition of rape, different kinds of evidence produced at trial, and ultimately a different "symbolic role" for the crime of rape.

Integrity talk thus runs the gamut in law and legal discourse, covering a wide range of conceptual models, types of actors, and normative aspirations. Often, such uses are unexplained and ungrounded in any particular theoretical construct. Given the central role integrity is said to play in various contexts, it is worth trying to discover its true meanings.[65]

BIBLIOGRAPHY

Ashworth, Andrew. "Exploring the Integrity Principle in Evidence and Procedure." In *Essays for Colin Tapper*, edited by Peter Mirfield and Roger Smith, 107–125. Oxford: Oxford University Press, 2003.

Audi, Robert, and Patrick E. Murphy. "The Many Faces of Integrity." *Business Ethics Quarterly* 16:1 (January 2006): 3–21.

Bloom, Robert M., and David H. Fentin. "'A More Majestic Conception': The Importance of Judicial Integrity in Preserving the Exclusionary Rule." *Journal of Constitutional Law* 13:1 (2010): 47–80.

Brien, Andrew. "Regulating Virtue: Formulating, Engendering and Enforcing Corporate Ethical Codes." In *Corruption and Anti-Corruption*, edited by Peter Larmour and Nick Wolanin, 62–81. Canberra: ANU Press, 2013.

Calhoun, Cheshire. "Standing for Something." *Journal of Philosophy* 92:5 (1995): 235–260.

Christman, John. "Autonomy in Moral and Political Philosophy." In *Stanford Encyclopedia of Philosophy*, edited by Edward N. Zalta. Stanford, CA: Stanford

---

65. An earlier version of this chapter was presented at the Conference on Integrity, Honesty, and Truth Seeking, at the University of Oklahoma Institute for the Study of Human Flourishing. I am grateful for the many helpful comments and questions I received. Special thanks to Stephen Galoob and John Leubsdorf for their helpful comments on an earlier draft, and to Christian Miller and Ryan West for their thorough and incisive editing.

University Press, 2011. Accessed October 2017, http://plato.stanford.edu/archives/spr2011/entries/autonomy-moral/

Cox, Damian, Marguerite La Caze, and Michael Levine. "Integrity." In *Stanford Encyclopedia of Philosophy*, edited by Edward N. Zalta. Stanford, CA: Stanford University Press, 2017. Accessed October 2017, https://plato.stanford.edu/entries/integrity/

Craig, Elaine. *Troubling Sex: Towards a Legal Theory of Sexual Integrity*. Vancouver: University of British Columbia Press, 2010.

Dolovich, Sharon. "Ethical Lawyering and the Possibility of Integrity." *Fordham Law Review* 70 (2002): 1629–1687.

Duff, Antony, Lindsay Farmer, Sandra Marshall, and Victor Tadros. *The Trial on Trial: Volume 3*. Oxford: Hart Publishing, 2007.

Galoob, Stephen R., and Adam Hill. "Norms, Attitudes and Compliance." *Tulsa Law Review* 50 (2015): 613–634.

Green, Stuart P. *Lying, Cheating, and Stealing: A Moral Theory of White Collar Crime*. Oxford: Oxford University Press, 2006.

Green, Stuart P. "Foreword: Symposium on Vice and the Criminal Law." *Criminal Law and Philosophy* 3 (2013): 3–9.

Halfon, Mark S. *Integrity: A Philosophical Inquiry*. Philadelphia: Temple University Press, 1989.

Kamisar, Yale. "The Right to Counsel and the Fourteenth Amendment." *University of Chicago Law Review* 30 (1962): 1–77.

Kramer, Matthew. *Torture and Moral Integrity: A Philosophical Inquiry*. Oxford: Oxford University Press, 2014.

Lacey, Nicola. "Unspeakable Subjects, Impossible Rights: Sexuality, Integrity and Criminal Law." *Canadian Journal of Law and Jurisprudence* 11 (1998): 47–68.

Luban, David. "Integrity: Its Causes and Cures. *Fordham Law Review* 72 (2003): 279–310.

McFall, Lynne. "Integrity." *Ethics* 98 (1987): 5–20.

McLeod, Carolyn. "How to Distinguish Autonomy from Integrity." *Canadian Journal of Philosophy* 35 (2005): 107–133.

Miller, Christian. "Integrity." In *International Encyclopedia of Ethics*, edited by Hugh LaFollette, 2640–2650. Oxford: Blackwell Publishing, 2013. https://onlinelibrary.wiley.com/doi/10.1002/9781444367072.wbiee242.pub2.

Miller, Seumas. "Corruption." In *The Stanford Encyclopedia of Philosophy*, edited by Edward N. Zalta. Stanford, CA: Stanford University Press, 2018. Accessed September 11, 2019, <https://plato.stanford.edu/archives/win2018/entries/corruption/>

Murphy, Erin. "The Mismatch between Twenty-First-Century Forensic Evidence and our Antiquated Criminal Justice System." *Southern California Law Review* 87 (2014): 633–672.

Roberts, Paul, Jill Hunter, Simon N. M. Young, and David Dixon. "Introduction: Re-Examining Criminal Process Through the Lens of Integrity." In *The Integrity of*

Criminal Process: From Theory into Practice, edited by Jill Hunter, Paul Roberts, Simon N. M. Young, and David Dixon, 1–34. Oxford: Hart Publishing, 2016.

Taylor, Gabriele. "Integrity." *Proceedings Aristotelian Society* (Supp.) 55 (1981): 143–159.

Williams, Bernard. "Integrity." In *Utilitarianism For and Against,* edited by J. J. C. Smart and Bernard Williams, 108–118. Cambridge, UK: Cambridge University Press, 1973.

California v. Minjares, 443 U.S. 916, 928 (1979)

Giordenello v. United States, 357 U.S. 480 (1958)

R. v. Grant [2009] 2 S.C.R. 355, para. 68–70

I.N.S. v. Lopez-Mendoza, 468 U.S. 1032 (1984)

Mapp v. Ohio, 367 U.S. 643 (1961)

National Federation of Independent Business v. Sebelius, 567 U.S. 519 (2012)

Pennsylvania Bd. of Probation and Parole v. Scott, 524 U.S. 357 (1998)

Salinas v. United States, 522 U.S. 52 (1997)

Schneckloth v. Bustamonte, 412 U.S. 218, 242 (1973)

State v. Bridges, 925 P.2d 357 (Hawaii 1996)

United States v. Calandra, 414 U.S. 338, 357 (1974)

United States v. Casere, 440 U.S. 741, 770 (1979)

United States v. Grayson, 438 U.S. 41, 54 (1978)

United States v. Janis, 428 U.S. 433 (1976)

United States v. McCrory, 930 F.2d 63 (D.C. Cir. 1991)

Patient Protection and Affordable Care Act, 42 U.S.C. §18001 (2010)

U.S. Senate Report No. 98-225 (1983–1984)

Additional Sources

American Bar Association, Model Rules of Professional Responsibility (2013)

Center for Public Integrity, https://www.publicintegrity.org/

U.S. Department of Justice, Criminal Division, Public Integrity Section, https:// www.justice.gov/criminal/pin

Chapter 3

Enacting Integrity

JENNIFER A. HERDT

"The supreme quality for leadership is unquestionably integrity," maintained Dwight Eisenhower.[1] Even those who regard other traits as more central to leadership will acknowledge that integrity is a virtue. How, though, is it to be cultivated? Developing the virtue of integrity is in many ways much like the process of developing any virtue. We receive direct moral instruction, and learn to empathize with those around us, but the process gets underway in earnest when we glimpse, however dimly, the special goodness of this particular virtue, and desire to instantiate it. Exemplars are studied and emulated. One's own successes and failures in emulation are scrutinized.

In order to discuss the process of developing integrity, then, we must begin by sketching its particular character, or what distinguishes it from other virtues. This turns out to be less than straightforward. While integrity's standing as a virtue is broadly acknowledged rather than contested, like that of humility and magnanimity, it has proven to be a slippery virtue to define. While the aim of this chapter is to

---

1. The quotation is often made, but without proper attribution; I have been unable to track down the original source; see, e.g., http://thehill.com/blogs/blog-briefing-room/news/360950-comey-tweets-eisenhower-quote-about-the-importance-of-integrity.

Jennifer A. Herdt, *Enacting Integrity* In: *Integrity, Honesty, and Truth Seeking*. Edited by: Christian B. Miller and Ryan West. Oxford University Press (2020). © Oxford University Press.
DOI: 10.1093/oso/9780190920487.003.0003

illuminate the processes by which integrity is cultivated, it will be necessary, first, to lay out a brief account of the nature of the virtue, which I define as excellence in standing for one's commitments. I will then proceed to discuss the development of integrity. I begin by considering the admiration and emulation of exemplars and the development of a more refined grasp of the distinctive goodness of integrity. I go on to consider the role of emotions of self-reflection (particularly those elicited by moral failures), supportive relationships and communities, and contexts of reason giving that break open insulated communities and the cognitive biases to which these are subject. In order to become persons of integrity, we rely on good (if imperfect) exemplars and supportive (if cognitively biased) communities; in becoming persons of integrity, capable of standing well for our commitments, we serve the ongoing communal pursuit of truth and goodness.

1. INTEGRITY AS STANDING WELL FOR ONE'S COMMITMENTS

I take the virtue of integrity to be a matter of virtuously standing for one's commitments.[2] The paradigmatic act of integrity is maintaining one's commitments at the risk of great cost, whether in terms of social standing or material well-being.[3] Think, for instance, of a whistleblower who reveals illicit activities going on within her company, thereby risking retribution, or someone who calls out a friend at a party for telling a racist joke.

---

2. This definition is particularly indebted to Calhoun 1995. While "commitment" refers in some contexts to an act of binding oneself to a specific course of action or policy, I will be using it in the broader sense of devotion or dedication to something or someone.
3. On the notion of the paradigmatic act of a virtue, indebted to Thomas Aquinas's approach to individuating the virtues, see Bowlin 2016: 118.

However, under some circumstances integrity is shown not in maintaining but in changing one's commitments, as perhaps when a lifelong faithful Catholic leaves the church, unable to countenance its persistent patterns of enabling and concealing sexual abuse. Hence, the virtue of integrity cannot be equated with the mere habitual disposition to perform its paradigmatic act. Integrity as a virtue, that is, cannot be equated with rigid adherence to principle. The fact that the virtue of integrity is not always displayed through its paradigmatic act does not, however, make integrity different from other virtues; while virtues are individuated in part by their paradigmatic acts, a virtue is a disposition to perform that act only in the right way and under appropriate circumstances. Facing death in battle may be the paradigmatic act of courage, but courage is displayed in many other ways, and it is not always courageous to charge into battle.

Commitments are varied in nature. One can be committed to human rights, or to one's neighborhood bowling association, or to one's writing. Integrity is not, though, a matter of standing for one's moral commitments as opposed to one's non-moral (aesthetic, political, etc.) commitments. Rather, commitments of *any* sort are subject to moral assessment, and the person of integrity is one who stands for his or her commitments in a good way, regardless of category or kind.

What is involved, then, in standing well for one's commitments? In part, this is an epistemic matter; it involves maintaining commitments thoughtfully, with proper responsiveness to evidence and awareness of one's own fallibility. Integrity can involve changing one's commitments, as noted, but only where this change is for good reasons. But standing for one's commitments is not just a matter of good judgment or belief; standing for something is expressed in how one acts. Further, being a person of integrity is not a matter of seeking to keep one's own hands clean, come what may; it is not a personal rather than a social virtue. To stand for one's commitments is to stand for them before others, to propose them as worthy of others' endorsement. It involves submitting one's judgment to others' critique. The person of integrity lives out his or her commitments in a way that seeks to commend them to others.[4] Integrity is, as Cheshire Calhoun has argued, "tightly connected to viewing oneself as a member of an evaluating community and to caring about what that community endorses."[5] The person of integrity thus contributes to the communal discernment of truth, beauty, and goodness, of all that is worth standing for. Our commitments are not simply a private concern, but matter to others; they contribute to a common project.

1.1 Integrity and Self-Integration

Defining integrity in terms of standing for one's commitments might, though, seem to ignore a core feature of integrity as ordinarily understood: that it has to do with wholeness, and in particular with the integration of various parts of oneself into a whole.[6] The "wanton" simply acts on whatever desire happens to be most psychologically salient at the moment and cannot properly be said to be or have a self at all. An integrated self, in contrast, is one in which certain desires are preferentially endorsed in a way that flows from a person's practical reasoning and so are ordered in relation to one another in a stable way.[7] Integrity so understood is not, however, an alternative to integrity understood as standing for one's commitments. In fact, some degree of wholeness or self-integration is a prerequisite for standing virtuously for one's commitments. Integrity is undermined by both

---

4. This does not mean urging all, say, to take up bowling, if that is a pastime to which one is personally committed; to commend something to others does not involve insensitivity to individual differences or to context. Bowling can be endorsed as a good pastime by those whose constellation of talents and predilections disposes them to other pastimes.

5. Calhoun 1995: 254.

6. Philosophical discussions of the integrated-self view of integrity often take their bearing from Frankfurt 1988.

7. See Taylor 1985: 116 and Watson 1975.

self-indulgence and weakness of will; the self-indulgent person is a wanton, acting on the whims of the moment, while the weak-willed person acts against her best judgment, is unable consistently to act according to her commitments, and so cannot be said to stand for them. The self-controlled or continent person, meanwhile, succeeds in standing for her commitments as would the person of integrity, but only with difficulty and inner conflict. She must, perhaps, remind herself how painful it would be to live with herself in the knowledge that she had not blown the whistle on her firm, even as she suffers many sleepless nights before she takes the decisive step. Such a person lacks both wholeness and the virtue of integrity but certainly is capable of standing for her commitments and cares about doing so in an excellent way. This situates her to begin to grasp the intrinsic goodness of integrity (beyond the attraction of being able to regard oneself as virtuous) and thereby to advance in developing the virtue, which will allow her to stand well for her commitments without this inner division.

Insisting that integrity is a matter of standing well for one's commitments, rather than simply of being an integrated self, highlights the social character of the virtue. Concern for integrity is not properly merely a concern for the quality of one's own character, but rather a concern for how one's commitments, and how they are lived out, influence others around us. Someone who is merely concerned with her own self-integration purely for its own sake is not thereby a person of integrity.

1.2 The Substantive Implications of Standing Well
     for One's Commitments

Understanding integrity in terms of standing well for one's commitments might seem to leave the matter of the content of these commitments entirely open; I might be a person of integrity if I stand for my commitment to white supremacy, say, so long as I do so thought-fully, open to counter-arguments and evidence, and so forth. In fact, though, robust constraints on the character of a person's commit-ments flow from what is involved in being capable of standing well for one's commitments. One must (implicitly, if not explicitly) con-sider acting on one's best judgment, arriving at one's best judgment through the reflective consideration of others' judgments, and taking into account relevant evidence, to be important goods, to be ranked above material gain, social approval, status, comfort, and the like.[8] One must be concerned about epistemic distortions introduced into practical reasoning by social injustice, power differentials, and the like. One's commitments must be consistent with one another, such that they do not pull one in conflicting directions. Arguably, in order to hold together as an agent, one needs in fact to be a *good* agent. That is, in order to have integrity in the sense of being consistently, stably integrated, one's commitments must be good, and one must stand for them well.

It has been maintained that the conceivability of "ideally coher-ent eccentrics" shows this not to be the case; that there certainly might be characters who accept some outlandish or morally repug-nant value and yet do so in a way that is perfectly consistent with all of their other values and with the facts. This might perhaps be an ideally coherent Caligula whose sole aim is to maximize the suffering of others, or someone who "given a choice, always prefers agony on a future Tuesday to the slightest pain on any other day."[9] When such hypothetical characters are fleshed out, however, it becomes evident just how alien they must be. Indeed, they must literally be aliens—nonhuman—given that their ideal coherence is possible only given

8. Calhoun 1995: 250.
9. Street 2009: 273–298. Street's Caligula example is taken from Gibbard 1999: 145; the exam-ple of the person with Future Tuesday Indifference originated with Parfit 1984: 124.

a lack of concern for sorts of things that human beings cannot but care about: avoiding pain, preferring happiness over misery, life over death, being loved over being hated.

Christine Korsgaard has mounted an even stronger argument to show that self-integration and goodness go hand in hand for any rational creature, arguing that "the moral law is the law of self-constitution."[10] As rational agents, human beings find themselves to be the sort of creatures who are expected to provide reasons for their actions. We find ourselves, then, confronted with the task of constructing a unified will. And, argues Korsgaard,

> in order to have a unified will, you must will in accordance with a universal law... [one that] ranges over all rational beings, that is, [that] commands you to act in a way that any rational being could act, because you could find yourself in anybody's shoes, anybody's at all, and the law has to be one that would enable you to maintain your integrity, in any situation, come what may.[11]

Korsgaard's argument is contentious, and I cannot fully defend it here. Critical to its success is showing that caring about consistency with one's future self is implicit in rational agency and that this is bound up with a rational requirement to care about responsibility to other persons as logically no different than responsibility to one's future self. If her argument succeeds, it sheds further light on the social character of integrity, in that the reasons that we give to ourselves are no different in principle from the reasons we offer to others: relating to ourselves at different points in time is like relating to other selves. If we cannot rely on ourselves, others cannot rely on us, and vice versa. Integrity, then, is far from mere volitional unity.

10. Korsgaard 2009: 214.
11. Ibid.

On the account just given, the perfected virtue of integrity seems to require not just that one stand virtuously for one's commitments, but that one have all and only harmoniously unified and good commitments. Indeed, it seems to require global goodness of character. This might be criticized as an impossible ideal. After all, we seem to have no problem picking out exemplars of integrity; none of these is globally good, and some are people with whom we deeply disagree. How could this be so? We can unravel this puzzle by recognizing that integrity, like other virtues, is not an all-or-nothing matter but rather is akin to a skill that is acquired gradually and by degrees.[12] That *perfect* integrity would require the presence of a broad array of other moral and epistemic virtues, as well as perfect wholeness and self-integration, does not mean that we do not regularly encounter instances of *imperfect* integrity, which remain exemplary given their comparative excellence. So, for example, we recognize excellence in standing for some range of one's commitments even where this is lacking in other domains; perhaps the staunch whistleblower remains silent in the face of racist jokes, unwilling to risk offending his old college buddies. He is imperfectly self-integrated and displays integrity only in a certain domain, but this is still admirable. Moreover, there is nothing incoherent about recognizing such exemplary imperfect integrity in those with whom we deeply disagree. We might praise the integrity of a politician who refuses to compromise her beliefs on abortion, or her concern for animal rights, even if we find her beliefs and commitments wrongheaded. Here we recognize that her commitments are not idiosyncratic but shared with reflective others, and we praise her ability to maintain her commitments in the face of significant challenges and temptations, even if we are convinced that she has failed fully to acknowledge some considerations that go against her convictions. Our praise will be highest where we take her to be

12. Annas 2011: 89–90.

justified in making and keeping the commitments she does, given her particular social-epistemic context, even where we take them to be objectively vitiated.[13]

1.3 Specifying Integrity by Identifying the "Difficult Good" It Secures

There is one final worry in the vicinity: that integrity has ceased on this account to be a distinctive virtue, as opposed to a name for a constellation of virtues, or indeed, for all-inclusive virtue.[14] Greg Scherkoske, responding to this concern, has argued that integrity is best understood as an epistemic virtue, where an epistemic virtue is "any stable cognitive trait, habit or process that reliably places its possessor in good epistemic position."[15] Excellences of epistemic agency, he adds, are not narrowly focused on maximizing true belief, but are "excellences of our shared life as practical and interdependent epistemic agents."[16] As an epistemic virtue, integrity need not, he argues, be identified by way of a characteristic thought or motivation. I have suggested, however, that integrity is adequately specified by its paradigmatic act: what Thomas Aquinas calls its object.[17] It being a difficult good to stand well for one's commitments, human beings need a virtue that enables us to do so.

I will not here attempt to determine whether integrity is best thought of as a moral or epistemic virtue. I note, though, that Scherkoske's account coheres well with the account I have given of

---

13. Here we apply to the case of commitment the important distinction between something's being true and someone's being justified in believing something. On truth and justification, see Stout 2004: 239, 248, 276–277.

14. See Miller's helpful discussion, 2013.

15. Scherkoske 2012: 196.

16. Ibid., 197.

17. Aquinas 1981: I–II.54.2, 60.1, II–II.27.1; on the object of a virtue and what she terms its "characteristic kind of action," see Porter 2016: 32.

integrity as virtuously standing for one's commitments, and of integrity's social significance, ably defended by Calhoun.[18] It also enables us to see how integrity can be a distinctive virtue while also, when perfected, involving the presence of all other virtues, moral as well as epistemic.

Integrity understood as standing well for one's commitments, then, is a distinctive virtue, individuated by the characteristic challenge it equips its possessors to meet. We stand well for our commitments when we maintain and live out our commitments in ways that are not swayed by threats or temptations, but that remain open to counter-arguments and counter-evidence; when we change our commitments only reflectively, for good reasons; when we show due regard for the judgments of others, and in a way alert to epistemic injustices and other distortions; when we live out our commitments in ways that show concern for advancing the communal recognition of truth, goodness, and beauty, and not simply concern for our own reputation or for maintaining clean hands; and when we do all this reliably, with ease rather than inner struggle.

2. DEVELOPING INTEGRITY: ACQUIRING NEW REASONS FOR ACTING

With this understanding of integrity in place, we can turn to the question of its acquisition. Several distinctive features require special attention here. First, we need to be able to make sense of the fact that we do pick out exemplars of integrity with whose judgment we disagree, as a way of distinguishing what we respect about them from

---

18. If integrity is an epistemic virtue, I would argue that it might fruitfully be understood, in Thomistic terms, as a "part" of prudence, perfecting practical intellect in reasoning and judging well concerning what ought to be done and how it is to be done.

what we disagree with. Second, we need to clarify how admiration and emulation can play a key role in the acquisition of a virtue like integrity, despite the fact that integrity has to do with a willingness to stand for one's own commitments and therefore for one's own best judgments. Third, the acquisition of integrity is special given that it is so intimately bound up with what it is to hold together as a mature self and thus to be a stable point for reason giving and character evaluation, so our account should illuminate these special features. In many respects, however, the acquisition of integrity is no different from the acquisition of any other virtue.

2.1 The Earliest Stages

The early stages of moral formation involve both direct instruction and behavioral conditioning. Small children are told what to do and what not to do, and learn that some ways of acting are "good" and others "bad," some "right" and others "wrong." This instruction, which employs a host of thicker moral terms, even with very young children—"nice," "mean," "nasty," "kind," "truthful," "generous," "brave," etc.—helps a child begin to acquire the moral concepts shared within her community. ("Integrity" is unlikely to be one of the moral concepts introduced early on in moral instruction, however, since small children cannot yet be said to have made commitments in a full-blown sense and thus are not expected to stand for them.) Reasons for compliance (or non-compliance) with such instruction are doubtless various and complex, even at this stage, but some degree of behavioral conditioning can be expected. After all, praise, approval, and social acceptance are pleasant; rebukes, disapproval, and punishment are not.

How, though, can someone begin to acquire the *virtues*, when these typically involve distinctive motivations and reasons for acting? To share a toy because Mommy will frown if you don't is not the same thing as sharing out of generosity. It is often thought that once a child develops habits of acting in ways positively reinforced by those around her, she will come to take pleasure in acting virtuously for its own sake. However, this is puzzling, as it seems to involve a shift from performing an action for the sake of the resultant pleasure, to performing an action for its own sake (with pleasure *supervening* on, but not motivating, that act). It is unclear what allows this shift to take place.

Alasdair MacIntyre's well-known discussion of how a child learning the game of chess moves from acting only for the sake of external goods to grasping the internal goods of chess is illuminating here.[19] Initially, the child plays chess only because she is given candy each time she does. Over time, having learned the game and played it, however, she is capable of grasping its distinctive goodness:

> So, we may hope, there will come a time when the child will find
> in those goods specific to chess, in the achievement of a certain
> highly particular kind of analytical skill, strategic imagination
> and competitive intensity, a new set of reasons, reasons now not
> just for winning on a particular occasion, but for trying to excel
> in whatever way the game of chess demands.

A virtue is like a skill or practice in that it similarly involves a distinctive form of perception and set of reasons for acting in a particular way.[20] However, just as direct moral instruction may not lead to the acquisition of a virtue, so bribing a child to play chess may not result in love of the game. A number of other contextual features are critical here. One might strongly motivate a child to master the game by

19. MacIntyre 1981: 188. I have discussed this in more detail in Herdt 2008: 26–30.
20. Julia Annas develops the skill analogy in depth in 2011.

punishing her each time she loses—but this is unlikely to lead her to love the game. Indeed, ample evidence indicates that the provision of rewards for participation makes individuals less rather than more likely to regard an activity as intrinsically worthwhile.[21] She is most likely to learn to appreciate the internal goods of chess when the one teaching her is someone she trusts and loves or respects, someone she regards as having in general a good handle on worthwhile forms of activity.

One critical feature of the formation of the virtues that is elided in the chess analogy as MacIntyre develops it is the fact that we have to do not just with a learner, a teacher, inanimate chess pieces, and rules of the game, but with other people who are affected by our actions—our fellow chess players, as it were. We cannot grasp what generosity, cruelty, etc. mean without grasping—understanding and caring about—how they affect others. A critical feature of early moral development has to do with empathetic perspective taking; early childhood moral instruction often seeks directly to elicit empathy, and empirical research supports a robust link between this kind of instruction and prosocial development.[22]

2.2 The Role of Imitation and Admiration

It is hardly sufficient, then, in order to inculcate a virtue, merely to engage a learner in a form of activity that in some salient respects is like the actions of the virtuous. Empathy plays a critical role in enabling learners to acquire an internal grasp of the goodness of core virtues such as kindness, generosity, and fidelity. Another core

21. Ryan and Deci have conducted empirical research in this domain for many decades; see, e.g., 2000.
22. I discuss the role of empathy in moral development in Herdt 2015 and 2016a; pathbreaking research on the connections between empathy and prosocial development was conducted by Martin Hoffman; see Hoffman 1982, 1991.

element of the process is imitation. Commonsense wisdom holds that the significance of modeling behavior dwarfs that of direct moral instruction, and there is growing empirical evidence to substantiate this view.[23] Aristotle emphasizes that human beings have a natural impulse to imitate, and that we derive pleasure from doing so.[24] Indeed, we often engage in imitation unreflectively, without forming any intention to do so. It has been suggested that this might help to explain the transition between merely associating pleasure with good action because external goods (like praise and approbation) have been attached to them, and acting as the virtuous do, which involves grasping the intrinsic goodness of so doing and acting for the sake that particular goodness.[25] Imitating an activity brings with it a pleasure inherent in successfully acting in the particular way that is sought after: "What is aimed at in the mimesis of an activity is that activity itself: mimetic pleasure in any performance is proper and intrinsic to that performance, and does not depend on what if anything follows upon it."[26] However, while in mimesis the agent sees the activity as an end in itself, this does not mean that mimesis itself enables an agent to act in the way the virtuous agent acts, and for her reasons. As Zagzebski notes, "The virtuous agent not only gets pleasure in the doing of the act, but the act must have the right motive for the kind of act that it is—for example, respect for others, in the case of honesty; caring for others' welfare, in the case of generosity."[27] Furthermore, the impulse to imitate is in itself non-discriminating; people can and do derive pleasure from imitating nasty, cruel, or pointless activity, not just virtue.

23. See, e.g., Rushton and Campbell 1977, Schnall, Roper, and Fessler 2010.
24. Aristotle 1987: 1448b4–10.
25. Fossheim 2006.
26. Ibid., 113.
27. Zagzebski 2017: 134.

While the impulse to imitate on its own fails to provide an adequate account of habituation in virtue, it can constitute an element in a fuller account. I noted in the previous section that learning to appreciate the internal goods of an activity is facilitated by relationships of trust and love.[28] In such a relationship, the learner trusts that the teacher has her good at heart, and that the activity is worthwhile even if it is challenging, even painful. This trusting relationship therefore disposes the learner to expect to find goodness in the activity. The learner is thus not simply acquiring concepts, not simply having her behavior conditioned by reward and punishment, and not simply imitating features of an action, but is actively engaged in seeking to discern goodness in the activity. This active engagement is critical for learning a skill, and likewise for acquiring a virtue. As Julia Annas argues,

> The learner needs to trust the teacher to be doing the right thing to follow and copy, and to be conveying the right information and ways of doing things. And further, from the start the learner of a skill needs also what I have called the drive to aspire, manifesting itself first in the need the learner has to understand what she is doing if she is to learn properly.[29]

Whence, though, comes this drive to aspire? There needs at some point to be the direct apprehension of the goodness of that to which we aspire.

Admiration may be one missing link. Linda Zagzebski has suggested that we detect excellence through the experience of the

---

28. Thus, I do not regard attending to the critical role of relationships, practices, communities, and a broader way of life as offering an alternative to an Aristotelian understanding of the development of the virtues, or as constituting an inside-out as opposed to an outside-in account of virtue development. See Porter and Baehr, chapter 7 of this volume.
29. Annas 2011: 17.

emotion of admiration. The emotion of admiration is a particular sort of response to something judged to be good, in that it typically elicits a desire to emulate the exemplar—to act as she has acted, and more basically, to become more like her, the sort of person who characteristically acts like this in similar circumstances.[30] Jonathan Haidt has conducted cross-cultural empirical research indicating that "elevation," an emotional response to (among other things) the display of virtue, is accompanied by distinctive physical effects: a sense of expansion in the chest, and a pleasurable feeling of being uplifted or elevated.[31] Admiration engages us in a holistic way, as embodied, feeling, thinking beings.

To admire someone is to see that person and his actions as good; admiration naturally elicits imitation. Our admiration for an action, and our desire to emulate the person who has performed it, lead us to examine both more closely. We look for features of the person that might help to account for his ability to act in this admirable way, seeking to identify relevant perceptions, emotions, and ends. We look in particular for acquired traits or dispositions, since it is these, rather than natural gifts or chance situational features, that we might be able to emulate—just as we might, in admiring a basketball champion, wish for his height but focus our attention on his ball-handling skills.[32] We seek, further, not simply to imitate our exemplar's external actions, but also the reasons and motives for which he acts. David

---

30. Zagzebski 2017: 33.

31. Haidt 2003: 281–283.

32. Christian thinkers traditionally distinguish between the acquired virtues and the infused virtues. The latter are gratuitously God given; like natural talent, they are not the result of effort and their possession is not meritorious. For our purposes here, however, the differences are not critical, for infused virtues, like acquired virtues, are understood as capable of growth and as requiring tending. Admiration leads us to examine religious exemplars, like any other exemplar, in order to discern their distinctive perceptions, emotions, and ends, and how these might be emulated. One might, for instance, adopt their faithfulness in attending worship, or their prayer practices.

Velleman has suggested that emulation proceeds through "wishfully picturing oneself in his image."[33] Doing so involves imaginatively adopting the exemplar's ways of perceiving and reasons for acting, and seeking to enact this imagined self-image. "These imaginative considerations," writes Velleman, "serve as narrative premises in light of which only some actions make sense as the continuation of his story. And when an agent does what makes sense in light of a narrative premise, or rationale, he is acting for a reason, albeit one that isn't true."[34] In so doing, what are not yet the agent's perceptions and reasons can come to be her own perceptions and reasons, as her "make-believe" reasons are experienced and inhabited and displace what were once her own reasons. Zagzebski suggests that "the model can work because even though imagining ourselves with a motivating feeling is not the same thing as having the feeling, imagining is very close to having, and an imagined feeling can cause an actual feeling, especially when we want to become a person with such a feeling."[35]

The process of developing integrity gets off the ground, then, when we observe examples of its paradigmatic act, admire persons who act in this way, and, seeking to emulate them, picture ourselves in their image or imagine an ideal self that is relevantly like them. We are likely to admire acts of integrity, and the people who perform them, long before we develop a concept of integrity, and likely even before we know the word.[36] Those we admire may or may not be persons who are offering us direct moral instruction or seeking to shape our behavior and character. Teenaged Julia might admire her friend Ben, who adopts a vegetarian diet after having learned about factory farming practices, and who maintains that diet even when some of

---

33. Velleman 2002: 101. Zagzebski drew my attention to the work of Fossheim and Velleman; see her discussion, 2017: 134–139.
34. Velleman 2002: 101.
35. Zagzebski 2017: 136.
36. See ibid., 60.

his friends ostracize him. She may admire him and wish she could be "like that" even if she does not feel moved to become a vegetarian and does not know what she finds so attractive in the way he is acting.

Religious communities frequently rehearse exemplary acts of integrity, often without identifying specific virtues enacted in them. Hearing such stories can also elicit admiration and inspire emulation. Take the story of Stephen, the first Christian martyr, narrated in the Acts of the Apostles. Christian communities hear this story of how Stephen was accused of blasphemy, and, when brought before the high priest to testify, how he defended his faith. They hear of how, while being stoned to death, he prayed that the sin of killing him not be held against his attackers, while charging his accusers with betraying Jesus, opposing the Holy Spirit, and failing to keep the law (Acts 6:8–7:60). Christians have for several millennia responded to this story with admiration, without necessarily possessing a theory of integrity or identifying Stephen as an exemplar of integrity.

2.3 Grasping the Special Goodness of Integrity

Of course, if picturing ourselves in the image of an exemplar is to foster the development of a virtue, it is necessary that we have at least a rudimentary grasp of that virtue's special goodness. Hence it is important that admiration and emulation powerfully focus our attention, leading us to scrutinize the objects of our admiration. This process of scrutiny has many dimensions. Comparing this paradigmatic act with others, and this exemplar to others, we begin to distinguish virtues from one another and to name them. We might say that Stephen had both integrity and forgivingness; integrity, insofar as he stood steadfastly for his faith in Jesus, forgivingness, insofar as he forgave those who regarded his faith as blasphemous and so stoned him. We may well become aware, too, of respects in which a person we admire is not exemplary and to distinguish these flaws and vices from his or her virtues. Admiring exemplars of integrity who are not kind, or habitually kind individuals who lack integrity, allows us to begin to distinguish these virtues and their associated patterns of perception, feeling, and intention more clearly from one another. We may also become aware of connections among various virtues. We may have difficulty identifying any exemplars of integrity who lack courage, for instance, even as we admire the courage of some individuals who do not obviously possess integrity—someone who risks his life to run into a burning building to save others, perhaps.

Our experiences of admiration, and the reflection elicited by our desire to emulate those we admire, are a personal matter. They also have important social dimensions. Many ordinary conversations focus on admirable actions and persons, often in fine-grained detail. Imagine those making fun of Ben's vegetarianism saying to Julia, "I can't stand that Ben—trying to make us all look bad with his hip vegetarianism!" "Well, I think what he's doing is pretty impressive," replies Julia. "After all, it isn't so easy to have to go with your friends to McDonald's and order the one vegetarian thing on the menu. And it's not as though he's trying to make you feel bad. He'll tell you why he became a vegetarian if you ask him, but he doesn't go around talking about it all the time. Remember how he always used to love burgers? It can't be that easy to stop eating something that tastes so good." It is in the course of just such exchanges that we refine our understanding of the virtues, articulating reasons for our admiration (or our contempt) and testing them out against the judgments of others. Indeed, much of what is slandered under the name "gossip" is in fact vital social reflection on character and virtue, assisting us in the fine discrimination of modes of perception, emotional response, and reasons for acting.

This is also a critical function of fictional narratives. Storytelling in traditional societies serves to preserve communal memory of important events, to be sure, but equally important is its function in holding up exemplars and eliciting shared reflection on their virtues. Today, conversations coming out of movie theaters (when not about the latest special effects) often consist in the fine-grained analysis of character.

2.4 Emulation, Self-Reflection, and Shame

We seek to act in ways that are like our exemplars. Of course, this is an enormously complex matter. Take a Christian who is inspired by the example of Stephen. She may long for an opportunity to display similarly steadfast devotion to the faith but lack any sense of how this might translate into her own social context. Emulation is rarely a matter of direct imitation. Perhaps her integrity as a Christian may be shown simply in explaining to friends why her son will miss the soccer game scheduled on Sunday morning. Or perhaps it will be shown even more fully in reaching out in solidarity with Muslims seeking to build a mosque in the neighborhood, when this initiative comes under fire.

Emulation of an exemplar is easiest when the exemplar's social context closely resembles our own. Julia may have quite a richly detailed sense of how to emulate Ben, should she become convinced that she cannot in good conscience continue eating meat. Should she recognize that what she admires is his integrity, not his vegetarianism, her task will be harder. Perhaps she defends an unpopular teacher, rightly discerning that the teacher is excellent but that his high academic standards are resented by her lazy peers. In order to see that defending the teacher would be an action relevantly similar to Ben's steadfast vegetarianism, she must have come quite a long distance in grasping the particular goodness that is involved in standing virtuously for one's commitments.

When we admire a person, or something she has done, not all of our attention is focused on her, or on our ideal self re-made in her image; some is directed toward ourselves as we presently are. This makes sense—insofar as admiration elicits the desire to emulate, it leads us to reflect also on the ways in which we are presently unlike our exemplars. This can elicit shame. Aristotle held that shame plays an important part in the acquisition of the virtues. It has been termed for him "the semi-virtue of the learner," insofar as one is capable of shame only insofar as one already loves what is fine and virtuous.[37] On Burnyeat's interpretation, the learner recognizes and admires virtuous action but sometimes pursues other ends that appear pleasant—friendship, comfort, power, influence. In effect, the learner is akratic, or rather, the akratic or incontinent person is someone who has gotten stuck at a stage of development natural for the well-brought-up young person on the way to developing the virtues. Having acted in a way that she judges her ideal self, made in the image of her exemplar, would not, she experiences shame.

How does shame enable the learner to develop the virtues? Aristotle's thought here seems to be that it disposes the learner to reflect on how she has fallen short, and this reflection can lead to a fuller understanding of the distinctive perceptions and motives of the virtuous. Imagine, for instance, that Julia forms a resolve to stand up for the unpopular teacher the next time she hears someone picking on him. However, when the occasion arises, she hesitates. The source of the offending comment happens to be the best friend of a boy she is hoping to date. "Maybe I should just keep quiet," she thinks. "I'll have another opportunity. And that last test really *was* hard—I can see why Jack was upset." Back in her room at home that evening, she is ashamed of herself. "I know I was just worried about what Jack would say to Leo. Ben would never have just kept his mouth shut in a situation like that. He would have found a way to say it that was fair to everyone." Julia, struck by her failure, arrives at a more fine-grained

37. Burnyeat 1980: 78; see Aristotle 1999: 1179b5–1180a5.

appreciation for what it would have meant to act "like Ben" in her own situation and renews her aspiration to emulate him more effectively next time.

However, recent empirical research offers evidence that shame may not in fact assist in the development of virtue, contrary to Aristotle's account. Or at least, it suggests the importance of distinguishing between guilt and shame as distinct emotions of self-assessment and making room for other emotions in this vicinity, such as contrition.[38] Where guilt is related to a specific action or behavior judged by the self to have been wrong, shame is a global negative reaction to the self. Guilt elicits empathy and concern for others and concern about the negative effects of one's actions on others. Shame, in contrast, is focused on others' negative assessments of oneself. Shame has been described as "egocentric" in orientation, while guilt is "other-oriented" in its concerns.[39] The two emotions are associated with distinctive patterns of behavior: shame, with denial, hiding, and efforts to escape, while guilt, with apology and reparation.[40] Shame as a negative global self-assessment is also linked with distinctive psychological tendencies: toward anger, withdrawal, depression, and anxiety.

This research does not so much discredit Aristotle's claims about the role of shame, and the scenario we have built around it for the development of integrity, as allow us to refine them. Often, when we act in ways that fail to emulate our exemplars and fall short of our ideal self, our emotions include elements of both shame and guilt. Julia can think both "I failed to stand up for my teacher as I think

38. Much of this research is associated with June Tangney; see Tangney, Stuewig, and Mashek 2007; I have discussed the role of empathy, guilt, and shame in moral development more fully in Herdt 2015 and 2016a. Robert Roberts develops an account of contrition in 2007: 97–113.

39. Tangney et al. 2007: 349.

40. Tangney, Miller, Flicker, and Barlow 1996, Wallbott and Scherer 1995.

I ought to have this afternoon" and "I'm the sort of person who is not able to stand up for my commitments." Insofar as the latter judgment and its associated negative emotion become entrenched, Julia no longer regards herself as a learner, someone on the road to virtue. She loses hope in becoming "like Ben." She ceases envisioning her ideal self in his image. Instead, she engages in negative self-talk that reinforces her *akrasia*—I don't have any backbone; I'm wishy-washy"—equating what she has *done* in this instance with who she *is*.

Now, one might argue that this is just being truthful. Julia really *is* akratic. She really did fail to stand up for her commitments, which undermines the sense in which she can be said to *have* commitments, and indeed, undermines the sense in which she can be said fully to be a self. What she is in one moment—her pattern of perception, desire, judgment—is not what she is in the next moment. But this will be true to some degree, as we have already pointed out, for anyone who does not possess perfect integrity. And no one can possess *perfect* integrity without possessing all of the other virtues (or if this is contested, at least without the possession of a related cluster of virtues—good judgment, courage, etc.).

Insofar as Julia is troubled by her failure and pinpoints it specifically as a failure to stand well for her commitments, we can characterize her as conscientious. She has now a sustained concern to be a person of integrity, the sort of person who stands well for her commitments, although she is not yet a person of integrity, for she lacks stable concern for (and the capacity to enact) the goods intrinsic to integrity (maintaining commitments thoughtfully, bearing steadfastly the costs of so doing, properly responding to evidence, being aware of one's fallibility, etc.).[41] Her conscientiousness may enable her to stand for her commitments in situations where she certainly

41. See the discussion of these distinctions, with reference to the virtue of honesty, by Roberts and West, chapter 4 of this volume.

would not have, absent the concern to be a person of integrity. And yet it does not itself constitute the virtue of integrity.

We would do well to note at this juncture that Julia's negative self-talk expresses only partial truths. A truer thought would be one that considers also her admiration for Ben and her aspiration to become like him—her imagined ideal self and her longing to approximate that self more fully. Insofar as her self-assessment takes all of this into account, it will no longer be the global negative self-assessment that researchers have identified as shame, but rather closer to what Robert Roberts has termed "contrition."[42] Like shame, contrition involves the perception not just that I have done something wrong, but that I have done something to spoil myself. Unlike shame, contrition involves the further perception that this spoiled self is not the full truth about me. As a specifically Christian emotion, contrition involves the judgment that I have offended against God, but that God is merciful and will forgive. Hence, contrition is a complex "seeing as" that generates a desire and intention to change and improve the self.

Christian contrition involves seeing oneself as having offended against a merciful and forgiving God, but a secular analogue of contrition is available to one who sees herself as having spoiled herself and culpably offended against her fellows even while recognizing that her deep desire for moral transformation reveals that she cannot be fully identified with that spoiled self. If Julia is contrite, she will not become so obsessed with her failure that she loses sight of the goodness of her exemplar and of her imagined ideal self. Her attention will be focused on achieving a more fine-grained grasp of what is involved in responding "like *that*," and her positive moral emotions will not be swamped by negative moral emotions. Given that contrition is both more truthful than shame and that it enhances the development of the virtues rather than miring persons in despair and isolation, we

42. Roberts 2007: 97–113.

should seek to move ourselves and one another from shame to contrition and guilt.

2.5 Community, Epistemic Authority, and Cognitive Bias

This is another point at which the broader social context plays a critical role in the development of the virtue of integrity, as for other virtues. It is not simply Julia's relationships with Ben, the teacher, and her classmates that matter here, but all of her relationships, and the kinds of community in which she is embedded. Julia will be more likely to be able to place her failure of integrity in a broader context supportive of ongoing aspiration, insofar as she has experienced secure attachment, and inhabits contexts—family relationships, friendships, religious communities, and/or her relationship with God—that offer support and acceptance.[43] If she is confident that she is known, accepted, and loved despite her failure to stand well for her commitments, she will be better able to admit and examine those failures, confident that they do not threaten her lovability, even if they reveal that she is not yet a fully coherent and stable self.

Importantly, such relationships and communities need not be sources solely of unconditional affirmation in order to play this critical supportive role in the development of integrity. They will assist in the development of integrity only insofar as they are also contexts in which agents are held responsible for their commitments and asked to give reasons for them and for their ways of standing for them. The support and affirmation they provide equip agents like Julia to take the risk involved in allowing themselves to be called into question, confident that their ultimate worth will not be undermined, regardless of how disintegrated they may be. Imagine parents with whom

43. See Porter and Baehr, chapter 7 of this volume, especially 196–197.

Julia regularly discusses such challenging situations, and who by their supportive listening and high expectations help her articulate just how she failed and why her choice to remain silent was so plausible in the moment. And contrast them with parents who *simply* affirm, who do not let Julia get her story out or help her get it right, but stop her in her tracks, "Oh honey, don't worry about it, you know we love you no matter what."

The process as I have outlined it helps us to make sense of how it is that we can admire someone's integrity while continuing to disagree with them and thus with their judgment. One might think that admiring someone would typically mean coming to agree with their judgments. However, this is not how either admiration or belief works. Admiration focuses attention and becomes progressively more differentiated; it is often not directed toward the judgments of the person one admires. And I cannot acquire beliefs through admiration alone, since I cannot believe something unless I think it is true. As Linda Zagzebski writes, "I can acquire the exemplar's motives of generosity or courage by wishfully picturing myself as generous or courageous, but I cannot acquire the exemplar's beliefs by wishfully picturing myself with her beliefs."[44]

However, when we admire someone's integrity, what we are admiring is in part an epistemic matter. We are admiring how she stands for her commitments, and this includes how she goes about defending them, offering reasons for them, listening to objections from others regarding them, acting on the basis of them, and so forth. Given that we admire these things about a person with integrity, we do have good reason to give special consideration to her judgments, in a way we would not in the case of someone we admire for her generosity, courage, fidelity, etc. Nevertheless, we can and do distinguish these things from the judgments themselves. Indeed, we are closer to

44. Zagzebski 2017: 147.

understanding the virtue of integrity insofar as we grasp that we need to stand by our own best judgment, not that of even our exemplars, if we are to develop integrity ourselves. To be sure, there are often cases in which we judge that someone else is more likely to have gotten at the truth about something than we have ourselves.[45] Standing by one's own best judgment does not mean refusing to trust epistemic authorities. What it does mean, though, is using our own best judgment about which epistemic authorities to trust.

There is complexity here, for it is not simply the case that we are as individuals prone to rationalization and cognitive bias. It is also the case that we are, as Jonathan Haidt has put it, less selfish than "groupish," with a tendency to favor our own groups and to dismiss or even demonize outsiders, isolating "ourselves within cocoons of like-minded individuals."[46] We are best able to overcome our confirmation biases and revise our beliefs in response to evidence insofar as we are held accountable by others.[47] But insofar as we hold ourselves responsible only to those who belong to our own identity groups, our exchanges of reasons will tend often to reinforce, rather than correct, some of our most deeply rooted cognitive biases. The development of integrity is thus greatly aided by exchanging reasons with those who do not share our identities or belong to our communities, as challenging as this often is. And this also means that grateful acceptance of communal affirmation should not legitimize the insulation of communal commitments from critique.[48]

There might seem to be something puzzling about insisting that admiration, emulation, and communal support and affirmation play such a key role in the acquisition of a virtue like integrity, when integrity has to do with a willingness to stand for one's own

45. See Zagzebski's discussion, ibid. and 2012.
46. Haidt 2012: 363; see also 92, 95.
47. Lerner and Tetlock 2003.
48. I discuss this in greater detail in Herdt 2016b.

commitments and therefore for one's own best judgments. However, as we have seen, the process also involves differentiating between what is admirable and what is not admirable in one's exemplars, and so of developing one's own judgments. In addition, as one progresses in the development of any virtue, further progress becomes less and less dependent on having others to look up to. While we may still admire Bob's patience and Mary's generosity and Sam's fidelity, much of our attention will be focused on how these might be integrated coherently in our own ideal self, situated as it is in a particular body and particular social context. This is not to say that the later stages in the development of integrity become more inward oriented. For integrity, as we said at the outset, is not simply a matter of standing for one's commitments for one's own sake in order to hold together as a self. It is a matter of standing for one's commitments for the sake of others, and for the sake of our common effort to live well by assisting one another to live according to the best possible commitments.

3. CONCLUSION

Julia may not yet be a person of integrity, but she is on the way. Intriguingly, she can draw closer to instantiating the virtue of integrity insofar as she becomes more aware of (and troubled by) the extent to which she is *not* yet a person of integrity. She grasps that standing up for this teacher is something that she must do, given her judgment of his excellence and how unfairly he is being treated. She *also* grasps that in order to stand excellently for this commitment, she must find a way to stand up for the teacher that her peers can grasp, a way that allows them to see and admire the special goodness of standing up for an excellent teacher who is being maligned, rather than dismissing her action as sycophantic. She is grasping that perfected integrity involves being adept at standing for one's commitments in a way that is finely tuned both to one's own embodied particularity and to the faults and foibles of those around one. So it is that we become more able to stand virtuously for our commitments precisely as we come to hold together better as selves, as stable sites of reason giving with others, and as committed to advancing the communal pursuit of the virtues. And this steady standing for our commitments will in turn be more possible for us insofar as we inhabit relationships and communities that give us a secure sense of our basic worth, while at the same time holding us responsible for our commitments and opening both individual and communal commitments up to reason-giving exchanges with outsiders or nonmembers.

We should not expect the development of integrity to be a neatly linear process. Given that some degree of coherent integration around the pursuit of vitiated ends is possible, as is the steadfast defense of such ends, we should expect that "progress" toward integrity often involves periods of *decreased* coherence, as we become aware of some set of goods toward which we had previously been insensitive, and work to integrate the proper recognition of these goods into our existing pattern of commitment and action. For instance, I might become persuaded of the justice of gender inclusivity, and then flounder in my efforts to stand well for this commitment, as long-standing habits of speaking and relating persist, and as I become aware in only a piecemeal way of tensions between my new commitment and other commitments that I hold—say, to the advancement of women through women's sports and women's colleges. Insofar as I already possess the virtue of integrity to some degree, supported by affirming but non-insulating relationships and communities, I will be well equipped to cope with such periods of incoherence and destabilization, able to move through them to arrive at a new equilibrium that is better or higher because it is more responsive to the full array of goods. Still, short of a perfect integrity that arrives only with perfect goodness, whatever integrity I acquire will not be immune to future destabilization. Indeed, one aspect of the virtue of integrity is an acceptance of finitude, and thus an attitude of openness to the possible need for new or changed commitments.[49]

BIBLIOGRAPHY

Annas, Julia. *Intelligent Virtue*. Oxford: Oxford University Press, 2011.

Aquinas, Thomas. *Summa Theologica*. Translated by the Fathers of the English Dominican Province. Westminster, MD: Christian Classics, 1981.

Aristotle. *Poetics*. Translated by Richard Janko. Indianapolis: Hackett, 1987.

Aristotle. *Nicomachean Ethics*. Translated by Terence Irwin. Indianapolis: Hackett, 1999.

Bowlin, John. *Tolerance Among the Virtues*. Princeton, NJ: Princeton University Press, 2016.

Burnyeat, Miles. "Aristotle on Learning to Be Good." In *Aristotle's Ethics: Critical Essays*, edited by A. O. Rorty, 69–92. Berkeley: University of California Press, 1980.

Calhoun, Cheshire. "Standing for Something." *Journal of Philosophy* 92:5 (May 1995): 235–260.

Fossheim, Hallvard J. "Habituation as Mimesis." In *Values and Virtues: Aristotelianism in Contemporary Ethics*, edited by Timothy Chappell, 105–117. Oxford: Oxford University Press, 2006.

Frankfurt, Harry. *The Importance of What We Care About*. Cambridge, UK: Cambridge University Press, 1988.

Gibbard, Allan. "Morality as Consistency in Living." *Ethics* 110:1 (1999): 140–164.

Haidt, Jonathan. "Elevation and the Positive Psychology of Morality." In *Flourishing, Positive Psychology and the Life Well-Lived*, edited by C. L. M. Keyes and J. Haidt, 275–289. Washington, DC: American Psychological Association, 2003.

Haidt, Jonathan. *The Righteous Mind: Why Good People Are Divided by Politics and Religion*. New York: Vintage Books, 2012.

Herdt, Jennifer A. *Putting on Virtue: The Legacy of the Splendid Vices*. Chicago: University of Chicago Press, 2008.

49. I am grateful to all of the participants in the Integrity, Honesty and Truth Seeking conference at which this paper was first presented, and in particular to Nancy Snow, our host at the University of Oklahoma's Institute for the Study of Human Flourishing, to the John Templeton Foundation for their enabling support, and to Ryan West and Christian Miller, conference organizers and highly attentive editors.

Herdt, Jennifer A. "Empathy Beyond the In-Group: Stoic Universalism and Augustinian Neighbor-Love." *Journal of Philosophy, Theology, and the Sciences* 2:1 (2015): 63–88.

Herdt, Jennifer A. "Guilt and Shame in the Development of Virtue." In *Developing the Virtues: Integrating Perspectives*, edited by Julia Annas, Darcia Narvaez, and Nancy Snow, 235–254. Oxford: Oxford University Press, 2016a.

Herdt, Jennifer A. "Secrecy, Corruption, and the Exchange of Reasons: Malesic Meets Haidt—and Yoder." In *Kierkegaard and Christian Faith*, edited by C. Stephen Evans and Paul Martens, 157–172. Waco: Baylor University Press, 2016b.

Hoffman, Martin L. "Development of Prosocial Motivation: Empathy and Guilt." In *The Development of Prosocial Behavior*, edited by Nancy Eisenberg, 281–312. New York: Academic Press, 1982.

Hoffman, Martin L. "Empathy, Social Cognition, and Moral Action." In *Handbook of Moral Behavior and Development*. Volume 1: Theory, edited by W. M. Kurtines and J. L. Gewirtz, 275–302. Hillsdale, NJ: Lawrence Erlbaum Associates, 1991.

Korsgaard, Christine. *Self-Constitution: Agency, Identity, and* Integrity. Oxford: Oxford University Press, 2009.

Lerner, J. S., and P. E. Tetlock. "Bridging Individual, Interpersonal, and Institutional Approaches to Judgment and Decision Making: The Impact of Accountability on Cognitive Bias." In *Emerging Perspectives on Judgment and Decision Research*, edited by S.L. Schneider and J. Shanteau, 431–457. New York: Cambridge University Press, 2003.

MacIntyre, Alasdair. *After Virtue*. Notre Dame: University of Notre Dame Press, 1981.

Miller, Christian. "Integrity." In *International Encyclopedia of Ethics*, edited by Hugh LaFollette, 2640–2650. Oxford: Blackwell, 2013.

Parfit, Derek. *Reasons and Persons*. Oxford: Oxford University Press, 1984.

Porter, Jean. *Justice as a Virtue*. Grand Rapids, MI: Eerdmans, 2016.

Roberts, Robert. *Spiritual Emotions: A Psychology of Christian Virtues*. Grand Rapids, MI: Eerdmans, 2007.

Rushton, J., and A. Campbell. "Modeling, Vicarious Reinforcement and Extraversion on Blood Donating in Adults: Immediate and Long Term Effect." *European Journal of Social Psychology* 7:3 (1977): 297–306.

Ryan, R. M., and E. L. Deci. "Self-Determination Theory and the Facilitation of Intrinsic Motivation, Social Development, and Well-Being." *American Psychologist* 55 (2000): 68–78.

Scherkoske, Greg. "Could Integrity Be an Epistemic Virtue?" *International Journal of Philosophical Studies* 20:2 (2012): 197.

Schnall, S., J. Roper, and D. Fessler. "Elevation Leads to Altruistic Behavior." *Psychological Science* 21 (2010): 315–320.

Stout, Jeffrey. *Democracy and Tradition*. Princeton, NJ: Princeton University Press, 2004.

Street, Sharon. "In Defense of Future Tuesday Indifference: Ideally Coherent Eccentrics and the Contingency of What Matters." *Philosophical Issues* 19 (2009): 273–298.

Tangney, J. P., R. S. Miller, L. Flicker, and D. H. Barlow. "Are Shame, Guilt, and Embarrassment Distinct Emotions?" *Journal of Personality and Social Psychology* 70 (1996): 1256–1269.

Tangney, J. P., J. Stuewig, and D. J. Mashek, "Moral Emotions and Moral Behavior." *Annual Review of Psychology* 58 (2007): 345–372.

Taylor, Gabrielle. *Pride, Shame, and Guilt*. New York: Oxford University Press, 1985.

Velleman, David. "Motivation by Ideal." *Philosophical Explorations* 5:2 (2002): 89–103.

Wallbott, H. G., and K. R. Scherer, "Cultural Determinants in Experiencing Shame and Guilt." In *Self-Conscious Emotions: The Psychology of Shame, Guilt, Embarrassment, and Pride*, edited by J. P. Tangney and K. W. Fischer, 465–487. New York: Guilford Press, 1995.

Watson, Gary. "Free Agency." *Journal of Philosophy* 72 (1975): 205–220.

Zagzebski, Linda. *Epistemic Authority*. Oxford: Oxford University Press, 2012.

Zagzebski, Linda. *Exemplarist Moral Theory*. Oxford: Oxford University Press, 2017.

PART II

HONESTY

Chapter 4

The Virtue of Honesty

A Conceptual Exploration

ROBERT C. ROBERTS AND RYAN WEST

Etymology: < Anglo-Norman *honest, onest,* Anglo-Norman and Middle French *honneste, honeste* (French *honnête*) honourable, virtuous, just, frank, commendable, appropriate, suitable, excellent, fine, estimable, conforming to the rules of polite society (from 11th cent. in Old French), courteous, civil, decent, respectable, (of a woman) irreproachable in conduct, chaste (13th cent.) < classical Latin *honestus* regarded with honour or respect, honourable, of high rank, worthy of respect, decent, fine, handsome < *honōs, honor* honour n. + *-tus,* suffix forming adjectives.

—*Oxford English Dictionary*

1. INTRODUCTION

In the minds of laypeople, the mention of virtue quickly evokes such ideas as kindness and honesty. Yet in a time when the examination of virtue concepts is a vigorous mainline philosophical activity, we find

Robert C. Roberts and Ryan West, *The Virtue of Honesty* In: *Integrity, Honesty, and Truth Seeking.* Edited by: Christian B. Miller and Ryan West. Oxford University Press (2020). © Oxford University Press. DOI: 10.1093/oso/9780190920487.003.0004

little philosophical discussion of honesty.[1] The OED's etymology suggests an explanation: the strong connection between 'honesty' and 'honor.' Honesty is just whatever is worthy of honor! Notice the unspecificity of most of the synonyms for the predecessors of 'honest.' Historically, we might say, to be honest was just to be virtuous, commendable, suitable, decent, of high rank, worthy of respect, etc. Perhaps philosophers have shunned honesty as a topic because it *isn't* a topic—or rather, it isn't *a* topic.

Still, in contemporary ethical discourse, it seems closer to being a topic than etymology would indicate. Christian Miller has suggested that in contemporary parlance honesty can be divided as follows:

(1) honesty as truthfulness;
(2) honesty as respect for property rights;
(3) honesty as proper compliance (playing by the rules, not cheating);
(4) honesty as fidelity to promises;
(5) honesty as forthrightness.[2]

These aspects or kinds of honesty seem to fall into two categories: a truthfulness category and a justice category. To be honest is to be a person who tends to tell the truth, and some situations that do not strictly require truth telling may be such that it would be a good thing to volunteer it. Forthrightness, when it is a kind of honesty, is truthfulness that is especially "open." For example, my marital situation may have some relevance to a potential employer's decision regarding me, though it is also, strictly, "none of his business." If I then volunteer a true description of my marital situation, I exemplify the truthfulness of forthrightness.

1. We are aware of only five extended treatments of the virtue in the recent philosophical literature: Miller 2017, Smith 2004, Carson 2010: chapter 14, Baier 1990, and Wilson 2018.
2. Miller 2017: 239–240. Miller does not intend his list to be exhaustive.

Truthfulness may also occupy certain contexts in which the utterer can manufacture truth by her action: she makes the claim true by bringing its truth about. The truthfulness of fidelity to promises belongs to this class. In promising Joe that I will water his houseplants during Christmas, I bind myself to make true the proposition *I water Joe's house plants during Christmas*. But to follow through on our commitments to another person is one of many ways to do justice by the other; by promising, I come to owe it to Joe to water his houseplants. If I promise and then fail, intentionally or negligently, to make that proposition true, I treat him unfairly. So this kind of honesty spans truthfulness and justice.

Honesty as respect for property rights is another kind of justice: for someone to have a right to a certain property is for others to owe him respect for or observance of that right. Honesty as playing by fair rules also seems to fall under justice. It would not be dishonest to fail to follow rules to which one has no (even implicit) commitment. So compliance with rules can also be seen as owed to the other participants, and thus as a kind of justice, where justice is basically giving others their due.

But again, honesty as respect for property rights and honesty as compliance with rules, like honesty as promise keeping, seem to involve a measure of truthfulness, for *candid* failures to respect property rights or play by the rules—say, the schoolyard bully who brazenly shakes you down for your lunch money before God and everyone—may seem to be unjust without being dishonest. Because of honesty's two-sidedness, our intuitions are fluid here, like our seeing of Jastrow's famous duck-rabbit. If we say, "he's unfair, but he's honest about it," we're loading our intuition from the truthfulness side (like thinking *duck*); if we say the bully's unfairness *is* dishonesty, we're loading the intuition from the justice side (like thinking *rabbit*).

To summarize: forthrightness is just a particularly open kind of truthfulness; promise keeping is a kind of truthfulness but also a kind of justice; and respect for property and compliance with rules are kinds of justice that may or may not involve truthfulness, depending on the case. So, although Miller's list of five categories offers a useful survey of the types of honesty, the diversity within the concept is less than the list makes it initially appear. Perhaps philosophers have neglected the virtue of honesty because it can be more elegantly treated under discussions of truthfulness and justice. Conceptually, honesty seems to lack a life of its own.

But as we've already begun to see, it would be a mistake to think that honesty consists in an unordered conjunction of two (or more) unrelated virtues. We think Rachana Kamtekar gives up too soon on the unity of honesty when she says:

> Although we use a single word, 'honest,' to describe the behavior of not lying, not cheating, and not stealing, it does not seem obvious that not lying, not cheating, and not stealing are the same sort of thing, or even that they are deeply connected. It may be that underlying this single word are three distinct and unrelated dispositions.[3]

Far from being strange bedfellows, truthfulness and justice are intimate partners in honesty. To tell the truth is often to give others their due; it is a way to treat them with the respect owed them as persons, or a way not to cheat them in various language-games of communal life. Think of the role of truth in business transactions, in marriage, in courts of law. In such contexts, justice depends on truth, and the concern for justice is often a central motive for telling the truth; you tell the truth, in part, because it would be unfair not to. Of course, truth is not the only thing we owe one another, so truth telling is not the whole of justice. And justice is not the only reason to tell the truth, so justice is not the whole of truth telling.

3. Kamtekar 2004: 468–469.

But even if they aren't coextensive, the virtues of truthfulness and justice overlap significantly, bound together, not by a single shared property, but by their high degree of relevance to one another. Having a shared property is not the only way that two things can be "unified."[4] Think of the way a person's right and left hands form an interdependent pair by the ways they function together. Neither hand is as useful by itself as each is in coordination with the other. The two hands are made for one another; they are highly "relevant" to one another. It's true, of course, that they have properties in common (e.g., *having fingers*) and that these properties facilitate their coordination. Justice and truthfulness also share properties (e.g., *being dispositions to interpersonal transactions, being in service of human well-being*). Our point is just that those common properties are not the only thing that unifies them. Like the left and right hands, the functional relevance of justice to truthfulness and of truthfulness to justice unifies them, and the field of their overlapping relevance constitutes the domain of the virtue that we call honesty.[5]

Accordingly, our exploration of the virtue of honesty will be divided into two topics: honesty as truthfulness and honesty as justice. However, we aim also to elucidate the interplay between them, as well as their relations with other virtues. Our approach supposes

---

4. See Miller's (2017: 240) "unification challenge."

5. It's not inevitable that a system of moral concepts have the concept of honesty that prevails in Western modernity. A system might make do with justice and truthfulness and their interactions, without having our concept of honesty. Virtues tend to be relevant to situations to which other virtues are also relevant. For example, situations that call for courage may also call for justice or compassion, and vice versa. It is hard to imagine a virtue that is specific to only a single kind of situation, and it would be utterly cumbersome to have a concept for every functional overlap of two virtues. The concept of honesty is a convenience, which probably also reflects the high rate and importance of these virtues' relevance to one another. Generosity and gratitude are also highly relevant to one another. It is easy to imagine a virtue that "unifies" them and expresses their functional interactivity (we might call it "gratigenosity" or "genergratositude"). The fact that our moral practices haven't yielded such a virtue category suggests that we haven't found it convenient in the way that we've found it convenient to have the virtue category of honesty.

that we can clarify the virtue of honesty by sketching its place in the surrounding geography of the virtuous life. In section 2 we will explicate truthfulness as a sensitivity to the values of truth, the relation of truthfulness as a virtue of caring to other virtues of caring, and its relation to two other kinds of virtues: humility and the virtues of passion control. In section 3 we will address questions about honesty as justice: Is all justice honesty? How is the virtue of honesty as justice related to conscientiousness about being honest?

But first, a note about virtues. This paper presupposes a "deep" conception of virtues. Virtues are not merely behavior dispositions, but are motivationally intelligent; in Rosalind Hursthouse's words, a virtue goes "all the way down."[6] To take truthfulness as an example, being disposed to tell the truth in a given kind of situation is not sufficient. One's disposition might be semi-rote, or it might be motivated by fear of consequences. In either case, the disposition would not be the virtue of truthfulness. To express the virtue, the truth telling would need to be generated from out of the agent in such a way that truthfulness characterizes that agent's *understanding* of the value of truth and truth telling. And that understanding needs to be an integral part of an emotional *appreciation* of truth and truthfulness. In a word, to be a *virtue*, truthfulness needs to be a characteristic of the "heart" of the agent, and truthful behavior an expression of that heart.

2. HONEST TELLING

2.1 *Truth and Its Values*

Bernard Williams divides the virtues of truth into Sincerity (truth telling) and Accuracy (truth seeking). The word 'truthfulness' seems more naturally to apply to Sincerity than to Accuracy, but as Williams points

6. Hursthouse 1999: 12.

out, Sincerity presupposes the seriousness about truth that is essential to Accuracy, and thus its carefulness about investigation.[7] If you are concerned that your communications to others be true, you will also tend to be serious about how you come to believe the claims that you convey, including implicit claims to be able to fulfill the promises you make. You won't be a victim of wishful thinking, or a person who says whatever he regards as convenient for himself that others believe. The untruths characteristic of an untruthful person sometimes stem less from the intention to deceive than from careless inquiry. The truthful person thus cares about truth both in the context of communication with other persons, and in the context of investigations and knowing.

So truthfulness is about truth. But what is truth? Truth, let us say, is how things are, not simply *as* they are, but considered *in relation to subjects' apprehension*, for example, by way of belief, claim, or perception. A belief is true insofar as its content states how things actually are (were, will be, would be); claims are true insofar as what they claim is how things actually are (etc.); and a perception is true insofar as what perceptually appears to the subject is how things actually are.[8]

What value does truth have for us? If the previous paragraph is correct, the value of truth will be the value of the faithfulness of our minds (beliefs, claims, perceptions, etc.) to the way things actually are. That faithfulness impinges on our lives in several ways.[9] For one thing, as William James points out, truth "works"; it makes for "*success*."[10] If you want to repair a malfunctioning engine, you will do much better if your beliefs about what is wrong with it are true than if they are false. But, as our account in the previous paragraph suggests, we don't think the truth of a proposition consists in its working,

---

7. Williams 2002, especially chapters 5 and 6.
8. This account is a paraphrase of Aquinas 1952: Question 1, Article 1, Reply.
9. The following list is not intended to be exhaustive.
10. James 1943; our italics.

but that it works because it's true—because it is taking reality into account.

As an important sub-species of truth's pragmatic value (and here the value of truth makes for the value of truth *telling*), truth (in the possession of each of two or more agents) promotes *interpersonal coordination.* The work of government is severely impeded if members can't depend on each other to tell the truth when asked and to be appropriately forthright about it when they aren't asked. Other things being equal, you will relate more expediently and more humanly to your partner if you have true beliefs about her mind than if you have false ones; for this reason (among others), you will value her truthfulness about her mind. Related to this is a person's relation to herself, so to speak. People who rationalize and deceive themselves in other ways tend to disable themselves for moral and other improvements, and for effectiveness in dealing with reality. Here the value of truth implies the value of truthfulness to yourself—of avoiding self-deception.

Truth's other values are also connected to its value in personal relationships.[11] Human relationships thrive on trust and ail on betrayal. Typically, a person feels devalued, insulted, belittled· by another (especially in a close relationship) when lied to, and truth telling is valued both as a *matter of justice*—something we owe to each other—and as a *cement of personal relationships,* a kind of fidelity of one person to another. Truth has value also, and in a way most fundamentally, because we humans are seekers of knowledge and understanding, for both of which truth is a necessary condition. So the truth of beliefs, perceptions, etc. has value for us as *epistemic contact with reality.*[12]

---

11. Compare Smith 2004.
12. In our view, the values of truth, knowledge, and understanding are mutually supporting: the value of truth helps explain (but does not exhaust) the values of knowledge and understanding, and the values of knowledge and understanding help explain the value of truth for epistemic agents like us.

2.2 Truthfulness Among the Virtues of Caring

In light of the sundry values of truth and its interactions with other value-laden features of situations, it is not always appropriate to tell truths, or even to know them. We might want to withhold truth from others because we don't want them to have the power of success that truth enables or because the success of our own action depends on not sharing the truth with others. Sometimes our relationships can be undermined by truth. It may be better, in some circumstances, for us not to have epistemic contact with reality (e.g., by listening to gossip). Thus, we need *circumspection* about the truth: good "vision" about circumstances, the ability to "see" the relevance of circumstances to an object of concern, and thus ideally to be concerned in the right way in the circumstances—in a way that is rationally measured to those circumstances.

Honesty as truthfulness is not merely a disposition to make true claims, or to seek the truth, or to face the truth (e.g., about oneself). It is a *character* trait, a habit of the *heart*, only if such a disposition originates in or is constituted by a caring about truth qualified by an appreciative understanding of truth's value—that is, some wisdom about truth and the way it interacts with other features of a human life (justice, the trust of others, promising, friendship, respect for others). For example, in some circumstances justice might be undermined by forthrightly telling the truth; so the person who is wise about the values of both justice and truth may withhold the latter. This is not to say that honest people need to have reflected on the values of truth in some abstract way, or that they consciously rehearse those values when they utter truths. Maxine, an honest person who understands the value of truth in relationships, may simply "see," without reflection, that when her son Clive asks her what she thinks Clive's motive was in questioning her authority, this is not a moment for forthrightness. And so she finds some way to avoid answering the question directly. If Maxine's truthfulness is deep and wise, then her perception at that moment is a product of what Daniel Kahneman calls her "System 1" thinking: not deliberate, discursive, time-consuming reflection (the work of "System 2"), but automatic, intuitive, and instantaneous insight.[13]

In short, we propose that the virtue of honesty as truthfulness is *circumspect concern for truth in communication,* and thus an *emotional sensitivity to the values of truth.* Let's unpack this sentence. 'Concern' is a general term for cares, desires, wishes, and loves. Concerns can be "negative"—for example, the desire (concern) to avoid being embarrassed in public. But when we speak here of a concern for truth, we mean a "pro-attitude"—what Robert Adams would call "being for" the truth: "loving it, liking it, respecting it, wanting it, wishing for it, appreciating it, thinking highly of it, speaking in favor of it and otherwise intentionally standing for it symbolically, acting to promote or protect it, and being disposed to do such things."[14] Thus, we are suggesting that truthfulness is a love of truth in the context of communication: the conveying of truth to other persons (or to oneself, thought of as a sort of "other"). A person who loves truth in this context will want, other things being equal, that his communications be true. But, because of the various values that truth has for us—the ways it affects our life—other things are not always equal. Sometimes the truth does not carry its usual goods. For example, though truth generally contributes to interpersonal harmony, in some circumstances (as in the Maxine and Clive case) it would disrupt.

---

13. See Kahneman 2011. Kahneman is less optimistic than we about the range of dispositions of System 1 thinking that can be shaped by learning. See Roberts and West (2015). We are grateful to Jay Wood for raising this issue. We don't mean to deny that System 2 thinking is part of Maxine's deep honesty. In circumstances that are less familiar to her than interacting with her son, she may need to deliberate long and hard about how forthcoming to be. And that deliberation will involve a skillful balancing of truth with justice, compassion, or other impinging values.

14. Adams 2006: 15–16.

Another point about concerns is that they always involve *some* understanding—correct or incorrect—of what they are about. My concern for my daughter's health involves an understanding of what health is, and of what health in her particular case would be. Similarly, when a person loves truth, she has some understanding of its import. When we say that honesty as truthfulness is a *circumspect* concern for truth in communication, we mean that the concern is qualified by a *good* understanding of the ways that truth impinges on and affects our lives (see section 2.1). The virtue of honesty as truthfulness is thus an *intelligent* love or caring about truth in the context of communication.

What about the claim that the virtue of honesty is therefore an *emotional sensitivity to the values of truth*? Roberts has argued that emotions are "concern-based construals," where a construal is a kind of conceptual perception or "seeing-as" (seeing one thing in terms of another).[15] (To refer again to Kahneman's vocabulary, we could say that emotions constitute an affectively charged form of System 1 cognition.) For example, if you care about your child, and you see that he is about to fall off a wall, you will see him as in danger, and that seeing-as will be fear for his safety. If honesty involves a concern for truth in the light of (in terms of) truth's various values in human life, then it is also a disposition to perceive with emotional sensitivity the situations in which truthful communication is (or is not) called for or has (or has not) been achieved. For example, if Maxine tells Clive what she thinks his motive was in resisting her authority, and Clive takes offense and shuts down communication with her for a time, Maxine may regret that she told Clive the truth. Or if, as in the original case, Maxine refrains from telling Clive the truth, it is her emotional sensitivity to the value (in this case, negative value) of truth that prevents her, wisely, from telling it.[16]

---

15. See, e.g., Roberts 2013.
16. For extensive discussion, see Roberts 2013: chapters 3–5.

The words of Joseph Conrad's Marlow in *Heart of Darkness* bear witness to the emotional implications of honesty's intelligent caring:

> I would not have gone so far as to fight for Kurtz, but I went for him near enough to a lie. You know I hate, detest, and can't bear a lie, not because I am straighter than the rest of us, but simply because it appalls me. There is a taint of death, a flavor of mortality in lies—which is exactly what I hate and detest in the world—what I want to forget. It makes me miserable and sick, like biting something rotten would do.[17]

If Marlow's honesty fits our formula, then his revulsion at a lie can be explained by reference to the values of truth. As an insult and devaluation of the deceived person, the lie often constitutes a personal breach with its purveyor. Thus, someone with a deep respect for others will find it repugnant, and even more so when the other is a friend or close acquaintance. A lie that succeeds in deceiving tends to reduce the other's ability to be effective in the world, perhaps by disabling her from coordinating with others. To commit the lie with open eyes (i.e., without self-deception) may require a cruel streak. And finally, the lie can put the deceived person out of epistemic contact with reality, sending her down a dark and fruitless path, even sowing chaos in the community—again, something a compassionate person would find distasteful in the extreme. Such deprivation of the goods of respect, interpersonal relation, agency, and contact with reality has, indeed, a flavor of death, at least for those who, in virtue of their wise concerns, are alive to truth's pragmatic, interpersonal, and epistemic values. The virtue of truthfulness is thus an affective affirmation of life—in particular and most immediately, the lives of the teller and receiver of truth.

---

17. Conrad 1960: 94. Marlow's "near lie" in this context consists in his not correcting another person's false beliefs about Marlow's influence in Europe.

That the values of truth are values of life suggests that the deep virtue of honesty will need to lodge in an encompassing virtuous character, for wise sensitivity to truth's values assumes wise sensitivity to the values characteristic of other virtues of caring, such as compassion, justice, generosity, and friendship. But this fact also helps explain why those with a circumspect regard for truth sometimes utter life-affirming falsehoods.

Around the fourth of July, Greg Boyle, a Jesuit priest who works with former and current gang members (known as "homeboys" and "homegirls" in the lingo of Boyle's world) in Los Angeles, hears a deafening volley of firecrackers from the bathroom near his office. He emerges in a rage: "By the time I get there, a homegirl, Candy, is a banshee, screaming in the *máscara* of the alleged culprit, Danny."[18] (Candy has been trying to preserve a peaceful atmosphere in the region of Greg's office.) He peels the two apart and heads to the parking lot with Danny for a little talk.

> Normally, I'd want to throttle this kid and give him, as they say, "what for." I manage something I rarely can. I morph into Mother Teresa *and* Gandhi. — "How ya doin?" I gently speak to Danny, on the hot asphalt of the parking lot. — "I DIDN'T DID IT!" Danny gives me both barrels, in perfect homie grammar. "I DIDN'T . . . DID IT!" — "I know," I say, . . . going against every grain in my being. "I know, I know. But I'm worried about ya," I say as quiet as I can be. "How ya doin?" — "Okay." — "Did you eat anything today?" — "No."— I give him five dollars. — "Why don't you go across the street and get something to eat." —Danny starts to walk away and mumbles loud enough to be heard, "Even though you don't believe me." I call him back. —"Danny, if you tell me you didn't do it, *mijo*, then . . . that's all I need." Danny

18. Boyle 2010: 45.

stands in the hot July sun and begins to weep. Cornered by shame and disgrace, he acquiesces to a vastness not mine.[19]

A couple of times in this interview Greg tells (or at least comes near to telling) Danny something that isn't true: that he believes Danny's denial of responsibility. (Despite Greg's assurances, and despite being off the hook and richer by $5, Danny seems to be concerned that Greg doesn't believe him—he understands that relationships thrive on trust!) If we assume, as indeed we can, that Father Greg has the honesty of truthfulness, we can see the circumspection of his honesty at work. One of the values of truthfulness is its function as cementing personal relationships. Here Greg's relationship with Danny is jeopardized by Danny's defensiveness and Greg judges (no doubt rather spontaneously—his System 1 at work) that it will not improve matters for him to deny Danny's denial, however lovingly he might thus speak the truth. So out of compassionate concern for his friend, he tells Danny an untruth, with the result that, in the power of his unconditional welcome of Danny's person, Danny himself truthfully reverses his denial, and their personal relationship—not to speak of Danny's with God—reaches a new plateau of maturity. In the circumstances, Greg recognizes that trimming the truth a little is needed to put his relationship with Danny on a firmer, more honest, footing, and Danny in closer epistemic contact with reality.

It isn't obvious, perhaps, that Father Greg's falsehood amounts to a lie, though, to borrow Marlow's language, it is "near enough" to one. Marlow himself, it turns out, goes all the way there. A year after Kurtz's death, Marlow visits Kurtz's "Intended," who is desperately in love with Kurtz, to give her some of Kurtz's belongings. Two things become evident immediately: first, the Intended is utterly ignorant of Kurtz's dishonorable character, esteems him above all others, and

19. Ibid., 45–46.

even prides herself on having "understood him better than any one on earth"; and second, time has not healed her wounds ("for her he had died only yesterday").[20] Seeking consolation, she presses Marlow to reveal Kurtz's dying words. Despite his aversion to deception, Marlow finds the truth "too dark" to speak. He tells the Intended that her name was the last utterance to pass Kurtz's lips, when in reality it was "The horror! The horror!" As he prepares to leave her house, his lie appalls him: "It seemed to me that the house would collapse before I could escape, that the heavens would fall upon my head."[21]

In a sense, both Father Greg and Marlow let compassion trump truth. Although Greg says that his falsehood went against every grain in his being, it seems clear that it falls far short of the momentousness of Marlow's lie. Plausibly, Greg spoke falsely in hopes that the truth would prevail in the end. And his interaction with Danny ultimately amounts to a quickly passing episode in the latter's adolescent journey toward honesty. Marlow, on the other hand, leaves the Intended in the dark about what appears to be the central concern of her life, so his lie feels like a deep betrayal of her trust. Some may think Marlow's lie indicates a lack of virtue; but we prefer to say that his compassion and honesty, combined with the facts of the world, make him tragic.

We've illustrated the dependence of the virtue of honesty as truthfulness on other virtues of caring. Next let us consider its dependence on humility.

2.3 Truthfulness and Humility

We're claiming that motivation is crucial to the virtue of honesty, and that not just any motivation to tell the truth will do. Williams seems momentarily to deny this when he says, "Sincerity at the most basic

20. Conrad 1960: 155 and 154.
21. Ibid., 157.

level is simply openness, a lack of inhibition. Insincerity requires me to adjust the content of what I say."[22]

Ponder Michael Jordan's famous induction speech into the Basketball Hall of Fame. On September 12, 2009, Jon Greenberg wrote of Jordan's speech, "It was a telling Jordan moment: honest, seemingly loving and full of hubris. It was not the words of a father, but of a competitor."[23] Jordan's speech was a litany of complaints against people who had underestimated his greatness, and the triumphs in which he had proved them wrong. "When Jordan . . . brought up his three children, he told them he felt sorry for them, because of the tall shadow they have to live with." In this "telling Jordan moment," Jordan tells, without evident inhibition, the truth about his own mind: he thinks he's extremely great. A person with lots of hubris, but less than Jordan, would probably be less "sincere" in baring his self-admiration and contempt for the blockheads who underestimated his grandeur. He would "adjust the content," as Williams predicts, to avoid giving an impression of small-mindedness to his audience. Jordan doesn't exhibit this caution, and so comes across, to many, as small-minded.

Jordan tells the truth about his self-admiration, and is thus "honest" in a purely behavioral sense, at least in this particular kind of case (namely, where the truth is something he relishes for reasons distant from the values of truth). But his "honest" behavior here does not exemplify the *virtue* of honesty because it is not motivated by a love of truth, but by his love of his greatness and its illustrations.[24] He speaks some truths because he personally likes them and relishes spreading them. Perhaps his sincerity's lack of caution also expresses arrogance: the extremity of my greatness overwhelms any need to guard against being thought small-minded. Or perhaps he's just so full of

22. Williams 2002: 75.
23. Greenberg 2009.
24. For more evidence that Jordan's "honesty" doesn't run deep, see Lake 2012.

himself that he's lost the empathic capacity to anticipate the effect his "honesty" will have on the affections of people like Greenberg.

We have emphasized that virtuous concerns enable evaluative vision; with Jordan we find illustrated the inverse phenomenon: vicious concerns distract, disorient, and otherwise disable the eyes of the heart. It is true, as Greenberg notes, that Jordan is plausibly the greatest athlete of his time. But the vanity, arrogance, domination, and invidious triumph that constitute the vices of hubris are distortions of humane perception.[25] They falsify one's own and other people's humanity, and so in that sense are contrary to honesty and the virtues of truth. To use Williams's expression, they are sources of "inaccuracy." They put Jordan in the dark with respect to some important truths. Greenberg gives an example of such inaccuracy in Jordan's case when he says that his words were "not the words of a father, but of a competitor." He seems to have processed his greatness as an athlete in such a way as to blind himself to himself and his children. Greenberg contrasts Jordan, in this regard, with David Robinson, who was inducted into the Hall of Fame on the same day as Jordan:

> I was at the gym during Robinson's speech, watching and listening on the elliptical. I'm not afraid to say I teared up. Robinson was often criticized for being too soft on the court, too cerebral. He was, in a lot of ways, the anti-Jordan, as a superstar. The Admiral spent the entirety of his speech thanking people. When he spoke of his family, he gushed over his three boys, calling them his best friends, encouraging them to reach their own goals.

The indebtedness to others expressed in those many thanks, and the acknowledgment of fundamental human equality in calling his

---

25. For more detail about the vices of pride, see Roberts and West 2017; and for more on their epistemic import, see Roberts and Wood 2018.

sons his friends, are truths of an order that ranks honesty, as an ability to appreciate such things, among the highest human virtues. Like Sincerity, fully virtuous honesty presupposes being equipped to acquire the truth about which one is sincere, honest, or forthright. And a person as deeply in the grip of hubris as Jordan is disabled for the personal evaluative truths that hubris obscures.

Narcissistic regard is just one of many motivations that can block a person's concern for the truth. Miller points out that empirical studies seem to show that most people are not unqualifiedly either honest or dishonest.[26] They sometimes behave honestly in honesty-relevant situations, and sometimes dishonestly.[27] You may have any of many reasons for lying, self-deceit, or shielding yourself from learning the truth—or for telling the truth! Maybe you gain money by lying. Maybe you anticipate that knowing the truth will make life more anxious or otherwise difficult. Maybe you don't want to give up your anger and vengeful projects. Maybe, like Marlow and Father Greg, you lie out of compassion or to protect someone from harm. Maybe you deceive as a strategy for getting another to see a truth about himself (Socrates in the *Euthyphro*).

But one especially common and significant class of truth-relevant motives is constituted by the vices of pride: conceit, vanity, domination, envy, racism, etc. You might tell either falsehoods *or* truths for reasons supplied by the vices of pride. Maybe you tell the truth about somebody out of an envious desire to "put him down"—or you lie about him for the same reason. To that extent, truth-telling behavior would not express virtuous honesty, though lie-telling behavior would usually express dishonesty.[28] Humility supports honesty by

26. Miller 2013: 294–297.

27. Miller calls the traits that most people have "mixed traits"—traits that are generically moral, but are neither virtues nor vices. See Miller 2013: 207–213.

28. It appears that the honesty of truthfulness shares a motivational feature that Bernard Williams has pointed out with respect to justice: just as there is no motive specific to

removing this class of motives, and relative humility mitigates them; and so humility liberates us to be virtuously honest.

We've seen humility diverge from "honesty" in the case of Michael Jordan's induction speech; but we have also disputed whether his "honest" behavior is an expression of the virtue of honesty. The vices of pride are all egoistic: they are all concerns for one's own importance in the sense of "narcissistic enhancement."[29] They are in strong friction with virtues that involve concern for, or commitment to, something beyond the self. Truth and justice, the objects of the virtuous concerns that make up the two sides of honesty, are both values beyond the self. Truth, we have said, is reality thought of in connection with a subject's apprehension of it; justice is everyone getting his due. The virtues of truthfulness and justice both require the subject to love something other than his own importance. For this reason, humility fits hand-in-glove with honesty. You can't have any genuine honesty without having some humility—that is, some openness to take an interest in things beyond your self, your own importance.[30] And the purer your humility, the readier, the more open you will be to devote yourself to truth and justice. Similarly in the other direction, the purer your honesty, the more complete will your humility be.

2.4 Truthfulness and the Virtues of Passion Control

So far, our sketch of the honesty of truthfulness has supposed a moral psychology of passional balance. That is, the picture has included only the concern for (sensitivity to, appreciation of) the values of

injustice (but injustices are to be explained by people's lack of the sense of justice), so there is no specific motive of mendacity, which is characteristically to be explained by a shortfall of the concern for truth. See Williams 1980: 197.

29. We found this felicitous, if somewhat clinical sounding, summary phrase for the vices of pride in Reimer 2009: 75.

30. See Smith 2004: 518: "An honest person is the antithesis of a pretentious person. A concern for appearances never overruns his concern for what is genuine."

truth on one side, and, on the other, the concerns that divert us from such values and obscure them from our awareness. If this were the whole picture of the moral psychology of honesty, then honest or dishonest action, emotion, and perception would be just a matter of the balance of these competing concerns. In people (or in moments) where the concerns for the values of truth outweighed the concerns for competing values, the action, perception, and emotion would be honest, and in the reverse case dishonest (or at any rate, not honest). Perhaps some people are so strongly moved by the values of truth that they resist "temptations" to falsehood as an efficient rain jacket resists the rain. But such people are rare at best. Even the most honest people are at times tempted to lie, and generalizing this picture of balanced motivations seems too simple.

In addition to our passions, we seem to have the capacity to stand back from our passions, to evaluate them, and to manage them in the interest of values that may not move us strongly enough to carry the day unaided—in other words, to undertake an *action* of resisting the adverse impulse. For example, if we find ourselves tempted to lie from vanity—say, fearing that our precious reputation for mastery of situations be tarnished—we can, by noticing that this desire is born of vanity and is contrary to the values of truth, resist the temptation, even if it is hot and intense in comparison with our "rational" and relatively cool commitment to truth.

The case just described would seem to exemplify courage, because the truth-resisting motive is fear; but since the fear arises from vanity, the courage functions as a substitute for humility: if you're without such vanity, you won't need to summon courage in a case like this. The temptation may come from elsewhere, of course. If you lie on your income tax return, the underlying vice is probably greed or stinginess, and the virtue that will stand in for a lack of greed (or for the virtue of justice or even generosity) is probably self-control: you see the justice of paying required taxes, and even though the impulse of greed is

strong, by effort of will you overcome it and write down the truth.[31]
While it is conceivable that a person be virtuously honest without any
virtues of passion control, we think it exceedingly unlikely, and so this
kind of virtue, like the virtues of caring and a degree of humility, will
be an aspect of the deeply honest person's character.

We have considered the truthfulness dimension of honesty, and
its fit with three kinds of virtues. Let us now turn to its justice dimension: the honesty of promise keeping, fair play, and respect for others'
property.

3. HONEST DEALING

Justice and injustice are properties of situations, institutions, personal relationships, court verdicts, laws, actions, and perhaps other
things. In saying so, we are talking, not about the virtue of justice, but
about what we might call "objective" justice. Justice in this sense is
the property of *being such that people get the good that is coming to them
and do not get the evil that is not coming to them.* For instance, a pay-
check is just when an employee receives the pay she's due; a prison
sentence is just when it fits the crime. What is due to people depends
on a variety of considerations, such as desert, status or role in a community, need, current possession, parity, positive law, and agreements such as promises.[32] The examples just noted illustrate some
of these considerations: a person is due adequate compensation for
work that she does, and a person may be due a penalty for criminal
or negligent actions (desert); equal work should receive equal pay
(parity); a prison sentence shouldn't go beyond what the penal code
allows (positive law); and so on.

31. For more detail about willpower and how it works, see West n.d.
32. This list is not intended to be exhaustive, but nothing else comes currently to mind.

To be just as a person—to have the virtue of justice—is to care intelligently about objective justice, where the caring is a deep disposition and 'intelligently' means understanding the various considerations on the basis of which goods and evils are due to people (desert, parity, and the rest) and having good judgment about their relative bearing in situations. This will include, indirectly, caring about the people involved; so something like benevolence or compassion stands in the background of justice. Among the wise, justice isn't simply a matter of evening scores.

We noted earlier that telling another the truth is often a matter of justice. It will be so in those cases in which one owes it to the other to tell him the truth. This debt might be in virtue of the other's deserving to be told the truth (he's been forthright with you, so you should be so with him), status or role in the community (he's a police officer), need (his well-being depends on your telling him the truth), agreement (you agreed to report to him), and perhaps other considerations. Concerned sensitivity to such considerations of justice is, of course, one aspect of truthfulness's circumspection, and helpfully illustrates honesty's two-handedness.

3.1 Is All Justice Honesty?

The three features from Miller's list that we have assigned to the honesty of justice are the keeping of agreements, complying with rules, and respecting others' property. To respect others' property is to observe the justice-principle that current possession gives a person a prima facie right to the property. Truthfulness could be expressed in such respecting, in case, for example, the respecting requires telling the truth about whom the property belongs to; but much respecting of property doesn't involve any immediate telling of the truth. However, if we think of the institution of property as presupposing an implicit "buy-in" by participants, we could see a remote connection to truthfulness here as well; we could think of thieves as liars about their buy-in. Admittedly, this is a stretch.[33]

By contrast, the promise keeping kind of justice seems to involve truthfulness essentially. Keeping promises falls under the kind of justice that we do when we keep our agreements. The just person is serious about her promises: concerned to make only ones she can keep, and to keep ones she has made; in so doing, she is expressing truthfulness as a necessary condition of doing justice.

Compliance with rules comes to be a kind of honesty when it is thought of as not cheating. Cheating is intentionally breaking duly constituted rules (e.g., of an athletic competition, a business arrangement, of test-taking, of a romantic relationship), usually to the supposed advantage of oneself or one's close associates, and usually to the disadvantage of other persons involved. If someone is cheated, it is the other participants. Compliance with rules may then be thought of as a way of keeping agreements, because even where no agreement is explicit, participation in the "game" (business, sport, debate, citizenship as in paying taxes) may be thought to constitute an implicit agreement to its rules (see Plato's *Crito*). But cheating is almost always (if not always) fraud. Fraud is injustice by deception. Think of contexts for cheating: cheating at games, cheating on one's income taxes, cheating on one's spouse, cheating in business, in politics. What should we think about a man who "cheats" on his wife, but does so openly? He is treating her unjustly, but perhaps not

33. Some thinkers have argued for a much tighter connection between truthfulness and respect for property rights than we deem plausible. For instance, William Wollaston (at least as interpreted by David Hume) seems to have thought that failures to respect property rights (as well as every other kind of "moral ugliness") are morally wrong when and because they cause false judgments. For Hume's refutation of Wollaston (whom Hume does not name, but refers to as "a late author who was fortunate enough to attain some reputation"), see Hume 2017: 237n1. Thanks to an anonymous reviewer for pointing us to the Hume/Wollaston debate.

dishonestly—because he doesn't deceive her. (That's why we feel that 'cheats' needs scare-quotes here.)

So honesty seems clearly to encompass the parts of justice having to do with respecting others' property, keeping agreements, and complying with constitutive rules. And each of these kinds of justice is connected in some way to truthfulness (rather loosely in the first case, essentially in the second, and somewhere in between in the third), which may help to explain their inclusion in honesty. What about other justice considerations? What about people's getting what they deserve? Is, say, not paying your employees a fair wage a breach of honesty? That seems dubitable, unless you agreed to pay them what they deserve. But again, if we tilt our intuition toward the justice side of honesty, underpaying them may seem more plausibly dishonest (thus the phrase, "honest wage"). Assuming that you owe your children a decent education because they have the status *your children*, would your failure to provide a decent education constitute dishonesty? Again, it would be unjust but probably not dishonest. Consider need. One might argue that it is unjust for some people in a community to go hungry when there is enough food to go around, if only it's rightly distributed.[34] Is anyone acting dishonestly in not providing the poor this food if he can? It seems that he is being unjust, but 'dishonest' seems the wrong word for his delinquency. Again, what if a father favors one of his children over another, and so violates the principle of parity? He is being unjust all right, but it seems wrong to call his error dishonesty. So it seems that not all justice is an aspect of honesty, but only the justice of agreements, constitutive rules, and property rights. But if you devise examples of any of the other kinds of justice so that they require the communication of truth, then they too become clear cases of honesty. For example, if what people need

---

34. St. Basil puts the point forcefully: "It is the hungry one's bread that you hoard" (cited in DeYoung 2009: 108).

from you is the truth, then if you withhold it, your injustice is a kind of dishonesty.

These considerations, together with those in the paragraph before last, seem to us to indicate that, while honesty is a two-handed virtue, it's not quite ambidextrous. Rather, honesty's dominant hand is truthfulness. Of the five kinds of honesty that Miller distinguishes, forthrightness is just a kind of truthfulness, keeping agreements essentially involves truthfulness, and compliance with rules can be thought of as involving implicit agreement. That leaves only respect for property rights as a kind of honesty that seems somewhat remote from truthfulness.

3.2 Honesty and Conscientiousness

Both truthfulness and justice, among other virtues (generosity, compassion), can be shadowed by conscientiousness about having them, and similarly a person can be conscientious about being honest. That is, a person can be conscientiously honest, where this virtue is not the same as honesty proper. We have said that the honesty of truthfulness is a circumspect concern for the values of truth in contexts of communicating it to others (truth *telling*). And we've said that the honesty of justice is a concern that objective justice prevail in contexts of regulated common activity, agreements, and property rights. Conscientiousness, like truthfulness and justice, is fundamentally an intelligent concern (it is one of the virtues of caring), but the concern differs by taking a subtly different object. Whereas justice and truthfulness take *objective justice* and *conveyed truth* as their objects (the subject being concerned about justice and conveyed truth), their shadowing conscientiousness takes *being just* and *being truthful* as their objects. Conscientiousness is about oneself, whereas the virtues that it shadows are about "the world"—such objects as truth (socially contextualized) and justice.

We have stressed that deep honesty depends on other virtues. Its dependence on conscientiousness seems to be primarily developmental. People who *lack* deep honesty typically need a measure of conscientiousness (together with the virtues of passion control) both to behave honestly in the face of temptation and to endeavor to deepen their honesty. After all, without a conscientious concern to be honest, less-than-honest folks will tend not to notice their lack of honesty with the kind of emotional pain that could move them to amend their lives.

Miller cites studies that seem to show that people's self-awareness as falling prospectively under negative moral descriptors ('cheater,' 'dishonest,' 'dishonorable') affects their inclination to cheat.[35] Bryan and colleagues found that causing subjects to think of themselves as *cheaters* if they cheated deterred cheating more than causing them to think of themselves as *having cheated*.[36] Mazar and colleagues found that having students sign a statement at the top of a questionnaire, "I understand that this short survey falls under MIT's [Yale's] honor system," significantly reduced cheating, despite a monetary reward for cheating, a guarantee not to be caught, and the fact that their university had no honor code.[37] The word 'honor' ('dishonor') identifies a status of a *self*, as does 'cheater.' To be honored is to have approving recognition directed at one's self. (You're honored *for* an achievement, say, but it's *you*, not the achievement, who receive the honor.) To be dishonored evokes shame in most people (a disapproving feeling toward oneself, a disposition to which is required for having a conscience).[38] Apparently, a college culture that construes cheating as lowering the cheater's status and keeps this evaluation before students' minds by reminders at opportune moments fosters

35. Miller 2014: 66–67.
36. Bryan et al. 2013.
37. Mazar et al. 2008.
38. On the developmental role of shame and related emotions, see Herdt (chapter 3 in this volume).

a motivating self-awareness about cheating.[39] We could say that priming with the honor code promotes, if only temporarily, conscientiousness about cheating (that is, repugnance for being a cheater).

Conscientiousness is not a fear of being caught. Another study examined how much money members of a staff contributed to the kitty on the "honor system" at an unsupervised office coffee station. On the wall behind the coffee pot was sometimes a picture of an arrangement of flowers, and sometimes a picture of a face (or merely eyes) gazing as if toward the coffee-patron. The picture of the face or eyes was found to improve the rate of paying by comparison with the flowers.[40] This set-up, in distinction from the college honor code and the provisional label 'cheater,' might be thought to appeal to patrons' fear of being *observed* ("caught") not paying for their coffee—in other words, to be thought *by others* to be dishonest. A genuine honor code, by contrast, carries some assurance that you needn't worry about being caught; instead, the code appeals to your conscience.

Miller points out that in situations where cheating is profitable and safe, we might expect cheaters to maximize gains by cheating to the maximum. But the vast majority of people in fact don't.[41] Instead, in conditions where they know they won't be caught, most people cheat, but only a little. Agreeing with the psychologists who ran the experiments, Miller hypothesizes that most people who cheat limit their cheating out of a concern to be able to continue to *think of themselves as honest*. The concern to be honest, which tends to involve the concern to think of oneself as honest, is what we call conscientiousness about honesty (that is, about being an honest person). If the participants in the studies (not to mention the rest of us) were a bit more

39. Strict accuracy might be better served by calling such codes "dishonor codes." But the circumspection of truthfulness prescribes a shading away from truth in this case, since considerations other than accuracy tell against such language.
40. A recent meta-analysis casts some doubt on this conclusion. See Northover et al. 2017.
41. Miller 2014: 68–72; see also Ariely 2012 and Leib and Shalvi (chapter 6 in this volume).

honest with themselves about their lack of honesty, perhaps their concern to be (or at least to think of themselves as) honest could be repurposed: rather than serving as a minor check on cheating and an abettor of self-deception, it could become an engine driving developmental effort.[42]

4. CONCLUSION

Is honesty a single virtue, or many? In a sense, we want to have it both ways. Honesty, we say, is a unified hybrid of truthfulness and parts of justice, a nearly ambidextrous virtue in which truthfulness takes the lead. But deeply reliable honesty is possible only when it partners with other virtues. As a virtue of caring, honesty involves circumspect concern for and sensitivity to the values of both truth in communication and objective justice. Such wise sensitivity depends on the wise sensitivities characteristic of other virtues of caring, such as compassion, generosity, and friendship, as well as humility's wise *freedom from* the sensitivities characteristic of vicious pride. And since no one's passions are perfectly put together, honesty must be patched up by virtues of passion control, such as courage, perseverance, patience, and self-control, as well as conscientiousness about honesty. Thus, although honesty proper is distinguishable from other virtues, our exposition has, in a way, confirmed the OED's etymological suggestion: the encompassing character of the honest person is well described as *being honorable*.[43]

---

42. On the development of honesty, see Porter and Baehr (chapter 7 in this volume).

43. We are grateful for support from the Templeton Religion Trust by way of the Self, Motivation, and Virtue Project at the Institute for the Study of Human Flourishing at the University of Oklahoma and the Beacon Project at Wake Forest University. The views expressed in this paper are those of the authors, and not necessarily the Templeton Religion Trust. Comments from participants at the workshop, "Integrity, Honesty, and Truth Seeking," held September 8–9,

BIBLIOGRAPHY

Adams, Robert Merrihew. *A Theory of Virtue: Excellence in Being for the Good.* Oxford: Oxford University Press, 2006.

Ariely, Dan. *The (Honest) Truth about Dishonesty.* New York: Harper Perennial, 2012.

Aquinas, Thomas. *De Veritate.* Translated by Robert W. Mulligan. Chicago: Henry Regnery Company, 1952. http://dhspriory.org/thomas/QDdeVer.htm.

Baier, Annette. "Why Honesty Is a Hard Virtue." In *Identity, Character, and Morality: Essays in Moral Psychology,* edited by Owen Flanagan and Amelie Rorty, 259–282. Cambridge, MA: MIT Press, 1990.

Boyle, Gregory. *Tattoos on the Heart.* New York: Free Press, 2010.

Bryan, C., G. Adams, and B. Monin. "When Cheating Would Make You a Cheater: Implicating the Self Prevents Unethical Behavior." *Journal of Experimental Psychology: General* 142 (2013): 1001–1005.

Carson, Thomas. *Lying and Deception: Theory and Practice.* Oxford: Oxford University Press, 2010.

Conrad, Joseph. *The Secret Sharer* and *Heart of Darkness.* New York: New American Library, 1960.

DeYoung, Rebecca Konyndyk. *Glittering Vices: A New Look at the Seven Deadly Sins and Their Remedies.* Grand Rapids, MI: Brazos, 2009.

Greenberg, Jon. "The Man Behind the Legend." 2009. http://www.espn.com/chicago/columns/story?columnist=greenberg_jon&id=4468210.

Hume, David. *Treatise of Human Nature.* Edited by Jonathan Barnes. 2017. https://www.earlymoderntexts.com/assets/pdfs/hume1740book3_1.pdf

Hursthouse, Rosalind. *On Virtue Ethics.* Oxford: Oxford University Press, 1999.

James, William. "Pragmatism's Conception of Truth." In *Pragmatism* and four essays from *The Meaning of Truth,* 131–53. New York: Meridian Books, 1943.

Kahneman, Daniel. *Thinking, Fast and Slow.* New York: Farrar, Straus, and Giroux, 2011.

Kamtekar, Rachana. "Situationism and Virtue Ethics on the Content of Our Character." *Ethics* 114 (2004): 458–491.

Lake, Thomas. "Did This Man Really Cut Michael Jordan?" *Sports Illustrated,* January 16, 2012. https://www.si.com/vault/2012/01/16/106149626/did-this-man-really-cut-michael-jordan

Lee, Kibeom, and Michael C. Ashton. *The H Factor of Personality.* Waterloo: Wilfrid Laurier University Press, 2012.

2017 at the University of Oklahoma, led to needed revisions. We are especially grateful to Christian Miller for very helpful comments on earlier drafts, and to Jason Baehr and Jay Wood for their feedback. Roberts thanks Michael Spezio, his co-PI on a research grant funded by the Self, Motivation, and Virtue Project, for stimulating discussions of the virtue of humility.

Mazar, Nina, On Amir, and Dan Ariely. "The Dishonesty of Honest People: A Theory of Self-Concept Maintenance." *Journal of Marketing Research* 45 (2008): 633–644.

Miller, Christian B. *Moral Character: An Empirical Theory.* Oxford: Oxford University Press, 2013.

Miller, Christian B. *Character and Moral Psychology.* Oxford: Oxford University Press, 2014.

Miller, Christian B. "Honesty." In *Moral Psychology (Volume 5): Virtue and Character*, edited by Walter Sinnott-Armstrong and Christian B. Miller, 237–272. Cambridge, MA: MIT Press, 2017.

Northover, S. B., W. C. Pedersen, A. B. Cohen, and P. W. Andrews. "Effect of Artificial Surveillance Cues on Reported Moral Judgment: Experimental Failures to Replicate and Two Meta-analyses." *Evolution and Human Behavior* 38:5 (2017): 561–571. doi: 10.1016/j.evolhumbehav.2016.12.003.

Reimer, Kevin. *Living L'Arche.* New York: Continuum, 2009.

Roberts, Robert C. *Emotions in the Moral Life.* Cambridge, UK: Cambridge University Press, 2013.

Roberts, Robert C., and Ryan West. "Natural Epistemic Defects and Corrective Virtues." *Synthese* 192:8 (2015): 2557–2576.

Roberts, Robert C., and Ryan West. "Jesus and the Virtues of Pride." In *The Moral Psychology of Pride*, edited by J. Adam Carter and Emma C. Gordon, 99–122. Lanham, MD: Rowman and Littlefield, 2017.

Roberts, Robert C., and W. Jay Wood. "Understanding, Humility, and the Vices of Pride." In *The Routledge Handbook of Virtue Epistemology*, edited by Heather Battaly, 363–375. New York: Routledge, 2018.

Smith, Tara. "The Metaphysical Case for Honesty." *Journal of Value Inquiry* 37 (2004): 517–531.

West, Ryan. "Willpower and the Cultivation of Virtues." Unpublished manuscript.

Williams, Bernard. "The Virtue of Justice." In *Essays on Aristotle's Ethics*, edited by Amélie Rorty, 189–200. Berkeley: University of California Press, 1980.

Williams, Bernard. *Truth and Truthfulness: An Essay in Genealogy.* Princeton, NJ: Princeton University Press, 2002.

Wilson, Alan T. "Honesty as a Virtue." *Metaphilosophy* 49:3 (2018): 262–280.

Chapter 5

Honesty as Ethical Communicative Practice

A Framework for Analysis

JANIE HARDEN FRITZ

1. A FRAMEWORK FOR HONESTY AS ETHICAL COMMUNICATIVE PRACTICE: CONTENT AND RELATIONSHIP DIMENSIONS OF MESSAGES

In both public and private relationships, the manner in which honesty is enacted matters. Communicating in a direct, explicit way barren of contextual considerations that can buffer the impact of potentially face-threatening information, such as criticisms or concerns about the other person, can be painful. For example, I can say, very directly and honestly, to one of my direct reports: "Your work is substandard and not up to the level we're expecting." However, expressing such concerns in a tactful, discerning way provides space for the receiver to come to terms with that information and make constructive meaning

Janie Harden Fritz, *Honesty as Ethical Communicative Practice* In: *Integrity, Honesty, and Truth Seeking*. Edited by: Christian B. Miller and Ryan West. Oxford University Press (2020). © Oxford University Press.
DOI: 10.1093/oso/9780190920487.003.0005

of it. The same general content, framed from an alternative perspective, carries a different tone: "I have noticed the care you've taken to learn a very complex set of operations required by this new accounting system. It's natural to make some mistakes while you're learning. We're hopeful that you'll show increased speed and accuracy over the next week to get your level of productivity high enough to meet our goals for the month. You're not there yet, but I believe you can do it."

The difference between these two approaches highlights a concern as important as the nature of the information revealed. These two elements—what is said and the manner, tone, and style characterizing how it is said—define two dimensions or aspects of interpersonal communication relevant to honesty: the content dimension and the relationship dimension of messages.[1] The content dimension references the information carried by a message; honesty is relevant to truthfulness regarding factual matters. The relationship dimension indicates feelings about the other person, the emotional state of the speaker, and/or the relationship. This dimension speaks to consideration for the human person as person-in-relation, is affectively valenced, and carries implications for power. The relationship dimension offers interpretive nuance and insight into the relative status and power of the persons conversing, as well as their feelings about themselves and each other. The relationship dimension's implications for honesty are shaped by culture and context. Both dimensions support the existence of human communities and the realization of the human being as an integral person-in-relation.

The purpose of this chapter is to highlight several research areas in the field of communication relevant to the content and relationship dimensions of messages, and to indicate briefly how they can contribute to a better understanding of honesty. My treatment explores several parameters of honesty in relationships across five research

---

1. Watzlawick and Beavin 1967, Watzlawick, Beavin, and Jackson 1967.

areas—self-disclosure and restraint, Grice's theory of conversational implicature, message design logic, communication competence, and civility, authority, and love—with one section devoted to each. But first, let me say a brief word about how I plan to use the phrase "interpersonal communication."

I define interpersonal communication broadly, to include two-person communication in all contexts.[2] An extensive body of interpersonal communication research identifies outcomes associated with communication practices in close relationships.[3] However, most relationships people engage in during the course of a typical day are not particularly close. Communication between two persons in non-intimate or public, role-bound relationships, such as work associates, neighbors, and members of social and civic groups, is a ubiquitous feature of daily life and invites enactment of communicative virtues contributing to human flourishing. The "weak ties"[4] of public association constitute the fabric of our social worlds and must be protected as much as the stronger ties that bind us to our close friends and family. A broad approach to interpersonal communication invites consideration of how the context of a relationship shapes the way honesty is textured and played out in tandem with goods other than that of the relationship (e.g., the good of an organization or institution, or the good of task-related work). Communication in these more distant relationships offers a context within which to consider honesty as a virtue driving communicative practice, with implications for the larger human community.

2. In the parlance of the field of communication, I am assuming a "situational approach," while others in the field—those who take a developmental approach—define "interpersonal communication" more narrowly, restricting it to communication in close relationships. See Miller 1978.
3. Knapp and Daly 2011.
4. Granovetter 1973.

2. SELF-DISCLOSURE

In this section, I consider principles of honesty related to self-disclosure and restraint in intercultural and public contexts. Some scholars find evidence for the existence of a minimalist set of ethical principles that hold across cultures, such as truth telling, honoring the dignity of human beings, doing no harm to innocents, valuing other human beings as persons, and protecting the weak.[5] Truth telling as a central element of honesty fits within this universal domain, although its enactment may take different forms in different cultures and across contexts and relationships. Here we see the importance of the relationship dimension of interpersonal communication serving as a set of background constraints on foreground content or informational honesty.

For example, expectations for honesty as forthrightness, frankness, and directness in communicative practice are shaped by culture. In high-context, collectivistic cultures, such as China, Japan, and Korea, communication functions as a social lubricant—that is, as a way to maintain social harmony by protecting face, or public presentation of others' selves, through ambiguity and indirectness in discourse—rather than primarily to impart information.[6] In such cultures, respect for another person may require honesty to be buffered through many layers of relational considerations and couched within carefully negotiated and indirect messages. The relational fabric of social life frays easily and cannot bear the direct approach of stark informational revelation. Such messages may be effective in the sense that the information is delivered, but the relational cost may be quite high. Concerns for the larger social unit, as well as the relationship itself and the face needs of persons in relation, point in the

5. Christians and Traber 1997.
6. Hall 2005.

direction of a tempered honesty gradually unfolding over time and in ways that permit adjustment to new understandings of one's social and personal world.

Consider, for instance, a relationship guided by a norm of honesty in a culture attentive to the face concerns of others. In considering addressing a concern to his friend Shana about her habitual lateness, Tim may choose not to state his concern directly. Instead, he may bring up the importance of the friendship and the demands of his own schedule. He may mention times when his own work was compromised by delays, and then, after offering appreciation for help Shana has given him in the past, ask her for help in accomplishing his own goals by arriving on time. Tim may not bring up Shana's lateness at all, and she may not articulate her intention to change her behavior. Instead, she may simply begin to show up on time. The issue would never be addressed directly. In this case, honesty as a virtue does not change, but its enactment through communication is carefully timed. The content of a message is structured to prepare the recipient for the eventual fullness of the message. Understood in this way, honesty's contribution to human flourishing is context dependent.

The Korean practice of nunch'I (playing things by eye, or being attentive to the unspoken) provides an illustration of concern for the relationship through the cultural specificity of self-disclosure norms.[7] A request for an evaluation of a performative act, such as hanging a picture, may be met with silence. The indirect honesty of this response provides maximum interpretive autonomy to the receiver, who may "hear" the "honest" response as indicating that the picture is askew, straighten it, and eliminate the need for further discourse on the matter, thus preserving the face of a picture-hanger of higher status than the potential critic. The modality of delivery of this "honest" message permits both content and relationship dimensions to contribute to

7. Robinson 2000.

the well-being of the relationship and the persons participating in it. In other cultural contexts, a direct response would send a message of acknowledgment of relational strength and the ability of both parties not to flinch at a relational partner's "raw" delivery of information. The relational message, in each case, derives its meaning from the cultural background, while the content dimension remains the same, although in the former case the content dimension is implicit or indirect.[8]

Another way that the relational message is contextually sensitive has to do with matters of authenticity and restraint in different relational contexts. In the 1960s, societal shifts in the United States against norms supporting institutional constraints on individual liberty and self-expression prompted increased informality and willingness to disclose the "true" self in a quest for transparency and openness when communicating with others interpersonally. Forthrightness and authenticity became the watchwords for interpersonal communication.[9]

A byproduct of this shift toward openness in the public sphere, coupled with an increasingly fragmented understanding of the "good" for human life, was the potential for disagreement and conflict when differences that once remained tacit emerged as topics of dispute (e.g., discussions of religious differences in the workplace). Furthermore, details of one's private life might create closeness when revealed in a private relationship, but might remove the focus of attention from tasks when shared in the workplace (e.g., information about a daughter's struggles with drug addiction). Norms for public discourse that limit self-disclosure with unfamiliar others, or others with whom one has a primarily role-based relationship, protect privacy and maintain social harmony.

8. Brown and Levinson's 1987 work on politeness theory offers an in-depth look at the phenomenon of face and request forms across several different cultures relevant to these issues.
9. Parks 1981.

These mid-century moves toward therapeutic openness and freedom of expression were countered two decades later with a renewed emphasis on the importance of restraint shaped by recognition of the value of privacy and respect in public contexts.[10] The workplace requires a focus of attention on work rather than on one's personal problems. Norms of respectful discourse create a sense of consideration between people occupying roles with differing levels of authority—say, a supervisor and a direct report. Far from the cold aloofness that some would associate with professionalism, the distance associated with formal, role-bound discourse can create space for strained relations in the work context to heal or take on a new form.[11] If I assume too much familiarity with someone I do not actually know well, my jokingly offered insult may be taken seriously, with serious consequences. Honesty, in this case, calls upon coworkers to function within the limits of professional roles rather than with feigned friendship.[12]

Working with distance involves limiting one's self-disclosure. If my coworker and I experience a severe disagreement that generates hard feelings, limited (but honest) responses to questions can create some measure of distance in the relationship. For example, I can respond to mundane questions (such as "How was your weekend?) with accurate, but limited, information ("Fine, thanks—and yours?"). I maintain relational respect through my reply, but limit involvement through limited content. Although previously in the relationship I might have offered more elaborate, detailed answers at a deeper level of informational honesty, restraint begins to reset relational boundaries, with the potential to redraw them in the future. Restricting the extent and depth of communication demonstrates a

---

10. Arnett 1981, 2006, Fritz 2013.
11. Scott 2017.
12. Hess 2006.

move toward concealment (i.e., restraint) rather than revelation (i.e., disclosure), two ends of a spectrum defining a dialectical tension that all relationships experience.[13]

Friends and romantic partners, as well as work colleagues, strive to balance the need to share personal information with each other and also keep some information to themselves. Because the dialectic of disclosure and restraint, of sharing thoughts and feelings but holding back some, is also connected to a sense of closeness or distance, one partner may limit what is said to the other partner in a particular time, place, or context in order to provide needed space. Honesty, in this case, is not abandoned, but is reserved for a moment in which a message can be heard with minimal relational damage. Honesty has a temporal quality. In this sense it characterizes a fitting response, in Calvin Schrag's language.[14] This is a response in which "fitting" marks the message as taking place at just the right time, in the right measure, and in the right context. Aristotle makes a similar point about virtues in general in the *Nicomachean Ethics*.[15] Honesty requires discerning, in each context, whether it is the right time to reveal, what is the right amount to reveal, and in what way the revelation should take place.

For example, when asked your opinion of your friend's new car, you may refrain from stating that you do not like its color, noting instead your favorable opinion of its safety features. The message is designed to protect the friend's feelings and maintain goodwill in the relationship. Since there are multiple possible domains of experience about which one might report or that might provide a space for rapport, one may communicate honestly—that is, accurately—in many ways without saying all that might be said.

Honesty as relational openness or authenticity takes the communicative form of revealing elements of oneself that the other person

13. Baxter and Montgomery 1993.
14. Schrag 1986.
15. Aristotle 1962.

would not otherwise know. In this sense, honesty points to a relation-ship of trust with another person. However, as Rawlins points out, the honesty of self-disclosure can threaten self and other.[16] When one discloses potentially damaging information, such as an infidelity, or a fear or weakness, one becomes vulnerable. Likewise, such disclosures place a burden or obligation on the other person to respond in par-ticular ways with contributions of time and other resources.

Honest self-disclosure in relationships is attentive to both the informational content and implications for the relationship, factors shaped by culture and context. In some cultures, direct, explicit mes-sages focused on the accuracy of the content may be honest in terms of factual information, but relationally damaging. Likewise, different locations for relational engagement, such as the workplace, require sensitivity to context when considering how much information to reveal at a particular time and in a particular place. In each case, hon-esty is shaped by attentiveness to relational concerns.

The next four sections explore insights for honesty based on Grice's maxims, message design logic, communication competence, and considerations of civility, authority, and love. These conceptual themes expand our understanding of how informational honesty and relational restraint work together in interpersonal communication.

3. CONVERSATIONAL IMPLICATURE: GRICE'S MAXIMS

H. Paul Grice presented a theory of conversational implicature to explain how people make sense of everyday utterances (e.g., a request for information, disclosure of private information, evaluative state-ments, and so forth), especially when those utterances seem not to

16. Rawlins 1983.

respond to the requirements of the context.[17] "Implicature" refers to the assumed implications of utterances that might, on the surface, appear not to be truthful, relevant, or appropriate—but that listeners assume to be truthful, relevant, and appropriate, given what Grice identified as the cooperative principle in conversation.[18] As a sociolinguist, Grice was interested in the rules people tend to follow in ordinary conversation. We assume that others are trying to be truthful, to offer relevant contributions to the conversation, and to provide as much information as is needed.

Grice offered the following four maxims to describe the rules people typically follow in conversation in order to accomplish their conversational goals:

Quantity: One should say no less and no more than is needed;
Quality: One should say what one knows to be true;
Relevance: One should offer comments relevant to the matter at hand; and
Manner: One should speak with clarity, in an understandable way.[19]

These maxims have implications for honesty. In the case of relevance, for instance, even if what I say does not appear to respond to the question or the point at hand, a listener still assumes that I am following the maxim. Imagine that you ask me whether I know where Stacey is, and I respond that I saw a red truck at Paul's house. On the surface, I appear to be responding in a way that is not relevant to the question. However, if we both know that Stacey drives a red truck, then you may assume from my comment that I am telling you that there is a good likelihood that Stacey is at Paul's house.

17. Grice 1975.
18. Ibid.
19. Ibid.

Another example suggests the potential for several types of implicature. If, in a letter of recommendation, I state that a candidate did everything asked of her, the statement is true regarding her performance in fulfilling her obligations. The unstated implication, however, is that the person did no more than was asked—did not take initiative, did not identify additional ways to be helpful, and so forth. Readers assume I am being honest about the recommended person's attributes. They also "read between the lines," picking up on the intended meaning by recognizing potentially relevant details that I chose to omit. The implications are that the writer has said all that can be said, no more and no less, has spoken truthfully, has offered information relevant to the purposes of the letter, and is intending to be clear. Through the work of implicature, one conveys a message that is honest on multiple levels but does not state directly all that might be said. Grice's maxims suggest that conversations work enthymematically—through unstated shared premises that require cooperative action by speaker and audience to be meaningful.

Grice's theory of implicature highlights the role of ambiguity in negotiating meaning between conversational partners in the service of relational harmony. Ambiguity avoids directness and immediacy but permits the possibility of revealing further details, should they be necessary. For example, when talking with a friend about a recipe I tried that turned out to be a colossal failure, my friend may ask, "When I prepare that dish, I use thyme, rosemary, and nutmeg. What did you put in it?" If I reply, "Oh, something like that," when I used basil and oregano, I am using ambiguity to avoid revealing my ignorance of spices in order to save face. If my friend is sensitive to my reluctance to confess culinary ineptitude, he may simply say, "Well, try using exactly the ingredients I used next time. It might work!" His response would be considered tactful in its recognition of my desire not to reveal more information or to offer an outright lie ("I used the ingredients you used, and it still turned out to be inedible!"). My friend's tactful response demonstrates concern for both the informational and relationship dimensions of messages at work in this level of honesty.

Grice's theory of implicature suggests that honesty at the level of content and relationship may take different forms. As conversational partners work to make sense of each other's messages, assumptions about the other's honesty permit interpretations that are similar enough to guide coordinated action but provide freedom for variations in specific understandings. Such variations provide protective space for differences to exist without disrupting the relationship.

4. MESSAGE DESIGN LOGIC

Grice's theory of conversational implicature focuses on how receivers make sense of others' utterances through assumptions about speakers' intentions. Another theoretical perspective relevant to relational honesty, which emerges from a different set of assumptions about language and conversation, is message design logic.[20] This framework for message creation focuses on the message sender. Message design logic assumes that a person generates messages, particularly goal-directed ones, according to a particular understanding of how communication works. These understandings, or underlying logics, yield different message forms. Expressive, conventional, and rhetorical design logics could be considered different implicit philosophies of interpersonal communication, each yielding different ways of understanding and enacting honesty with respect to the content and relationship dimensions of messages. I will address each in turn.

Expressive design logic.[21] Expressive design logic focuses on the speaker's emotional state without taking into account the speaker's

20. O'Keefe 1988.
21. Ibid.

or the listener's goals, the way the speaker's and listener's goals might be seen as compatible, or the contextual constraints of the event (e.g., expectations for discourse established by common practice). For example, if a work colleague arrives late for a meeting, and I feel frustrated, I may say, "Why did you bother coming at all? I'm sick and tired of waiting for you time and time again!" Authentic expression is the goal of the speaker working from an expressive design logic. The implicit purpose is to have the listener know how the speaker feels, although the assumption of the theory is that the speaker does not necessarily have that goal in mind at the moment of the utterance. Within this design logic, honesty could be understood as accurate portrayal of feelings, whether positive or negative, marked by expressing what one feels without editing or restraint. But since neither the content nor the relationship dimension of messages receives its due, honesty would not be operating as a virtue in most instances of expressive design logic.

Conventional design logic.[22] Conventional design logic assumes the rule-governed nature of conversation. That is, we learn rules for appropriate discourse in formal contexts, such as employment interviews, and informal contexts, such as casual conversation with friends over lunch. Standard, culturally accepted forms of politeness mark conversation carried out according to conventional design logic. For example, when trying to convince a colleague to swap shifts at work, Toya might offer to work extra hours for that colleague in exchange for his help. Instead of focusing on her own goals or states ("I'm just worn out and need the night off!"), she would make reference to conventionally accepted rules of interaction, such as, "When asking a favor, offer a favor in return."

Honesty, from the approach of conventional design logic, might work at the level of accuracy of self-disclosure. I may describe what I hope you will do and identify what you may expect to happen if you

22. Ibid.

take, or fail to take, the desired action. Honesty becomes functional or pragmatic. That is, honest utterances work to fulfill or support some purpose or goal identified by the generator of the message. Both the content and relationship dimensions of messages receive attention in this design logic, focusing on the sender's desires or wishes, with attentiveness to generally shared expectations for interaction.

Rhetorical design logic.[23] Rhetorical design logic works to reshape the context itself, with the aim of reconciling the goals of both parties. This work is done through reframing the situation to invite new understandings or meanings for both content and relationship. For instance, if a colleague has not completed the expected work for a group project, instead of expressing outrage ("I knew you wouldn't follow through—you're unreliable!") or offering a formulaic response ("We agreed that those who do no work get no credit; we're taking your name off the project"), someone working from a rhetorical design logic perspective might say, "Everyone falls behind sometimes. If you can bring what you've done so far, we'll pair you up with someone who can assist. We will make it work."

Honesty from a rhetorical design logic perspective would be situated within a broader perspective, such that considering another's goals would be part of the context of honest discourse. If honesty has accuracy as one of its attributes or features, then an honest utterance would be an informed utterance based on perspectival information relevant to one's interlocutor as well as to oneself. In the example of the nonperforming colleague, the speaker frames the colleague not as a lazy group member, but as someone subject to what all humans experience—failure despite good intentions and the need for occasional consideration and assistance. The relational message is one of concern, understanding, and consideration. Accuracy requires adequate knowledge or information regarding both facts and feelings. It

23. Ibid.

is possible to be inaccurate about one's own state of being or possibilities through self-deception, even when one thinks one is communicating accurately and honestly. From the perspective of rhetorical design logic, part of the moral virtue of honesty involves being honest with oneself, taking responsibility for conscientious consideration of even difficult truths that go against a preferred position.

Message design logic illustrates how honesty relevant to the content and relationship dimensions of messages may take different forms, depending on one's assumptions about the purpose of communication. Expressive, conventional, and rhetorical design logics offer progressively more complex understandings of the way language works.

5. COMMUNICATION COMPETENCE

Grice's theory of conversational implicature and the message logic framework focus on specific ways speakers make sense of others' utterances or construct messages in order to accomplish goals. The construct of communication competence works from a broader perspective, addressing attributes of effectiveness and appropriateness in communicative practices.[24] Because communication competence has been approached from a social science point of view, the issue of ethics has not been an explicit part of the discussion.[25] I will discuss appropriateness and effectiveness as the two facets of communication competence and then address some of the implications for honest communication in relationships.

Whereas effectiveness involves accomplishing one's goal in an interaction (e.g., convincing a friend to help with a move to new living quarters), appropriateness calls for attending to contextual

24. Spitzberg and Cupach 1984.
25. Fritz 2016.

concerns relevant to the other and to the relationship surrounding an interaction in constructing a message. Do I remind my friend of all the times I have helped her and state that she owes me? Do I compliment her on her long-standing helpfulness to everyone? Effectiveness is judged instrumentally and is based on the accomplishment of an intended outcome or goal, considered the primary goal. The primary goal could be considered an external good, corresponding generally to the content or informational dimension of messages. For example, when someone attempts to gain compliance from another—perhaps to provide assistance on a task or perform a favor, as in the example of convincing a friend to help me move—the primary goal is that desired outcome.[26] The goal can be achieved in a number of different ways; these different approaches point toward appropriateness. Appropriateness attends to secondary goals, such as preserving the relationship or protecting the image of self or other, which may or may not be achieved in pursuit of a primary goal. Appropriateness attends to concerns related to ensuring that the relationship remains stable or secure and is therefore directed toward relational flourishing.

I offer here an expanded view of honesty, taking into account both effectiveness and appropriateness. For example, if I provide an honest account of my own productivity to my supervisor, even when I have not produced as much as expected, she can take action to supplement the shortfall by other means, thereby protecting the larger unit and/or organization. I can be honest about my performance in at least two different ways. If I provide only information about my lack of productivity, that would be sufficient to meet the criteria of effectiveness and meet the standard of informational honesty. If, however, in my report, I include an explanation of the failure and an action plan to remedy it, I have also met the criteria of appropriateness—that is, if

26. See Dillard, Segrin, and Harden 1989 for a discussion of primary and secondary goals in influence attempts.

the culture of the organization is one that emphasizes solving problems constructively rather than focusing on failure.

This latter action, which could be called holistic honesty, provides my supervisor with a rationale for continuing my participation in the work of the organization. If the organization has invested time and money to hire and train me, and I show the promise of doing good work, then my honest action will assist my supervisor in making a case for my continuing in the position and will support the culture of the organization. Furthermore, if the supervisor was my advocate at the time of hiring, then my eventual success as an employee will benefit more than my own career; my supervisor will be shown to have made a good decision in providing support for me. This accompanying good of appropriate honesty that honors my relationship with the organization and my supervisor enhances and enriches the effectively content-driven, or informationally honest, response.

From this perspective, honesty includes the enactment of communicative practices marked by an ideal balance of effectiveness and appropriateness, placing honesty as a virtue within the scope of practical wisdom. Honesty is virtuous communication when it takes the entire relevant context into account. The goodness of honesty itself as a virtue speaks to the status of human beings as relationally connected, with the need to attend to material and temporal features of the world and social and relational well-being.

Honesty in a relationship has implications for the communities of which the people in the relationship are a part, extending the conceptualization, or at least the expected reach, of communication competence beyond the relational partners and the relationship. Both persons and relationships are embedded in larger social units and are accountable to those encompassing entities. Hence, communication within interpersonal relationships ripples out to the larger sphere and shapes it. For example, if relationships among colleagues in my department are marked by honesty that is both tactful, or sensitive to relationships, and information-rich, or descriptive of real concerns and disagreements, then the entire unit will foster productivity and the possibility for enjoyable work, despite the inevitable differences and conflicts that emerge in the course of everyday interaction.

In sum, honesty as an element of communication competence takes both the content and relationship dimensions of messages into account. Holistically honest communication is attentive to multiple goals, seeking both effectiveness and appropriateness in all interactions. Holistic honesty has implications for the larger community, such as an organization, within which relationships are situated. Communication in relationships shapes both the relationship itself, and by implication, the culture and climate of the host organization, such that positive or negative communication influences others' expectations and communicative practices.[27] The extent to which honesty as a virtue characterizes persons in relation at the proximal or individual relationship level shapes distal features of larger communities and fosters beneficent practices at the level of the larger unit.

6. CIVILITY, AUTHORITY, AND LOVE

Communities, in order to function well, need communicative practices that permit discussion and resolution of disagreement—or some procedural means to move forward in the face of unresolved disagreement. The communicative virtue of civility has been considered a necessary element of a well-functioning public sphere, despite disagreement over its definition and characteristics—including the degree of honesty appropriate for conversations between persons holding differing views of the good.[28] In the workplace, professional

27. Fritz 2013.
28. Bejan 2017.

civility is a communicative virtue for interpersonal interaction with implications for honesty.[29] In contexts of instruction or apprenticeship, honest evaluation of performance from a position of authority contributes to the good of others. This section considers how civility and honesty work creatively when oriented toward love and concern for another in public settings. I begin with the context of the workplace.

Human goods in the workplace include proximal goods, such as respect, worth, and support for others, as well as distal goods, such as productivity and the health of an organizational culture or environment. In the workplace, professional civility supports those goods. Communicative practices of casual communication about the weather, greetings, and uplifting comments about one's surroundings create contexts in which honesty in various forms protects and promotes productivity, place, and persons. These conversational practices provide connection among persons regardless of relational closeness, indicating a willingness to associate cordially with both friends and strangers.

Professional civility supports honesty responsive to the good of persons and the larger organizational unit and provides a richer rationale than communication competence for the workplace and an explicit focus on ethical practice in specific domains of work: productivity, place (the organization), and persons. As in the case of communication competence, but originating from a virtue ethics perspective, the honesty of professional civility attends to both content and relationship dimensions of messages. For example, performance appraisals function well when honesty touches several areas. Just as in the previous example of an employee's honesty about meeting production goals when self-reporting to a supervisor, honesty matters when supervisors provide performance appraisals.

29. Fritz 2013.

One may be honest about contextual matters—for instance, if every new worker experiences challenges when first learning a set of tasks, honesty may require a supervisor to disclose that information for the relational or affective goal of shoring up a new employee's self-perception and hope for success at the job. If the new employee is making errors, it is honest to inform the employee of the gap between expectation and performance and of the relative seriousness or typicality of these errors in the broader context of work. Simply reporting that errors are made, and performance is not up to standard, does not provide a holistic or meaningful picture of performance relative to others and with regard to temporal expectations. In this sense (as well as in others), phronesis, as Aristotle notes, is necessary for the work of the virtues, for phronesis guides their enactment in particular situations. Honesty as a virtue, from this perspective, is holistic, complex, and textured. In other words, professional civility offers honest critique that considers the need for support for the person receiving the message. The need for improvement is shared against a background of confidence in the other's ability and concern for the other's well-being.

This example of a performance evaluation in relation to holistic honesty and professional civility can be understood within a framework that considers the role of legitimate authority in evaluative discourse. Offering criticism of another's performance when one has no authority to offer such comments or when there are no defined criteria for evaluation could be understood as uncivil discourse or rudeness, even if the comments are accurate or honest. Many contexts of decision making have minimal public standards for evaluation. For example, if (a) no participant has greater expertise or authority than another, (b) implicit or explicit understandings of decision making are democratic in nature, and (c) there is general agreement on broad external standards governing the rightness or wrongness of a course of action, then statements portraying oneself as superior in

knowledge, expertise, or power may provoke defensiveness in others.[30] Examples of such decisions include designing a park, developing a strategic plan for an organization, or figuring out how an office
space will be configured. There are criteria of cost and workability
and other similar considerations, certainly; however, there is a wide
range of options that could be pursued. The understanding, in this
context, is that everyone's opinion carries equal weight. Attempts to
position one's own ideas as superior to those of others, or to place
oneself in an authoritative role without a legitimate basis for doing
so, shut down conversation and create resentment from others in the
group. Such comments, even if honest and accurate, may come across
as inappropriate and not be received well.

However, in contexts where standards are in force and for which
someone holds authority from expertise (or position, in many cases),
such honest statements carry a different implication. They should be
received without defensiveness and, indeed, with gratitude, even if
the message carries negative evaluative content. After all, the person
providing the comments is in a position to assist or help the learner
or apprentice or, in many cases, a team member who is equal in skill
and authority but who may have made an error and, for the sake of
the product or project, needs correction. The shared goal of excellence subordinates other, potentially face-threatening meanings to
a meaning directed toward a common understanding and commitment to the good. When criticism is accompanied by encouragement, honesty is holistic. The content and relationship dimensions of
the message work together to generate an honesty that is both realistic and hopeful.

Consider, for example, the case of an instructor helping a student to learn how to play a musical instrument. The student would
like to play skillfully, but perhaps is growing weary of hours and

30. Gibb 1961.

hours of practice and constant correction from the instructor. The burden is made lighter when the instructor offers supportive comments about how the student is improving, as well as corrective reminders about a hard-to-extinguish bad habit that keeps cropping up in the student's technique. The instructor's authoritatively honest (but not authoritarian) comments, although painful to hear at times, promise the fruit of excellence. Without such comments, the student would never achieve the level of excellence necessary to master the instrument.

This understanding of honesty works in tandem with love's creativity, in Caroline Simon's framework. Simon addresses love in multiple contexts (love for neighbor, friend, romantic partner, and spouse).[31] Love, on Simon's view, involves imagination and a disciplined heart that has learned to see and understand another person's potential despite her flaws and failings. To speak accurately of what is and what might be requires insight into another's potential—or, in Simon's terms, "destiny"—and a thorough, non-superficial knowledge of who another person both is and might become if that person is to reach full potential. Even if that person were not fulfilling her destiny and not manifesting the fruits of what the loving imagination presents, an honest message related to content could also work at the relationship level (with the meaning of the message relevant to concern and care rather than to rebuke and insult) to call forth the potential rather than repeating or reflecting what is at the moment. Honesty might work at the factual level of what is, but only tied (according to Simon) to the potential or future manifestation of what will, in hope, be the case. This calling forth through an honest appraisal ties the present and future together, building a bridge from what is not yet to what will be—or can be—manifested as reality in the life of excellence of another person.

31. Simon 1997.

However, honesty requires a realistic appraisal of what is actually the case in order to avoid the trap of naïve optimism[32]—an insistence that all is well when all is not well, founded on expectation rather than responsiveness to the real.[33] Honesty, conceptualized holistically and as encompassing the content and relationship dimensions of messages, can point to hope rather than naïve optimism. A central kind of hope is the conviction of things not seen immediately, but envisioned as a future reality emerging from a potential discerned through imagination. Honesty based on hope would avoid fantasy, or fiction making, when what one desires another to become is not within the horizon of possibility for that person but merely wishful thinking on one's own part. Hopeful honesty rightly informed by imagination might recognize another's superior skill, despite one's wishes to the contrary. This honesty would avoid the bad faith of self-deception.[34] Honesty must discern whether what is not yet manifested is actually possible and within another's potential.

This section has considered an understanding of honesty in relationships that accounts for the good of relationships, persons in the relationship, and their associated communities. Honesty takes account of more than factual information on the basis of which true or false statements can be made. A holistically honest message attends to the potential of persons in relationships, providing concern and consideration when potentially painful or unwanted content, such as criticism, must be given. Such holistic honesty from an authoritative source can be rooted in love for the human person, even for those with whom one is not close. Holistic honesty recognizes the complexity of the human person-in-relation and the potential for ongoing growth and flourishing of persons and communities.

32. Lasch 1991.
33. Arnett, Fritz, and Bell 2009.
34. Sartre 1953.

7. CONCLUSION

In sum, honesty is a communicative virtue for interpersonal relationships. Honesty's specific form is sensitive to cultural expectations, the nature of the relationship, and the setting within which the relationship is situated. Honesty acknowledges the importance of assumptions we make about others' intentions as we cooperate to create shared meaning in conversation. Honesty acknowledges the goals of oneself and others, and works responsively to discover new possibilities for the flourishing of self, other, and the larger social groups of which relationships are a part. What I am calling holistic honesty is more than the reporting of accurate information. Honesty includes sensitivity to others and attentiveness to the context within which conversation takes place.[35]

BIBLIOGRAPHY

Aristotle. *Nicomachean Ethics*. Translated by M. Ostwald. Indianapolis, IN: Bobbs-Merrill, 1962.

Arnett, Ronald C. "Toward a Phenomenological Dialogue." *Western Journal of Speech Communication* 45 (1981): 201–212.

Arnett, Ronald C. "Professional Civility." In *Problematic Relationships in the Workplace*, edited by Janie M. H. Fritz and Becky L. Omdahl, 233–248. New York: Peter Lang, 2006.

Arnett, Ronald C., Janie M. H. Fritz, and Leeanne M. Bell. *Communication Ethics Literacy: Dialogue and Difference*. Thousand Oaks, CA: SAGE, 2009.

Baxter, Leslie A., and Barbara M. Montgomery. *Relating: Dialogues and Dialectics*. New York: Guilford Press, 1996.

Bejan, Teresa M. *Mere Civility: Disagreement and the Limits of Toleration*. Cambridge, MA: Harvard University Press, 2017.

Brown, Penelope, and Stephen C. Levinson. *Politeness: Some Universals in Language Use*. New York: Cambridge University Press, 1987. Original work published 1978.

---

35. I would like to thank Christian B. Miller and Ryan West for their extensive and helpful feedback on this chapter.

Christians, Clifford G., and Michael Traber, eds. *Communication Ethics and Universal Values*. Thousand Oaks, CA: SAGE, 1997.

Dillard, James P., Chris Segrin, and Janie M. Harden. "Primary and Secondary Goals in the Production of Interpersonal Influence Messages." *Communication Monographs* 56: 19–38.

Fritz, Janie M. H. *Professional Civility: Communicative Virtue at Work*. New York: Peter Lang, 2013.

Fritz, Janie. M. H. "Interpersonal Communication Ethics." In *International Encyclopedia of Interpersonal Communication*, edited by Charles R. Berger and Michael L. Roloff, 889–902. Hoboken, NJ: Wiley-Blackwell, 2016.

Gibb, Jack R. "Defensive Communication." *Journal of Communication* 11 (1961): 141–149.

Granovetter, Mark S. "The Strength of Weak Ties." *American Journal of Sociology* 78 (1973): 1360–1380.

Grice, H. Paul. "Logic and Conversation." In *Philosophy of Language*, edited by A. P. Martinich, 165–175. New York: Oxford University Press, 1975.

Hall, Bradford 'J'. *Among Cultures: The Challenge of Communication*. 2nd ed. Belmont, CA: Wadsworth, 2005.

Hess, Jon. "Distancing from Problematic Coworkers." In *Problematic Relationships in the Workplace, Vol. 2*, edited by Janie M. H. Fritz and Becky L. Omdahl, 205–232. New York: Peter Lang, 2006.

Knapp, Mark L., and John A. Daly, eds. *The SAGE Handbook of Interpersonal Communication*. 4th ed. Thousand Oaks, CA: SAGE, 2011.

Lasch, Christopher. *The True and Only Heaven: Progress and its Critics*. New York: Norton, 1991.

Miller, Gerald R. "The Current Status of Theory and Research in Interpersonal Communication." *Human Communication Research* 4 (1978): 164–178.

O'Keefe, Barbara J. "The Logic of Message Design: Individual Differences in Reasoning about Communication." *Communication Monographs* 55 (1988): 80–103.

Parks, Malcolm R. "Ideology in Interpersonal Communication: Off the Couch and into the World." In *Communication Yearbook 5*, edited by Michael Burgoon, 79–107. Beverly Hills: SAGE, 1981.

Rawlins, William K. "Individual Responsibility in Relational Communication." In *Communications in Transition*, edited by Mary S. Mander, 152–157. New York: Praeger, 1983.

Robinson, James H. "Communication in Korea: Playing Things by Eye." In *Intercultural Communication: A Reader*, edited by Larry A. Samovar and Richard E. Porter, 74–81. 9th ed. Belmont, CA: Wadsworth, 2000.

Sartre, Jean-Paul. *Being and Nothingness: An Essay on Phenomenological Ontology*. Translated by Hazel E. Barnes. New York: Washington Square Press, 1953.

Scott, Kim. *Radical Candor: Be a Kick-Ass Boss Without Losing Your Humanity*. New York: St. Martin's Press, 2017.

Schrag, Calvin. *Communicative Praxis and the Space of Subjectivity*. Bloomington: Indiana University Press, 1986.

Simon, Caroline J. *The Disciplined Heart: Love, Destiny, and Imagination*. Grand Rapids, MI: Eerdmans, 1997.

Spitzberg, Brian H., and William R. Cupach. *Interpersonal Communication Competence*. Beverly Hills, CA: SAGE, 1984.

Watzlawick, Paul, and Janet H. Beavin. "Some Formal Aspects of Communication. *American Behavioral Scientist* 10 (1967): 4–8.

Watzlawick, Paul, Janet H. Beavin, Janet H., and Don D. Jackson. *Pragmatics of Human Communication*. New York: Norton, 1967.

Chapter 6

Justifications as a Threat to Honesty

A Behavioral Ethics Approach

MARGARITA LEIB AND SHAUL SHALVI

People often face ethically challenging situations where they need to choose between behaving honestly and lying for profit. Some challenges are rather small, arguably having no dramatic consequences. For example, should I let the cashier know he accidently gave me too much change, or should I keep the extra dollar? Other challenges are more serious and can have life-threatening consequences. Consider the recent Volkswagen scandal. Instead of providing regulators with the correct results of an emissions test, Volkswagen's engineers intentionally altered their engines so that during testing (but not otherwise) the vehicles released low enough levels of emissions to meet U.S. standards. The engineers' actions saved Volkswagen money by not forcing them to reduce the *actual* emission rates. However, this unethical action also released on U.S. roads vehicles with emission rates that are 10 to

Margarita Leib and Shaul Shalvi, *Justifications as a Threat to Honesty* In: *Integrity, Honesty, and Truth Seeking.* Edited by: Christian B. Miller and Ryan West. Oxford University Press (2020). © Oxford University Press. DOI: 10.1093/oso/9780190920487.003.0006

40 times above the U.S. Environmental Protection Agency's standards. After the scandal was exposed and the dust had settled, the damage caused by the heavily polluting cars was estimated at 59 early deaths and 450 million dollars.[1]

In light of such potentially extreme consequences, systematically studying the mechanisms that allow people to engage in dishonest behaviors is important. Uncovering when and why people break the rules or lie should help policymakers to design interventions and environments that curb dishonesty and, importantly, encourage honest behavior.

One line of research in the field of ethics focuses on normative questions concerning how people *should* behave in ethically challenging situations.[2] Several chapters in this volume provide examples of this approach (Roberts and West, chapter 4; Scherkoske, chapter 1). In the last decade, however, another line of research has developed, focusing on the descriptive task of mapping how people *actually* behave in ethically challenging situations. This approach—known as "behavioral ethics"—assumes, as well as finds evidence for, the malleability of honesty. That is, while there might be a small proportion of individuals who will behave completely honestly (or dishonestly) over time and across situations, for most individuals, (dis)honest behavior is not consistent but rather flexible and dependent on a variety of factors.[3] Questions like "What are the factors that push people to engage in dishonest behavior?," "What are the underlying psychological processes behind such behaviors?," and "How can dishonest behavior be curbed?" are the main focus of the behavioral ethics approach, and of this chapter. Cheating and lying—which we define as violating well-defined rules and/or intentionally misreporting

1. Barrett et al. 2015.
2. Bazerman and Gino 2012, Greene 2012, Haidt 2007, and Trevino and Weaver 1994.
3. Gibson, Tanner, and Wagner 2013.

the truth, regardless of motivation or circumstances—are the main forms of dishonest behavior we examine.[4]

To tackle the questions mentioned in the previous paragraph, behavioral economists, management researchers, and social psychologists employ diverse methodologies. A small but growing body of work attempts to assess (dis)honest behavior in "real life" environments.[5] But most research is conducted in lab settings, using experimental tasks designed to isolate the specific factors that affect (dis)honesty.[6] The "clean" nature of lab experiments provides big advantages in terms of control. But do tasks in the lab generalize to real-life settings? Some recent research suggests that they do. For instance, dishonest behavior in experimental tasks predicts riding in public transportation without paying, not returning an undeserved payment, and the diluting of milk with water by milkmen in Indian dairy markets.[7] Similarly, lying in experimental tasks also correlates with other socially deviant behaviors, such as misbehaving in school and skipping work without a reason.[8] Thus, although we must exercise caution here, we have reason to believe that findings obtained in the lab can be generalized to real-life behavior.

This chapter provides evidence suggesting that when facing ethically challenging situations, people often rely on justifications to free themselves to engage in dishonest behavior. These justifications fall into two main categories—self-serving justifications

4. There are many alternative definitions of dishonest behavior (see Miller 2017). For instance, Roberts and West (chapter 4 in this volume) suggest that motivational considerations are essential when evaluating behavior as honest or not, and that virtuously honest people wisely break the rules and misreport the truth under certain circumstances. Arguably, even though our definitions of dishonesty diverge, most of the behavior considered in this chapter would count as dishonest on either definition.

5. For a review, see Pierce and Balasubramanian 2015.

6. For a review, see Abeler, Raymond, and Nosenzo 2019, Moore and Gino 2015.

7. Dai, Galeotti, and Villeval 2017, Potters and Stoop 2016, and Kröll and Rustagi 2016.

8. Cohn and Marechal 2015, Hanna and Wang 2017.

and socially motivated justifications—and we devote one section to each. Then, in the last section, we focus on one context where socially motivated justifications are particularly common—namely, settings in which people can collaborate on joint unethical acts—and discuss how corrupt collaboration emerges, spreads, and, importantly, can be curbed.

1. THE ROLE OF JUSTIFICATIONS IN UNETHICAL BEHAVIOR

Classical economic theory suggests that the decision to break the rules and lie or follow the rules and remain honest depends on a simple cost-benefit analysis.[9] On one side of the scale, individuals weigh the profits they will obtain from breaking the rules or from lying; on the other side, they weigh the probability of getting caught and the punishment that might follow. If the gains outweigh the costs, people will break the rules and lie. If not, they will remain honest.

In the last decade, however, research suggests that people also take other considerations into account when deciding between being honest or lying. In particular, people care about their moral self-image, and are motivated to see themselves as good and honest people.[10] Since cheating can threaten individuals' perception of themselves as moral human beings, people do not lie to the full extent, even when they can and rely on justifications to free themselves to lie.[11]

In her seminal work, Kunda proposed that people's motivations shape the way they access and evaluate information.[12] When people

9. Becker 1968.
10. Mazar, Amir, and Ariely 2008.
11. Abeler, Raymond, and Nosenzo 2019.
12. Kunda 1990.

prefer a certain outcome over another, their motivation leads them to prefer an interpretation of reality that is aligned with their preferences, helping them to arrive at their desired conclusions. However, this process is constrained by individuals' ability to create reasonable justifications. In other words, in order to maintain a moral self-image and simultaneously profit from dishonesty, people need to be able to find convincing justifications that will free them to engage in dishonest behavior. These justifications, which can be seen as sources of rationalization, are internal, as they help individuals to explain their behavior to themselves and not necessarily to others.[13] Justifications allow people to change their evaluations of their dishonest behavior in such a way that dishonest behavior no longer reflects poorly on their moral self-image, thus reducing the threat of seeing themselves as dishonest, immoral persons.[14]

Here we propose two main types of dishonesty-enabling justifications: self-serving justifications and socially motivated justifications. Self-serving justifications allow individuals to process information in ways that benefit themselves, pushing them to bend ethical rules. For example, ambiguous settings or rules allow individuals to take advantage of such ambiguity and make more self-serving (and less self-hurting) mistakes, even when such mistakes have clear ethical implications. Socially motivated justifications apply when unethical acts are thought to serve a purpose that benefits others as well. The prosocial "side effects" of dishonesty make people think of their unethical acts as rather ethical, freeing them to engage in such behavior more. In the next two sections, we review both kinds of justifications, beginning with self-serving justifications.

---

13. Mulder, Jordan, and Rink 2015.
14. Shalvi et al. 2015. Whereas in some settings lying may be more objectively justifiable by society, we focus on people's subjective feeling of having a justification to lie.

2. SELF-SERVING JUSTIFICATIONS: INTERPRETING REALITY IN A SELF-BENEFITING WAY

Some factors that can prompt self-serving justifications are external cues in one's surroundings, such as counterfactual information. Counterfactual information amounts to "what could have been," if things were just a bit different. Imagine, for example, that you get a phone call from a friend asking you to help him move from his apartment this Sunday afternoon. You do not want to help. But since bluntly saying so is not socially acceptable, you are now looking for a good excuse to get you off the hook. As the conversation continues, you notice on your calendar that your sister has a birthday party on Saturday afternoon. If only the birthday party were on Sunday, it would have been the perfect excuse! But wait—maybe it is good enough. Would you be tempted to say, "Sorry, my sister has a birthday party on Sunday that I have to go to, so I can't help you move," even though the party is a day earlier? After all, it is not a big lie, but rather a small stretch of the truth.

In order to assess systematically whether people use counterfactual information to justify lying, Shalvi, Dana, Handgraaf, and De Dreu had participants engage in a die-under-cup task.[15] In this task, participants were asked to roll a die under a cup three times, each time looking at the outcome of the die roll. Before starting the task, participants learned that they had to report the outcome of the *first* die roll they observed, and that their payoffs would be determined by the outcome they report, with higher outcomes corresponding to higher pay (specifically, reporting a 1 would lead to a payoff of $1, 2 = $2, 3 = $3, 4 = $4, 5 = $5, and 6 = $6). Since the cup concealed the die, the outcomes were completely private. Thus, participants could

15. Shalvi, Dana, Handgraaf, and De Dreu 2011.

lie to boost their pay. Imagine a participant in this situation: her first roll yields a 3, the second a 2, and the third a 5. Reporting the first outcome, as instructed, would secure her $3, which is not too bad. But reporting a 5 is much more profitable. Would she report a 5 instead of a 3? After all, she really did roll a 5; it was just on the third roll, not the first.

If most people use the extra outcomes to justify their lying and indeed report the highest roll out of three, instead of the first one as instructed, the distribution of participants' reports should reflect this reporting strategy. Specifically, this would mean that most participants would report a 1 only if in all three rolls they saw a 1. Such a situation is highly unlikely, being predicted in less than 1% of cases. The report of a 6 would mean that a participant saw at least one 6. This case is much more likely, predicted in 42% of the cases. Continuing this pattern, the researchers created a theoretical distribution representing what participants would report if they reported the highest of the three outcomes, and compared it to the distribution of participants' actual reports. Results revealed that the actual distribution of reports did not differ from the theoretical distribution of reporting the highest of three outcomes ($p > .05$), suggesting that people tend to use counterfactual information to justify their lies. Most people do not seem to invent new facts (e.g., report rolling a 6 without having observed one), but just stretch the truth and shuffle facts for profit (e.g., report rolling a 6 on the first roll, when they rolled it on the second or third roll). In a control condition, participants rolled the die only once and reported it. This distribution of reports did not differ from the distribution of honest reports, where the chance of reporting each outcome is 1 in 6. Taken together, the researchers found that after seeing more profitable die roll outcomes, the majority of people will use these counterfactuals to justify their lies.

To understand why people use counterfactual information as a justification, Shalvi et al. asked a different group of participants to evaluate the degree to which they perceive various reporting patterns as lies, on a scale from 1 ("not at all") to 7 ("very much").[16] Results showed that reporting an outcome that was observed on a roll not eligible for pay was perceived as less of a lie ($M = 5.57$, $SD = 1.59$) than reporting an unobserved outcome ($M = 5.87$, $SD = 1.47$). That is, reporting a 5 as the first roll is seen as less of a lie when the first roll is a 3 and the second roll is a 5, than when the first roll is a 3 and the second roll is a 4. It seems like misreporting on the basis of observed counterfactual information is perceived as less of a lie, it threatens people's moral self-image less, thus freeing them to lie.

The conclusion that *observing* counterfactuals is what frees people to lie, however, might be criticized. After all, in the die-under-cup task, participants not only *observe*, but also *create* the counterfactual information. While they might be thinking, "I *saw* a 5 on the third roll, so it is OK to report a 5 as the outcome of my first roll," it is just as plausible that they're thinking, "I *rolled* a 5 on the third roll, so it is OK to report a 5." So the question is: Do people need to *create* the counterfactuals, or is merely *observing* them enough to justify lying? To answer this question, we conducted a follow-up study.[17] In our experiment, all participants saw three die roll outcomes and were asked to report the first one, with higher reports securing higher payoffs. Participants were divided into three groups. Those in the "combined condition" rolled the die three times, as in the original task, thus both observing and creating all three outcomes. Participants in the two experimental conditions, by contrast, rolled only the first die; the second and third were rolled by another participant in the room. In the "observing, own die" condition, the other participant rolled the second and third outcome using the original participant's die. In the "observing, other's die" condition, another's die was used.

16. Shalvi et al. 2011.
17. Bassarak et al. 2017.

Results revealed that people lie to the same extent in all three conditions, supporting the conclusion that merely observing counterfactual information is a sufficient justification for lying.

We've seen that *seeing* "what could have been" frees people to lie; as it turns out, so can merely *imagining* "what could have been." Individuals who can generate more information about "what could have happened if..." when asked to write about an imagined experience also can generate more lies.[18] Similarly, creative people are more likely to lie than are non-creative people, and are less likely to rely on external cues such as counterfactual information to do so.[19] Creative people do not need to *observe* counterfactuals; they can rely on their own imaginations to *generate* them.

An additional factor that allows individuals to justify their dishonest behavior is ambiguity. In ambiguous situations, people can intentionally interpret the situation in a self-serving rather than self-hurting way, thus justifying self-serving dishonesty. In vague settings, it is easy to tell yourself (as well as others, if suspicion arises) that you merely misunderstood or made a mistake and did not intend to do something wrong. If these mistakes are systematic, and more likely to benefit rather than hurt oneself, it is reasonable to assume that people use the ambiguity as a justification for dishonesty.

To assess how ambiguity affects dishonesty, we designed the ambiguous die paradigm.[20] In this task, participants saw an "X" on a computer screen (for one second), followed by an image of six die roll outcomes (for two seconds; see Figure 1). Then participants were asked to report the die roll outcome that appeared closest to the X (the "target die"), with higher reports corresponding to higher payoffs. Participants engaged in this task for multiple trials. Across

18. Briazu et al. 2017.
19. Gino and Ariely 2012, Bassarak et al. 2017.
20. Pittarello et al. 2015.

trials, we varied the outcome of the die appearing second closest to the X ("outcome next to the target"). Specifically, in half of the trials the outcome next to the target was higher than the target die, whereas in the other half of the trials the outcome next to the target was lower than the target die. For example, in Figure 1 (adopted from Pittarello et al. 2015) you can see that the target die is 3 and the outcome next to the target is 5. In such a trial, making a mistake and reporting the outcome next to the target instead of the target is profitable. However, if the outcome next to the target was 2 instead of 5, making a mistake and reporting the outcome next to the target instead of the target would be unprofitable. We assessed the proportion of profitable and unprofitable mistakes participants made.

Across trials we manipulated ambiguity. In particular, we varied the location of the X to be closer to or farther away from the target die. As can be seen in Figure 1, in the medium-ambiguity trials (in black), the X appeared on the side of the target die. In the low-ambiguity trials (in light gray), the X appeared 20 pixels (0.5 cm) closer to the center of the target die, making the target die very easy to identify. In the high-ambiguity trials (in dark gray), the X appeared 20 pixels (0.5 cm) away from the side of the target die, and 30 pixels (0.8 cm) away from the side of the outcome next to the target, making the target die rather difficult to detect. Importantly, in all ambiguity levels, the X was always objectively closest to the target die.

Arguably, making genuine mistakes in this task is both possible and probable. But genuine mistakes would not be affected by the outcome next to the target. That is, if participants make only genuine mistakes, unprofitable mistakes should be as common as profitable ones. Alternatively, if participants' mistakes are self-serving, we should see a different pattern. Will participants be more likely to make profitable mistakes, as compared to unprofitable ones? Furthermore, will this tendency increase as the ambiguity of the task increases? The answer to both questions was yes.

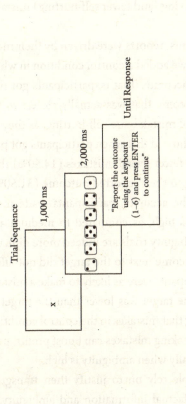
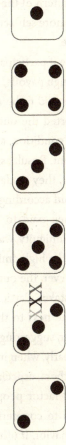

Figure 1 Illustration of the experimental procedure adopted from Pittarello et al. 2015. In the example, the target outcome is 3, and the outcome next to the target is 5. Ambiguity was manipulated to be low (light gray), medium (black), or high (dark gray) by changing the location of the X.

Overall, participants mistakenly reported the outcome next to the target more often when it was higher than the target die (31.20%) than when it was lower (7.20%). That is, people were more likely to make self-serving mistakes that secured higher pay, than self-hurting mistakes that secured lower pay. Importantly, ambiguity affected the pattern of the biased mistakes: the more ambiguous the trial was, the more self-serving (and fewer self-hurting) mistakes participants made.

In order to see if participants' reports were driven by their motivation to secure high payoffs, we added a control condition in which participants were paid to be accurate. That is, participants got paid only if they reported the outcome that was actually closest to the X. In the control condition, all mistakes are self-hurting, as they do not secure payment. Results showed that when participants got paid for being accurate, they made fewer overall mistakes (14.50%) than when they got paid according to their reported outcome (31.50%). Furthermore, when paid to be accurate, participants made more mistakes when ambiguity was high, as compared to medium and low, proving that the high-ambiguity trials are indeed more difficult. Importantly, however, the outcome next to the target did not affect the pattern of mistakes. Participants were as likely to make a mistake when the outcome next to the target was lower than the target as when it was higher, suggesting that mistakes in the control condition were genuine. Clearly, when making mistakes can boost profits, people tend to make them, especially when ambiguity is high.

An additional factor people rely on to justify their transgressions, in addition to counterfactual information and ambiguity, is other people's behavior. If others break the rules, even if those rules are reasonable and well known, people might think that doing so is justifiable. For example, Keizer, Lindenberg, and Steg conducted a series of field experiments assessing how rule violation spreads. One experiment was conducted in Groningen, a northern city in the

Netherlands, where bikes are a main form of transportation.[21] In one alley, used for parking bikes, the researchers posted a sign reading "No Graffiti." Despite the sign, the researchers covered the alley with graffiti, establishing an environment where rules are violated. On the handlebars of each bike parked in the alley, the researchers hung an advertisement flyer. Since there were no trash cans around, in order to get rid of the flyer, bike owners either had to take the flyer with them, keeping the alley clean, or throw it on the ground, littering the alley. Results revealed that rule violation is contagious. In the setting with graffiti, 69% of people littered. This was twice as much as in a control condition: when there was no graffiti on the wall only 33% of people littered. Seeing that others break the rules seems to free many people to do so as well.

Further evidence for the effect of exposure to rule-violating behavior can be found in a large-scale experiment conducted by Gächter and Schulz.[22] The researchers had 2,568 young participants (mean age = 21.7, standard deviation = 3.3) in 23 countries around the world engage in a modified version of the die-under-cup task in which they were instructed to roll a die two times and report the first die roll, with higher reports corresponding to higher payoffs. The authors further measured the extent to which rules were violated in each country by constructing an index of the "Prevalence of Rule Violations" (PRV). The index was composed of each country's levels of political fraud, tax evasion, and corruption. The authors found that the higher a country's PRV score, the more likely were participants from that country to stretch the truth and lie in the die-under-cup task. As the PRV scores were based on data from at least eight years before collecting participants' reports, it is safe to say that the young participants did not affect the scores. Rather, participants

21. Keizer, Lindenberg, and Steg 2008.
22. Gächter and Schulz 2016.

were exposed to corruption, tax evasion, and political fraud in their countries, and this in turn affected their level of (dis)honesty.[23] While being exposed to corruption can turn some people against it and thereby increase honesty, the results reported here show that such exposure can also corrupt.[24]

Further work suggests that even being reminded of *one's own* rule-breaking behaviors may facilitate lying. Cohn, Maréchal, and Noll had inmates in Switzerland's largest maximum security prison for male adults (Pöschwies) engage in a task in which they could earn money by lying.[25] All inmates received ten coins worth 0.5 Swiss francs each. Participants were asked to flip each of the ten coins and report the outcome: "heads" or "tails." Participants could keep every coin that they reported landing on "heads," but had to return any that they reported as landing on "tails." Before conducting the task, half of the inmates were asked to answer questions that reminded them of their criminal past, such as "What were you convicted for?" The other half answered neutral questions that lacked such reminders, such as "What is your favorite activity when you do not have to work?" Inmates who were reminded about their rule-violating behavior reported a higher proportion of "heads" (66%) than did inmates who were not reminded about their criminal past (60%). Although the differences are rather modest, the small reminder and increase in saliency of inmates' criminal identity seem to play some role in their lying behavior.

To sum up, seeing counterfactual information, being in vague settings, and being exposed to one's own or others' rule-violating behavior all serve as justifications for dishonest behavior. These factors allow individuals to reframe rule-violating behaviors as less

23. For more information on the PRV index and additional analysis providing further support for a causal relationship, see Ibid.
24. See also Kocher, Schudy, and Spantig 2017, Soraperra et al. 2017, and Shalvi 2016.
25. Cohn, Maréchal, and Noll 2015.

dishonest, thus protecting their moral self-image when engaging in unethical behavior for profit.

3. SOCIALLY MOTIVATED JUSTIFICATIONS: LYING FOR THE GREATER GOOD

Unlike self-serving justifications, which affect only one's own pay-off, socially motivated justifications free people to behave dishonestly because doing so not only benefits the self, but also results in a socially desirable outcome. The prosocial consequences of dishonesty allow people to do wrong but feel moral. After all, when dishonesty serves a greater good, it seems easily justifiable.

In his influential work, Uri Gneezy sought to understand whether, and to what extent, people take into account others' outcomes when they can deceive.[26] In his experiment, participants engaged in a deception game, where a sender and a receiver are paired together. The sender learns that there are two possible ways in which money can be split between himself and a receiver: options A and B. Option A is more profitable to the receiver and less profitable to the sender, whereas option B is more profitable to the sender and less profitable to the receiver. Only the sender knows the actual monetary consequences of each option, but it is the receiver's job to choose which monetary split, A or B, will be implemented. Thus, the sender can either send an honest message, saying "option A will earn you more money than option B," or a dishonest message, saying "option B will earn you more money than option A." Because the receiver does not know the monetary consequences of the options, the sender can trick the receiver into choosing the monetary split that favors the sender.

26. Gneezy 2005.

Gneezy assigned participants to three different conditions. In the first condition, sending a dishonest message and tricking the receiver to choose option B instead of A increased the sender's pay by $1 and decreased the receiver's pay by $1. In the second condition, it increased the sender's pay by $1, but decreased the receiver's pay by $10. In the third and final condition, it increased the sender's pay by $10 and decreased the receiver's pay by $10. Each sender knew only about the payoffs associated with the condition to which she was assigned. Assessing the proportion of dishonest messages sent revealed that senders were sensitive to receivers' payoffs. Only 17% of senders sent a dishonest message when the receiver could lose $10 and the sender could earn only $1. By contrast, 36% of senders sent a dishonest message when $1 was at stake for each, and 52% sent a dishonest message when $10 were at stake for each. Clearly, people take others' outcomes into account when they consider whether to deceive.

In line with this work, further research found that people lie for a variety of prosocial reasons. When making a decision in a group, rather than alone, people lie more.[27] Furthermore, people lie to benefit the less wealthy, to restore equality, to benefit (harm) others after being benefited (harmed) themselves, and to secure high pay for charity.[28] A growing body of work also found that people lie more when it benefits both themselves and others, as compared to benefiting only themselves.[29]

Wiltermuth, for example, had participants complete a task in which they needed to unscramble nine words.[30] The more *consecutive*

---

27. Cohen et al. 2009.
28. Gino and Pierce 2009b, Okeke and Godlonton 2014, Gino and Pierce 2009a, Gino and Pierce 2010, Atanasov and Dana 2011, Leib, Shalvi, and Moran 2019, Lewis et al. 2012, and Ayal 2015.
29. Gino, Ayal, and Ariely 2013, Wiltermuth 2011, and Conrads et al. 2013.
30. Wiltermuth 2011.

words participants managed to unscramble, the higher their payoff was. Thus, if a participant managed to unscramble the first, second, third, and fourth words, he would get $4. However, if he managed to unscramble the first, second and fourth, but not the third, he would get only $2. After completing the task, participants reported the number of consecutive words they unscrambled. Because no one verified their actual performance, participants could lie to boost their pay. All the scrambled words in the task were solvable, but the third word was so obscure and rare that none of the participants in a pilot study managed to solve it. Thus, if a participant reported solving more than two consecutive words, he was most likely lying. In one condition, participants' performance in the task affected only their own pay. In another condition, it affected both their own and someone else's pay. Results showed that participants in the prosocial condition were more likely (36.7%) to report unscrambling the third word, as compared to those who were responsible for only their own pay (26.7%).

Gino, Ayal, and Ariely further found that increasing the number of people who can benefit from one's lies increases lying.[31] In their experiment, participants were given 20 matrix problems, where each matrix consisted of twelve three-digit numbers (e.g., 3.23). To solve a matrix, participants had to find the two numbers, out of the twelve, that exactly summed to 10. They had five minutes to solve as many matrix problems as they could, and were paid $0.50 for every matrix they reported solving. The researchers set up three conditions and gave participants the entire instructions for the experiment before they started the task.

In the individual condition, participants counted their solved matrices, shredded them, and wrote down the number of matrices they solved on a separate piece of paper. They then handed that paper to the experimenter and were paid accordingly. The other two

31. Gino, Ayal, and Ariely 2013.

conditions involved two- and three-person groups. In these conditions, participants shredded the matrices, wrote down the number of matrices they solved, and then were instructed to find their partner (in the dyad condition) or two partners (in the triad condition) who were also in the room. The groups then approached the experimenter, who summed up the total number of matrices the group solved, divided it by two or three (depending on the group size), and paid each participant. Thus, in the group conditions, participants' reports affected not only themselves, but also one or two other participants. Results suggested that impacting others' payoff increased reporting: participants in the triad condition reported solving 15.92 matrices on average, those in the dyad condition, 13.83 on average, and those in the individual condition, 11.07 on average.

An alternative explanation for these results might be that participants did not lie more, but rather were more motivated to succeed when their performance affected others, which led to better performance in the matrix task. In order to rule out this explanation, the researchers added three control conditions. These paralleled the individual, dyad, and triad conditions from the previous iteration of the experiment, except that this time, after completing the task, participants handed the matrices to the experimenter, who counted the solved matrices and paid them accordingly. Thus, lying was impossible in the control conditions. On average, participants solved around seven matrices in the control conditions, with no differences between the individuals, dyads, and triads.

Moreover, Gino et al. showed that people report feeling less guilty and evaluate themselves as better people when their lies benefit someone else as well as themselves, as compared to when their lies benefit only themselves.[32] Further, lying to benefit both oneself and another person (versus only oneself) was evaluated as less unethical.

32. Ibid.

Surprisingly, in a more recent study, participants evaluated people who lied to benefit both themselves and others as more moral, benevolent, and trustworthy than people who behaved honestly but benefited only themselves.[33] Indeed, many people judge unethical acts to be rather ethical if these acts have prosocial consequences, thus reducing the threat to the moral self-image of those who engage in them.[34]

4. THE ETHICAL HAZARD OF COLLABORATION

So far, we have shown that working *for* others can increase lying. But how might people behave when they need to work *with* others? Might cooperative settings increase dishonesty? If so, how might we curb such collaborative corruption? Since people collaborate with others on a daily basis, at home as well as at work, it is important to understand the ethical hazards that collaboration can impose and how these hazards might be addressed.

In various organizational settings, people face a dilemma: collaborate with their peers, or follow ethical rules of conduct. The Volkswagen scandal with which we began is a good example. Volkswagen's engineers did not wake up one morning and decide, as separate individuals, to alter the engines' emission rates. Rather, their unethical conduct was a joint effort. Each engineer faced a choice between collaborating with his or her fellow engineers or adhering to clear ethical standards. It is a difficult dilemma, and recent work suggests that when facing it, collaboration often trumps ethicality.

33. Levine and Schweitzer 2014, 2015.
34. For a discussion of cases in which social considerations might objectively justify the telling of falsehoods, see Roberts and West (chapter 4 in this volume).

To assess how collaborative settings affect dishonesty, Weisel and Shalvi devised a sequential dyadic die-rolling task in which participants were paired and assigned the role of A or B.[35] In each round of the task, participant A rolled a die and reported the outcome on a computer screen. Then participant B learned about participant A's report, rolled her own die, and reported the outcome on a computer screen as well. Then both participants saw a summary of both reports and their associated payoffs. Participants engaged in this task for 20 rounds.

Participants were assigned to one of several conditions. In the "align outcomes" condition, if both players reported the same outcome (a "double"), they both got paid according to the double's worth (i.e., a double 1 = 1 euro; double 2 = 2 euros, etc.); if they reported divergent outcomes (a "non-double"), they earned no money. Before starting the task, participants learned about this incentive scheme. Results showed that when incentives were completely aligned, people lied a lot. Specifically, participants reported doubles in 81.5% of the trials, which was much more than the 16.66% expected if participants were honest. In an "individuals" control condition, where participants engaged in the task alone and played the roles of both A and B, the proportion of doubles was 55%, significantly lower than in the "align outcomes" condition.

In an attempt to curb joint unethical acts, Weisel and Shalvi tested a series of additional conditions in which they changed the incentive scheme, and reduced or completely removed A's or B's interest in a double.[36] In two conditions, A (or B) received a fixed payment *regardless* of whether the dyad reported a double, while B (or A) was paid according to the original incentive scheme. In additional conditions, A (or B) received a fixed payment per double, regardless of

35. Weisel and Shalvi 2015.
36. Ibid.

the double's numerical value, while B (or A) was paid according to the original incentive scheme. Results revealed that reducing one partner's interest in reporting a double has an effect. The proportion of doubles in the additional conditions was lower (ranging between 41.5% and 76.5%) than the proportion of doubles when participants' incentives were aligned. Collaborative settings are a fertile ground for corruption, and disentangling people's incentives when they work together seems like a promising way to decrease joint unethical acts.

Often, however, people not only collaborate with others, but can also choose with whom to collaborate. As such, it is highly important that we seek to answer at least three further questions. First, when given a choice, with whom do individuals choose to collaborate: honest or dishonest others? Second, does giving individuals the ability to choose their collaborators affect corruption? And third, does giving individuals the ability to choose their collaborators have a financial impact? In a recent project we addressed these questions by implementing a modified version of the sequential dyadic die-rolling task.[37] In the modified version of the task, participants engaged in the task for 30 rounds. This time, all participants observed digital die rolls on the computer screen instead of rolling physical dice privately, which allowed us to compare the actual outcomes with the reported outcomes, and to categorize participants as honest (if they reported the actual outcomes) or dishonest (if they didn't).

Participants were assigned to one of three conditions. In the "choice" condition, after every three-round "block," participants indicated whether they would prefer to stay with their current partner or switch to a new partner. If at least one partner in a dyad wanted to switch, the dyad would split and both members would get new partners. In two additional conditions we removed participants' ability to choose a partner. In the "forced stay" condition, participants

37. Gross et al. 2018.

stayed with the same partner throughout the task, and in the "forced switch" condition, participants had to switch partners every three-round block.

To assess with whom individuals prefer to work we focused on the "choice" condition, and categorized individuals as "honest" (if they accurately reported the actual outcome in all three rounds in a given block) or "dishonest" (otherwise). As we might have expected, results reveal that dishonest participants seek and find a "partner in crime." Dishonest As and Bs were much more likely to ask to switch partners when their partner was honest, rather than dishonest. Further, when both dyad members were dishonest, the dyad was very stable, and its members asked to switch in only 3.5% of the cases.

The more interesting question concerns what honest individuals do. Do they ask to switch from a dishonest partner and seek a non-corrupt relationship? Alternatively, do they prefer to stay and profit from such a relationship? Think of yourself in the "choice" condition, taking the role of A. You see different die roll outcomes on the screen: the potentially profitable fives and sixes (if matched), but also the less profitable ones and twos. As an honest person, you report accurately regardless of the outcomes presented on the screen. Your partner, however, seems less honest. B matches every single one of your reports, securing payment for both of you. Of course, if B would match every now and then, you might think it was just a coincidence; but the more rounds B matches, the more you realize you are working with a corrupt partner. Now, after working with that partner for a while, you are asked, "Do you want to stay with your partner, or would you like to switch to a new partner?" This is, arguably, a dilemma. You care about honesty to some degree; indeed, you have proven it by reporting honestly in every round. But do you care about your partner's dishonesty, especially when his dishonest reports benefit you as well? Would you engage in ethical free riding (i.e., the intentional benefiting from others' rule-violating behavior without engaging in such behavior oneself)? After all, you (supposedly) did nothing wrong!

Our results reveal that many people do indeed engage in ethical free riding. Honest As asked to switch partners much more often when they were paired with an honest B, as compared to a dishonest B. Honest As switched in 46% of the cases when B did not match their reports at all, but only in 11% of the cases when B matched all three reports. Ethical free riding allowed participants to maintain their "honesty," and keep their moral self-image intact.

Additional analyses revealed that out of all participants in the "choice" condition, the majority (70.6%) are classified as dishonest, with the large majority of the dishonest participants seeking dishonest partners (89.4%) and a minority staying with truth tellers (10.6%). Among the honest participants in the sample (29.4%), the majority engaged in ethical free riding (63.9%) and a minority showed preference for honest partners (36.1%). Both dishonest and honest people exploited the opportunity to select a partner and preferred to interact with corrupt others, showing that providing individuals with the freedom to choose whom to work with comes with a moral hazard.

Given that people are affected by others' behavior, as we showed in the previous section of the chapter, it is also valuable to assess to what extent dishonesty is contagious when people work together, and how the ability (or lack of ability) to select a partner affects the contagiousness of dishonesty. Results show that overall dishonesty is contagious. In two conditions, participants were more likely to lie if their partner lied in the previous round than if their partner was honest in the previous round. In the "forced stay" condition, the likelihood of a participant lying increased by 39% if his partner had lied in the previous round. Similarly, in the "choice" condition, the likelihood of a participant lying increased by 38% if his partner had lied in the previous round. In the "forced switch" condition, however, the likelihood of a participant lying *decreased* by 8% if his partner had lied, suggesting that constantly forcing people to switch their partners helps to curb the contagiousness of dishonesty.

Lastly, we assessed the overall financial impact of joint unethical acts by comparing the proportion of fully honest dyads, and the financial damage dishonest participants cause across the three settings. Looking at both factors is important as they may (or may not) cancel each other out. A setting with a lot of honest dyads, but where liars have a large financial impact (lies are effective) may produce as much financial damage as a setting with fewer honest teams, where liars have a small financial impact (lies are ineffective).

We found that in the "forced stay" condition only 4.6% of dyads were fully honest (both A and B report honestly). The rate more than doubled in the "forced switch" condition (9.9%), and more than tripled in the "choice" condition (14.5%). Effectiveness of lies, on the other hand, showed a different picture. In the "choice" condition, 31% of the lies resulted in the highest profit possible, which is similar to the 38% of lies in the "forced stay" condition. However, forcing people to switch partners led to much less effective lies. In the "forced switch" condition only 9% of lies resulted in the highest profit possible. Allowing individuals to choose their partners, as well as letting dyads develop long-term relationships, increased the dyad's ability to coordinate and tell effective lies that caused more financial harm to others.

All in all, the prevalence of fully honest dyads and the efficiency of lies seemed to cancel each other out, as the overall accumulated effects of corruption in terms of monetary cost did not vary greatly, especially between the "choice" and "forced switch" conditions. In the "forced stay" condition the average (per dyad, per block) earning from lying was €12.08. The average was somewhat lower in both the "choice" and "forced switch" conditions (€10.79 and €10.23, respectively; the differences between the three averages did not reach statistical significance). When considering whether to provide individuals the freedom to choose their partners, one has to consider the corrupt dynamics that such freedom enables.

5. CONCLUSION

Honest behavior is complex. While most people want to think of themselves as honest individuals, many are willing to bend ethical rules for profit as long as they can justify their acts. This chapter surveyed both self-serving and socially motivated factors that can provide such justifications. The systematic study of the mechanisms underlying (dis)honest behavior is of great interest and importance both within and outside of academia. Understanding what liberates people to violate rules may also enable us to understand what makes people obey them. Insights from the behavioral ethics field are useful when crafting environments and policies aimed at curbing corruption and encouraging honest behavior.[38]

BIBLIOGRAPHY

Abeler, Johannes, Collin Raymond, and Daniele Nosenzo. "Preferences for Truth-Telling." *Econometrica* 87:4 (2019): 1115–1153. doi:10.3982/ECTA14673.

Atanasov, Pavel, and Jason Dana. "Leveling the Playing Field: Dishonesty in the Face of Threat." *Journal of Economic Psychology* 32:5 (2011): 809–817. doi:10.1016/j.joep.2011.07.006.

Ayal, Shahar. "Strategic Altruism: Cheating in Monetary Donations to Social Organizations." Inequality, Trust and Ethics Conference: London, 2015. https://papers.ssrn.com/sol3/papers.cfm?abstract_id=2607652.

38. We would like to thank Christian Miller and Ryan West for their insightful and helpful comments on this chapter. This project has received funding from the European Research Council (ERC) under the European Union's Horizon 2020 research and innovation program (grant agreement ERC-StG-637915).

Barrett, Steven R. H., Raymond L. Speth, Sebastian D. Eastham, et al. "Impact of the Volkswagen Emissions Control Defeat Device on US Public Health Impact of the Volkswagen Emissions Control Defeat Device on US Public Health." *Environmental Research Letters* 10 (2015): 114005.

Bassarak, Claudia, Margarita Leib, Dorothee Mischkowski, Sabrina Strang, Andreas Glöckner, and Shaul Shalvi. "What Provides Justification for Cheating-Producing or Observing Counterfactuals?" *Journal of Behavioral Decision Making* 30:4 (2017): 964–975. doi:10.1002/bdm.2013.

Bazerman, Max H., and Francesca Gino. "Behavioral Ethics: Toward a Deeper Understanding of Moral Judgment and Dishonesty." *Annual Review of Law and Social Science* 8:1 (2012): 85–104. doi:10.1146/annurev-lawsocsci-102811-173815.

Becker, Gary S. "Crime and Punishment: An Economic Approach." In *The Economic Dimensions of Crime*, edited by Nigel G. Fielding, Alan Clarke, and Robert Witt, 13–68. London: Palgrave Macmillan UK, 1968. doi:10.1007/978-1-349-62853-7_2.

Briazu, Raluca A., Clare R. Walsh, Catherine Deeprose, and Giorgio Ganis. "Undoing the Past in Order to Lie in the Present: Counterfactual Thinking and Deceptive Communication." *Cognition* 161 (2017): 66–73. doi:10.1016/j.cognition.2017.01.003.

Cohen, Taya R., Brian C. Gunia, Sun Young Kim-Jun, and J. Keith Murnighan. "Do Groups Lie More than Individuals? Honesty and Deception as a Function of Strategic Self-Interest." *Journal of Experimental Social Psychology* 45:6 (2009): 1321–24. doi:10.1016/j.jesp.2009.08.007.

Cohn, Alain, and Michel André Marechal. "Laboratory Measure of Cheating Predicts School Misconduct." CESifo Working Paper Series No. 5613. 2015.

Cohn, Alain, Michel André Maréchal, and Thomas Noll. "Bad Boys: How Criminal Identity Salience Affects Rule Violation." *The Review of Economic Studies* 82:4 (2015): 1289–1308. doi:10.1093/restud/rdv025.

Conrads, Julian, Bernd Irlenbusch, Rainer Michael Rilke, and Gari Walkowitz. "Lying and Team Incentives." *Journal of Economic Psychology* 34 (2013): 1–7. doi:10.1016/j.joep.2012.10.011.

Dai, Zhixin, Fabio Galeotti, and Marie Claire Villeval. "Cheating in the Lab Predicts Fraud in the Field: An Experiment in Public Transportation." *Management Science*, January 2017. INFORMS, mnsc.2016.2616. doi:10.1287/mnsc.2016.2616.

Gächter, Simon, and Jonathan F. Schulz. "Intrinsic Honesty and the Prevalence of Rule Violations across Societies." *Nature* 531:7595 (2016): 1–11. doi:10.1038/nature17160.

Gibson, Rajna, Carmen Tanner, and Alexander F. Wagner. "Preferences for Truthfulness: Heterogeneity among and within Individuals." *The American Economic Review* 103:1 (2013): 532–548. doi:10.2307/23469653.

Gino, Francesca, and Dan Ariely. "The Dark Side of Creativity: Original Thinkers Can Be More Dishonest." *Journal of Personality and Social Psychology* 102:3 (2012): 445–59. doi:10.1037/a0026406.

Gino, Francesca, Shahar Ayal, and Dan Ariely. "Self-Serving Altruism? The Lure of Unethical Actions That Benefit Others." *Journal of Economic Behavior and Organization* 93 (2013): 285–292. doi:10.1016/j.jebo.2013.04.005.

Gino, Francesca, and Lamar Pierce. "Dishonesty in the Name of Equity." *Psychological Science* 20:9 (2009a): 1153–1160. doi:10.1111/j.1467-9280.2009.02421.x.

Gino, Francesca, and Lamar Pierce. "The Abundance Effect: Unethical Behavior in the Presence of Wealth." *Organizational Behavior and Human Decision Processes* 109:2 (2009b): 142–155. doi:10.1016/j.obhdp.2009.03.003.

Gino, Francesca, and Lamar Pierce. "Robin Hood Under the Hood: Wealth-Based Discrimination in Illicit Customer Help." *Organization Science* 21:6 (2010): 1176–1194. doi:10.1287/orsc.1090.0498.

Gneezy, Uri. "Deception: The Role of Consequences." *American Economic Association* 95:1 (2005): 384–394.

Greene, Joshua. 2012. *The Moral Brain and How to Use It.* New York: Penguin Group.

Gross, Jörg, Margarita Leib, Theo Offerman, and Shaul Shalvi. "Ethical Free-Riding: When Honest People Find Dishonest Partners." *Psychological Science* 29:12 (2018): 1956–1968.

Haidt, Jonathan. "The New Synthesis in Moral Psychology." *Science* 316:5827 (2007): 998–1002.

Hanna, Rema, and Shing-Yi Wang. "Dishonesty and Selection into Public Service: Evidence from India." *American Economic Journal: Economic Policy* 9:3 (2017): 262–290. doi:10.1257/pol.20150029.

Keizer, Kees, Siegwart Lindenberg, and Linda Steg. "The Spreading of Disorder." *Science* 322:5908 (2008): 1681–1685. doi:10.1126/science.1161405.

Kocher, Martin G., Simeon Schudy, and Lisa Spantig. "I Lie? We Lie! Why? Experimental Evidence on a Dishonesty Shift in Groups." *Management Science* 64:9 (2018): 2995–4008. doi:10.1287/mnsc.2017.2800.

Kröll, Markus, and Devesh Rustagi. "Shades of Dishonesty and Cheating in Informal Milk Markets in India." *SAFE Working Paper Series 134.* Frankfurt: SAFE—Sustainable Architecture for Finance in Europe, 2016. https://www.econstor.eu/handle/10419/130760.

Kunda, Ziva. "The Case for Motivated Reasoning." *Psychological Bulletin* 108:3 (1990): 480–498. http://ovidsp.tx.ovid.com/sp-3.27.2b/ovidweb.cgi?QS2=434f4e1a73d37e8c106b2a94fb1982bbe3fab61159d0d391737496da4f48f7d-c7f4c555537b6423066fd1494baf5f1ea9e7149d973b485d0c80f32a836ea8fcf016bd25a3d4be6368b1ae45c38ed52e2db5c819d34b518a52cc96efddf09f2f-94c8468a0e3.

Leib, Margarita, Shaul Shalvi, and Simone Moran. "Dishonest Helping and Harming After (Un)fair Treatment." *Judgment and Decision Making* 14:4 (2019): 423–439.

Levine, Emma E., and Maurice E. Schweitzer. "Are Liars Ethical? On the Tension between Benevolence and Honesty." *Journal of Experimental Social Psychology* 53 (2014): 107–117. doi:10.1016/j.jesp.2014.03.005.

Levine, Emma E., and Maurice E. Schweitzer. "Prosocial Lies: When Deception Breeds Trust." *Organizational Behavior and Human Decision Processes* 126 (2015): 88–106. doi:10.1016/j.obhdp.2014.10.007.

Lewis, Alan, Alexander Bardis, Chloe Flint, Claire Mason, Natalya Smith, Charlotte Tickle, and Jennifer Zinser. "Drawing the Line Somewhere: An Experimental Study of Moral Compromise." *Journal of Economic Psychology* 33:4 (2012): 718–725. doi:10.1016/j.joep.2012.01.005.

Moore, Celia, and Francesca Gino. "Approach, Ability, Aftermath: A Psychological Process Framework of Unethical Behavior at Work." *The Academy of Management Annals* 9:1 (2015): 235–289. doi:10.1080/19416520.2015.1011522.

Mulder, Laetitia B., Jennifer Jordan, and Floor Rink. "The Effect of Specific and General Rules on Ethical Decisions." *Organizational Behavior and Human Decision Processes* 126 (January 2015): 115–129. doi:10.1016/J.OBHDP.2014.11.002.

Okeke, Edward N., and Susan Godlonton. "Doing Wrong to Do Right? Social Preferences and Dishonest Behavior." *Journal of Economic Behavior and Organization* 106 (2014): 124–139. doi:10.1016/j.jebo.2014.06.011.

Pierce, Lamar, and Parasuram Balasubramanian. "Behavioral Field Evidence on Psychological and Social Factors in Dishonesty and Misconduct." *Current Opinion in Psychology* 6 (December 2015): 70–76. doi:10.1016/J.COPSYC.2015.04.002.

Pittarello, Andrea, Margarita Leib, Tom Gordon-Hecker, and Shalvi Shalvi. "Justifications Shape Ethical Blind Spots." *Psychological Science* 26:6 (2015): 794–804. doi:10.1177/0956797615571018.

Potters, Jan, and Jan Stoop. 2016. "Do Cheaters in the Lab Also Cheat in the Field?" *European Economic Review* 87: 26–33. doi:10.1016/j.euroecorev.2016.03.004.

Shalvi, Shaul. "Corruption Corrupts." *Nature*, 531:7595 (2016): 456–458. doi:10.1038/nature17307.

Shalvi, Shaul, Jason Dana, Michel J. J. Handgraaf, and Carsten K. W. De Dreu. "Justified Ethicality: Observing Desired Counterfactuals Modifies Ethical Perceptions and Behavior." *Organizational Behavior and Human Decision Processes* 115:2 (2011): 181–190. doi:10.1016/j.obhdp.2011.02.001.

Shalvi, Shaul, Francesca Gino, Rachel Barkan, and Shahar Ayal. "Self-Serving Justifications: Doing Wrong and Feeling Moral." *Current Directions in Psychological Science* 24:2 (2015): 125–130. doi:10.1177/0963721414553264.

Soraperra, Ivan, Ori Weisel, Ro'i Zultan, Sys Kochavi, Margarita Leib, Hadar Shalev, and Shaul Shalvi. "The Bad Consequences of Teamwork." *Economics Letters* 160 (November 2017): 12–15. doi:10.1016/J.ECONLET.2017.08.011.

Trevino, Linda Klebe, and Gary R. Weaver. "Business ETHICS/BUSINESS Ethics: One Field or Two?" *Business Ethics Quarterly* 4:2 (1994): 113–128. doi:10.2307/3857484.

Weisel, Ori, and Shaul Shalvi. "The Collaborative Roots of Corruption." *Proceedings of the National Academy of Sciences* 112:34 (2015): 10651–11056. doi:10.1073/pnas.1423035112.

Wiltermuth, Scott S. "Cheating More When the Spoils Are Split." *Organizational Behavior and Human Decision Processes* 115:2 (2011): 157–168. doi:10.1016/j.obhdp.2010.10.001.

Chapter 7

Becoming Honest

Why We Lie and What Can Be Done About It

STEVEN L. PORTER AND JASON BAEHR

1. INTRODUCTION

This chapter addresses the question of how we become the kinds of persons who do not lie. While there are morally justifiable lies (e.g., lying to save a life), in many cases in which lying is an attractive option, morally justifying reasons are nowhere in sight.[1] What often is in sight is our own personal benefit—we commonly lie to gain an advantage or avoid some disadvantage. This chapter argues that one path to becoming honest is to develop an underlying sense of relational safety, well-being, and acceptance that undermines, or at least significantly weakens, self-serving motivations to lie.

We begin by isolating the nature of lies told to benefit oneself. We then identify a weakness with a direct approach to virtue formation, which motivates the development of an alternative pathway of

---

1. For the remainder of this chapter, when we speak of becoming the sort of person who refrains from lying, we are assuming cases of morally unjustified lies.

Steven L. Porter and Jason Baehr, *Becoming Honest* In: *Integrity, Honesty, and Truth Seeking*. Edited by: Christian B. Miller and Ryan West. Oxford University Press (2020). © Oxford University Press. DOI: 10.1093/oso/9780190920487.003.0007

virtue formation. Our alternative proposes a set of practices embedded in an overall way of life as the means to undercut some central motivations of self-serving lies. These central motivators to lie—self-protection, self-preservation, and self-enhancement—can be weakened by practices aimed at a relationally connected way of life. These relational connections (i.e., secure interpersonal attachments) provide the social-emotional support that brings about safety (protection), well-being (preservation), and acceptance (enhancement) that can enable truth telling. We conclude by considering one practical objection to this alternative account of the formation of honesty.

2. WHY WE LIE

One common way to manage information that others possess is to lie.[2] When we lie we affirm a statement that we believe to be false with the intention that others take what we say as true or treat us as if it were true.[3] This is an imprecise definition in that it does not cover all putative cases of lying. For instance, the "bald-faced lie" is an assertion made with full knowledge that everyone knows it is false. While the assertor does not intend others to take what he says as true or even to treat him as if it were true, his false statement nevertheless counts as a lie.[4] Nonetheless, persons typically lie with the intention to deceive. Indeed, it is this intention that on many occasions plays a part in *why* persons lie.

2. The social psychologist Bella DePaulo's research found that, on average, persons lie 1.5 times a day. See DePaulo 2004: 306.

3. On this definition, asserting what one believes to be false with the intent to deceive is sufficient to count as lying even if what one asserts turns out to be true. On other definitions, asserting a false statement is a necessary condition for lying, such that a person can intend to lie but fail to do so if the statement they believe false is actually true. Nothing in this chapter hangs on this debatable point. For further discussion, see Carson 2010: 17–26.

4. See Sorenson 2007.

For instance, when a child says she has brushed her teeth and she knows she has not, she intends that her parent believe her claim or at least treat her as if it were true. In the latter scenario, the parent may suspect the child of lying but decide not to make her brush her teeth, which is good enough for the child.[5] The intention to have others believe what one says is true—or treat one as if what one says is true—exposes a common motivation for lying: we frequently lie due to some perceived benefit to ourselves that we judge the deceit will likely bring about. For example, we lie about the age of our child to save money on a movie ticket, or to a friend about why we are late for an appointment to avoid our friend's disappointment, or about having read a certain book to maintain the appearance of being well read.

Bella DePaulo's research on lying found that the distinction between self-serving motives and other-oriented motives helpfully categorized her participants' motivations for lying. DePaulo observed that self-serving lies "are told to protect or enhance the liar psychologically, or to protect or promote the liar's interests. . . . The more instrumentally oriented self-centered lies are told in the service of the liar's personal gain or convenience."[6]

In many situations, of course, telling the truth is what brings personal gain or convenience and is, therefore, the easy thing to do. "Would you like fries with that?" "When would you prefer to meet?" "In order to be paid, please provide your social security number." In

---

5. There are many cases like this. I might tell the police officer who pulls me over that I haven't had any alcohol to drink even though I did have one drink. The police officer may not believe me, but he treats me as if what I said were true because he does not suspect me of being intoxicated.

6. DePaulo 2004: 309–310. For a similar distinction, see Leib and Shalvi (chapter 6 in this volume). While other-oriented motives for lying are significant, this chapter's focus is on self-serving motives. DePaulo did find that self-serving lies outpaced other-oriented lies two-to-one, and that more serious lies were more likely to be of the self-serving sort (DePaulo 2004: 311, 317). For a discussion of the other-oriented motive, see DePaulo 2004: 310–311 and DePaulo 2017: 287–294. See also Miller 2013: 286–305 for further discussion of DePaulo's research and motivations for lying.

such instances, truth telling is deeply habituated and lying is the fur-thest thing from our minds. But when there is a perceived benefit in getting others to respond to us by means of a falsehood, truth telling is often difficult, and lying is often tempting. The truth, as the say-ing goes, hurts. And when veracity is going to hurt the speaker, the desire to lie can arise. To be sure, undetected lying can save us from loss, increase our fortunes, and guard our reputation, when to tell the truth in such instances comes with a cost in these areas of our lives.

3. A WEAKNESS WITH DIRECT APPROACHES TO BECOMING HONEST

Truth telling in situations in which lying is tempting can bring about costly repercussions, and those costs can be painful disincentives to truth telling. The problem is not simply that the cost-benefit analy-sis in some cases favors lying. Acting viciously can often lead to per-sonal gain of some sort. The problem we have in mind attaches itself to direct approaches to virtue acquisition. By "direct approaches" we mean formative pathways that recommend practicing actions in accordance with virtue as the primary means to bring about virtu-ous dispositions. In other words, these direct approaches operate on the basic notion that persons become just primarily by direct efforts to act in just ways, that persons become honest primarily by direct efforts to act in honest ways, and so on.[7]

These direct approaches typically depend upon the idea that prac-ticing actions in accordance with virtue must be accompanied by an

---

7. It is important to note that Aristotle's utilization of direct efforts to acquire virtue would not count as a "direct approach," in that Aristotle emphasized other necessary ingredients (e.g., a good upbringing, a good city, good laws, friendship, etc.) in the development of virtue. The "direct approaches" we have in mind here are reductions of Aristotle's view.

incipient experience of appropriate or proper pleasure in doing good that serves to reinforce the inclination to act in the virtuous manner again.[8] For instance, as Nancy Sherman observes:

> On Aristotle's view, practice would be neither necessary nor sufficient for acquiring states and abilities if it did not yield derivative pleasures. For it is the pleasure proper to a particular activity that impels us to perform that activity the next time with greater discrimination and precision.[9]

On this understanding, acting virtuously is by nature pleasant, and it is in tasting the pleasures of virtue that persons learn to enjoy virtue for what it is. This experience of appropriate pleasure in acting virtuously serves to reinforce and refine the underlying motivational psychology characteristic of the virtue.

One problem for—or better, weakness of—these direct approaches is that at times the experience of appropriate pleasure when acting virtuously is overridden by the painful consequences of so acting.[10] In such a case, acting according to virtue is not reinforced by the pleasure of so acting. For instance, the attempt to courageously protect the one being bullied can end up with both the bully and the one bullied turning on the courageous protector, such that the courageous one finds herself feeling more pain in her courageous act than proper pleasure. Instead of being left with a desire to

8. See, for instance, Burnyeat 1980: 75–78 and Sherman 1989: 184–190.

9. Sherman 1989: 184.

10. A further problem is that it is questionable whether virtuous-persons-in-training (versus those who are already virtuous) actually have the capacity for deriving pleasure from virtuous actions. See Curzer 2004: 148–150 for more on this point. Curzer goes on to question whether even virtuous persons usually find virtuous action pleasurable *on balance* (150–154). These concerns compound the present challenge for direct approaches inasmuch as they threaten to further disincentivize the practice of honesty. See Porter 2012: 136–138 for a related discussion.

repeat her courageous action, she finds herself thinking, "I'll never do that again." Thus, it seems that for direct approaches to work, enough needs to go right in the practice of virtue that an experience of proper pleasure is likely to arise without an overriding experience of pain.

While appropriate pleasure can be overridden by pain in the attempt to form any virtue, the formation of honesty (especially where lying is expected to bring a benefit to oneself) is particularly vulnerable to this problem. When the truth is told on occasions when lying is tempting, money can be lost, friends can be disappointed, and reputations can be tarnished. Whatever appropriate pleasure inheres within the practice of truth telling on such occasions, the overriding felt experience can be one of pain, loss, or embarrassment.

The negative felt experience in refraining from lying is perhaps particularly prevalent among children, who are regularly testing boundaries under the seemingly omniscient eye of parents or guardians. Even though a young child may not yet be adept at lying ("I didn't eat the cookie," said with crumbs on the sides of the child's mouth and the half-eaten cookie gripped tightly in his hand), the child is often adept at predicting what will happen if the parent learns the truth of the matter. The parent's discovery of the truth often leads to some painful consequence for the child (e.g., loss of dessert for the rest of the week) and so the child is attracted to the possibility of lying. The lie becomes an efficient means to avoid negative consequences, and if there is a family dog or pre-verbal sibling to blame for the missing cookie, the lie can be effective as well. This is why some parents adopt the following strategy when they suspect their children of lying about having done x (e.g., who ate the cookies?): the parent says to the child, "if you tell the truth about x, you won't get in trouble." These parents realize that the consequences of telling the truth loom so large for the child that lying seems worth the risk. The parent who promises no negative consequences not only eliminates the cost of telling the truth, but also helps clear the way for an experience of proper pleasure in truth telling that thereby helps to habituate honesty.

Unfortunately, not all parents (or police officers, tax accountants, teachers, employers, insurance adjustors, neighbors, spouses, friends, and others to whom persons are tempted to lie) promise no negative consequences to help elicit the truth. Rather, the painful consequences for letting the truth be known are often waiting to flood in, and the experience of appropriate pleasure is liable to get lost in the mix. This is not to say that the proper pleasure of truth telling fails to arise at all when one tells the truth, but rather, whatever proper pleasure arises gets swamped by the overall experience of loss and embarrassment, especially when the stakes are high. When a costly truth has been told and the truth teller, awash in the pain, is asked, "But doesn't it at least feel good to have told the truth?" a plausible response is, "No, the whole thing feels horrible." Thus, when it comes to refraining from lying, it can be difficult to prime the virtue formation pump with the experience of appropriate pleasure.

4. AN ALTERNATIVE PATH TO BECOMING HONEST

But the direct approach is not the only available pathway for acquiring virtue. Another option is what might be thought of as an indirect approach to virtue formation. This approach is "indirect" in that it does not directly practice the acts in accord with virtue, but instead, first, seeks to identify the underlying psychology of virtuous behavior (and/or the underlying psychology of vice) and, second, pursues an overall way of life that is conducive to bringing about this underlying psychology. This way of life is not a direct attempt to practice the behavior in accord with virtue; rather, the practices involved in the way of life are indirectly related to the acquisition of the virtue in question. These practices provide what Nancy Snow has referred to as the "personality scaffolding" for the formation of virtuous dispositions. Snow understands "personality scaffolding" as "the psychological structures and mechanisms that can help or hinder the development, sustenance, and exercise of virtue."[11] This is to say, the indirect formative process looks to a set of activities that constitutes an overall way of life, and this way of life engenders the beliefs, valuations, desires, emotions, and attitudes that make up at least some of the requisite underlying psychology conducive to acquiring the virtue in question. On this indirect approach, the virtue formation pump is primed prior to the practice of behavior that accords with virtue.

In this way, the indirect pathway meets the direct approach half-way in that indirect formation is complemented by the actual practice of behavior in accordance with virtue, with the latter serving to rein-force the underlying psychology as well as the way of life that preceded it. What indirect formation adds is an alternative way of approaching virtue formation. In particular, it helps cultivate the personality scaf-folding that makes the experience of appropriate pleasure more likely in the process of virtue acquisition, and is thereby particularly suited for the formation of honesty when the pain of acting honestly would otherwise outweigh the felt experience of pleasure.[12]

In order to pursue an indirect formation process when it comes to refraining from self-serving lies, we first identify the underlying moti-vations for these lies as well as a set of activities that would under-mine these particular motivations. One plausible conceptualization of the liar's underlying motivations is that lying, especially when due to a perceived personal benefit, springs from a personal orientation to the world that centers on certain deeply entrenched human concerns

11. Snow 2013: 131.
12. For more on this notion of personality scaffolding, see Snow 2018: 75–78.

such as self-protection (will I be able to keep the goods that I have?), self-preservation (will I be able to obtain the goods that I need?), and self-enhancement (will I be able to ensure that others will think well of and accept me?). This is to say, the perception of a personal benefit to oneself can be understood as a judgment based on desires to avoid the loss of goods already possessed (self-protection), gain goods for oneself going forward (self-preservation), and maintain or improve others' view of oneself (self-enhancement). While there is nothing wrong in principle with these concerns, when the fulfilment of them is threatened by truth telling, lying can be a tempting means to protect against loss, gain goods, and enhance one's standing. As long as we see ourselves as under threat in terms of protection, preservation, and enhancement, we can be tempted to lie.[13] While there are no doubt other motivations for self-serving lies, a large class of such lies plausibly stems from one or more of these desires.[14]

This analysis suggests that a way to become honest, at least when it comes to refraining from lying due to a perceived personal benefit, is to engage in a process of reorienting oneself to the world such that one does not experience oneself as under as much threat in terms of protection, preservation, and acceptance by others. In particular, this reorientation involves an alternative way of seeing oneself such that

13. Of course, this analysis presses the question of the morality of lying. Do certain types of threat to one's own (or another's) well-being morally justify lying in order to avoid the threatened outcomes? Even on a positive answer to that question, many types of threat to one's own (or another's) well-being are presumably inadequate to morally justify lying.

14. For comparison, Gillath and colleagues consider three motivations for lying: achievement, power, and intimacy. See Gillath et al. 2010: 849. DePaulo's research found that many lies, including the most serious lies, are told for self-centered motives. See DePaulo 1994: 309–311, 317. Moreover, Kashy and DePaulo found that lies are more frequently told by persons who care deeply about what others think of them. See Kashy and DePaulo 1996: 1050. Annette C. Baier discusses similar motivations for lying that she refers to as our "self-protective and self-assertive ends." See Baier 1993: 281. Of course, another powerful motivation for truth telling would be an increase in empathy for the way lying disregards and harms the one lied to. See Staats et al. 2008.

one's protection, preservation, and acceptance by others are judged as sufficiently secure apart from lying. This sort of secure sense of self is not a guaranteed constant. Thus, a set of practices that make up such a way of life would need to be engaged in order to develop the sense that one will be able to maintain the goods that one has, obtain the goods that one needs, and ensure that others think well of and accept one. This underlying psychology will diminish the motivation to lie in order to protect, preserve, and enhance others' view of one-self. Indeed, to the degree that this alternative sense of self emerges, the desire to lie can fade away since being honest in this way no longer erodes one's secure standing in the world. In other words, whatever perceived cost might come from truth telling will not be sufficient to override one's secure sense of self.

For instance, consider Sam, who tried to get a few additional things finished at the office and once again left late. Still far from home, his spouse phones and says, "You said you'd be home by 5:30. It is 6:00. You knew I needed the car. What happened?" Sam has a choice. He could either tell the truth and own up to his decision to stay late, or he could lie, blaming his lateness on heavy traffic. It seems plausible to suppose that what is at stake here is Sam's self-protection, self-preservation, and self-enhancement. That is to say, if Sam tells the truth he stands to lose certain goods he currently has (harmony with his spouse), he puts in jeopardy future goods he hopes to gain (an enjoyable evening with his spouse), and he sets up his spouse's disappointment and rejection. With these goods under threat, the temptation to lie looms large. But if Sam feels generally secure regarding these goods, then he stands a better chance—due to that state of mind—of having the capacity to tolerate the negative fallout of telling the truth.

It is important to note that what we are calling a "secure sense of self" is not primarily a sense of material or physical security, but instead a sense of relational security. This is a secure sense that when

I am unable to hold onto what I have, when I don't have what I need, and/or when I am rejected by some, there are one or more others who will help restore what has been lost, provide for me, and/or stand by me. Often, these are the sorts of relational goods that are under threat; but even when material and physical goods are under threat, a sense of relational safety, security, and acceptance can serve to diminish the temptation to lie. So, on this pathway of virtue formation, it is the *relational* way of life that Sam has cultivated in previous days, weeks, and months that shapes his way of being in the world and that heavily influences his capacity to tolerate the pain of truth telling.

5. A RELATIONALLY CONNECTED WAY OF LIFE AND BECOMING HONEST

Within philosophy, the recent return to seeing philosophy as involving the cultivation of an overall way of life helps promote this indirect, relational pathway of virtue acquisition.[15] For instance, Pierre Hadot has argued that all ancient philosophical schools (e.g., Platonism, Aristotelianism, Epicureanism, Stoicism, etc.) envisioned philosophy as consisting "not merely in speaking and discoursing in a certain way, but also in being, acting, and seeing the world in a specific way . . . . Philosophy is not merely discourse but a choice of life, an existential option, and a lived exercise."[16] Within these philosophical schools, acquiring virtue involved immersion in a form of life which included exercises (e.g., dietary regimes, meditation, contemplation, etc.) that formed the inner life of the subject and predisposed him or her for the acquisition of virtue. On this conception of virtue formation, virtuous action springs from an overall personal orientation to

15. See Hadot 1995, 2004, Cooper 2012, and Snow 2016b.
16. Hadot 2004: 220.

reality that is maintained by the practices that constitute a particular way of life.

For instance, ancient Stoicism is an overall way of life that encourages the practice of meditating on one's inevitable death as a means to eradicate fear and worry about the conditions that would hasten one's death.[17] By meditating on one's death through the lens of Stoic doctrine—according to which one's death, like everything else that happens, is simply part of the unfolding of God's perfectly rational will for the universe—one can become rightly indifferent to continued existence.[18] In this way, the Stoic attempts to detach from her self-concerns, re-envisioning her life from a God's-eye point of view. In this regard, Epictetus writes,

> Why don't you reflect, then, that for man the source of all evils, and of his meanness of spirit and cowardice, is not death itself, but rather the fear of death? It is to confront this that you must train yourself, and it is towards that end that all your reasonings, all your studies, and all your readings should be directed, and then you'll recognize that it is in this way alone that human beings can attain freedom.[19]

On this conception of Stoicism, virtuous action springs from an overall personal orientation to reality that is maintained by indirect practices that constitute a Stoic way of life.[20]

Confucianism is another example of indirect virtue acquisition by means of an overall way of life. Snow writes, "Confucian paradigms

17. Robertson 2010: 165–168.
18. There is an important distinction in Stoicism between "preferred indifferents" and "non-preferred indifferents," where becoming rightly indifferent to a naturally valuable thing is not to deny that one still prefers that thing. See Reydam-Schils 2006: 59–69.
19. Epictetus 2014: 216 (*Discourses* 3.26.38–39).
20. See Cooper 2012: 214–225, Gill 2018.

stress virtue cultivation as structured immersion into a way of life . : . . This focus on the outer life is meant to structure attention in specific ways so as to create a kind of inner life. We cultivate the inner by attending to the outer."[21] In particular, intentional engagement with various kinds of ritual propriety (or *li*), music, classic texts, and other "situational factors" are meant to shape affect and cognitions "in ways intended to elicit virtuous response, and, eventually, through habituated practice, virtuous dispositions."[22] Snow concludes that this "total immersion in a way of life . . . is deliberate and a more global form of virtue development" than other more standard paradigms of virtue development.[23]

On these indirect models of virtue acquisition, the practice-habituation process is not directed toward practicing the virtuous behavior itself, but is directed toward immersion in an overall way of life that brings about the inner states and dispositions underlying the virtuous response. However, it is important to note that it is not that the direct pathway of practice-habituation is wrongheaded as much as it is truncated when considered separately from an overall way of life. Indeed, what Aristotle thought of as the importance of a "good upbringing" for the development of virtue can be helpfully extended to include a good way of living throughout one's life.[24] This is to say, one way of understanding the importance of a good upbringing is that it tills the psychological soil in which direct practice of virtuous acts takes root. And yet, within contemporary psychological theory and research, it is widely maintained that the social-emotional benefits

21. Snow 2016a: 149.
22. Ibid., 151.
23. Ibid. Snow juxtaposes Confucian virtue formation with her own "folk" approach to virtue acquisition and Julia Annas's broadly Aristotelian "expertise" paradigm.
24. Aristotle writes, "That is why we need to have had the appropriate upbringing—right from early youth, as Plato says—to make us find enjoyment or pain in the right things; for this is the correct education" (1999: 21; *Nicomachean Ethics* 1104b11–13).

of a good upbringing are not an all-or-nothing childhood affair, but rather a lifelong developmental task sensitive to a person's choices.[25]

To illustrate, let us assume that some subset of lies for personal benefit is motivated by the fear that if the truth were known, others would view us negatively, leading to our being relationally rejected. On this assumption, social-emotional practices that reinforce the unconditional positive regard of significant persons in our lives would mitigate this fear. So, if Sam is confident in the unconditional acceptance of significant others in his life (perhaps including his spouse), then he will find it easier to face up to his spouse's negative feelings and tell the truth regarding his lateness. The way of life Sam needs to practice in order to be prepared to keep from lying is a relationally connected one. In psychological terminology, the sort of relationship in question can be helpfully characterized as a "secure attachment."[26]

Rooted in the research of John Bowlby, a secure attachment is understood as a type of interpersonal relationship in which the one who is securely attached possesses an abiding confidence in the emotional availability, attunement, and care of significant others. Attachment theory is:

> built on the core observation that security-enhancing caregivers or "attachment figures" (usually beginning with parents or other primary care providers in childhood) help a child develop positive mental representations of self and relationship partners. They also support the development of effective means of regulating emotions and coping with threats and stressors. Children and adults with a history of supportive attachment relationships are notably less defensive, more mindful of their feelings, more

25. See, e.g., Thompson 2015: 297.
26. For more on attachment theory, see Cassidy 2008, Thompson 2016, and Bowlby 1988.

genuinely empathic, and more open in communicating with relationship partners.[27]

Conversely, persons with an unreliable and neglectful relational history tend to develop insecure attachments that bring about attachment anxiety and attachment avoidance. Anxiously attached individuals have a negative evaluation of self that includes chronic anxiety about intimacy/closeness, jealousy, fears of abandonment/neglect, and a high need for approval from close others, rather than a secure sense of self.[28] Attachment avoidant individuals possess a negative evaluation of others that includes fears of intimacy/closeness and a lack of trust in the availability of others, rather than a confidence in the acceptance and support of close others.[29]

The crucial idea on this social-emotional formative path is that through the help of others securely attached individuals have become confident of the protection of others in times of loss (i.e., protection), of the care of others in times of need (i.e., preservation), and of the acceptance of others in the face of rejection (i.e., acceptance). This is to say, through secure attachment to others, individuals can come to have a habituated sense of self that involves the internalized meaning that because I am cared for by competent others "I will be protected," "I will be alright," and "I will be accepted." This secure sense of self militates against the fear that "I will lose too much," "I won't have enough," and "I will be rejected," thereby undermining the central motivations to lie for personal benefit.

Consider the example of the temptation to cover-up a sex scandal out of the fear of losing one's job, spouse, and reputation. The temptation to lie is fierce precisely because protection, preservation, and enhancement are on the line. How should one counsel the one

27. Gillath et al. 2010: 842.
28. Ibid.
29. Ibid.

facing the temptation to engage in a cover-up? Does the wise counselor recommend the direct practice of honest behavior in the face of
the massive temptation to lie? Or does the wise counselor say, "You
are never going to be able to face up to the truth without some help.
I will gather a group of your closest friends and we will stand by you
no matter what and help you face up to the truth."

Of course, such an indirect move is possible only if there is a wise
counselor to call and close friends to gather, as well as openness to
being aided in this way. The practices required to develop and maintain a secure relational context are varied, and much depends, according to attachment theory, on one's early relational experience—that
is, whether or not one had a good or "good-enough" upbringing.[30] If
one's upbringing was not "good enough," then corrective relational
experiences are needed, and there are practices whereby persons can
seek these out (e.g., therapy, trust-building exercises, practices related
to post-traumatic growth, intentional friendship, etc.). Once a person
is committed to the value of being known and accepted by safe others,
a way of life that involves self-awareness, transparent communication,
confession and forgiveness, mindfulness of the other, meaningful relational interaction, and so on can be intentionally cultivated. Practices
such as these help establish a relationally connected way of life leading
to a way of being in the world—a habituated personal orientation to
reality—that gradually sublimates self-protection, self-preservation,
and self-enhancement to an alternative way of seeing oneself so that
one's protection, preservation, and reputation are sufficiently secure
apart from lying. A fundamental aspect of this new orientation is an
emerging willingness to relinquish control over the perceived disadvantages of honesty. So, on this view, lying (and perhaps other forms
of dishonesty) is largely unnecessary when the costs of truth telling
are no longer seen as a threat to one's secure standing in the world.

30. For the notion of "good-enough" parenting, see Winnicott 2005: 144–148.

6. EMPIRICAL EVIDENCE FOR THE RELATIONSHIP BETWEEN SECURE ATTACHMENT AND HONESTY

This theoretical connection between secure attachment to others and truth telling has had limited but promising empirical investigation. Several studies have found significant associations between insecure attachment and increased frequency of lying.[31] For instance, Ennis and his team hypothesized that in many cases persons lie to influence and make a good impression on others, and that insecurely attached individuals have a particular need to utilize deception to accomplish these social interaction goals.[32] Based on a self-report measure of frequency of lying and a measure that assessed attachment style, Ennis et al. found a significant positive correlation between relational attachment anxiety and the frequency of telling self-centered lies to both strangers and best friends.[33]

Building off previous studies, Omri Gillath and his colleagues conducted a series of studies that demonstrated both an association between insecure attachment and lying as well as an association between secure attachment and truth telling. In summarizing their research, Gillath et al. write, "Taken together, the studies indicate that attachment security allows a person to forgo various kinds of defenses and be more open and honest with others and more true to oneself."[34] While more empirical work is needed to demonstrate a

31. Cole 2001, Vrij et al. 2003, and Ennis et al. 2008.
32. Ennis et al. 2008: 106.
33. Ibid., 113. It should be noted that the positive correlation found with anxiously attached individuals was not as strong with an avoidant attachment style. Since avoidant attachment is characterized by independence and autonomy, this weaker correlation could be due to the tendency for relationally avoidant individuals to lack concern about how they are perceived by others.
34. Gillath et al. 2010: 853. While the research exploring the role of attachment in predicting virtuous behavior more generally is not extensive at this point, some studies have found a

causal connection between secure attachment and truth telling, these empirical studies showing a significant correlation between the two provide additional support to the proposed theoretical connection.

7. AN OBJECTION TO THE ALTERNATIVE INDIRECT PATHWAY

Despite the conceptual and empirical connection between secure, social-emotional support and not lying, a worry remains. The proposal offered is that the development of securely attached relationships brings about social-emotional support that aids one in refraining from lies that are perceived to benefit oneself. But, of course, the development of those very types of relationships would surely require that one refrain from lies that are perceived to benefit oneself. In other words, refraining from lying to others is needed to develop the secure attachments that are purported to enable one to refrain from lying to others. As Aristotle himself worries: it can appear that to do what it takes to develop a given virtue, one must already possess that virtue.[35] If so, virtue formation doesn't get off the ground.

Further, if one has to be honest in order to enter into a relational way of life that cultivates honesty, then the empirical correlation between secure attachment and honesty does not support the notion that secure attachment is causally connected with honesty. Instead, the explanation of why securely attached persons lie less than insecurely attached persons is that honest people already tend to be

meaningful connection. For instance, Carissa Dwiwardani and her fellow researchers found a significant relationship between secure attachment and self-reported behaviors associated with humility, gratitude, and forgiveness. See Dwiwardani et al. 2014.

35. *Nicomachean Ethics* II.4. See Porter 2012: 137–138.

securely attached. If that is correct, the presence of the virtue of honesty is what explains the correlation, not any sort of causal connection between secure attachment and honesty.

But is honesty (or a lack of dishonesty) required to develop the sorts of securely attached relationships that have been conceptually and empirically linked to honesty? While there is no doubt that lying to benefit oneself breaks down relational trust and security, there are several ways that relational connections of the required sort could be developed. First, a minimal amount of honest behavior that falls short of fully formed honesty is sufficient to begin developing friendships of the requisite sort. Over time, these gradually maturing friendships might incrementally support the development of honesty both in the friendships themselves as well as in other relational contexts. Much like an alcoholic can be sober enough to commit to an Alcoholics Anonymous group that then helps him maintain and develop sobriety, someone struggling with lying can be honest enough to commit to practices of friendship that then help him maintain and develop his honesty.

Second, parents and other adult caregivers often deal with regular self-serving lies amongst children with whom they are nevertheless able to form close interpersonal connections. In these cases, the parent is able to tolerate the lies and provide relational encounters that promote a sense of relational safety, well-being, and acceptance. Such relational encounters can even include confronting the child with his or her lies with the aim of repairing the rupture in the relationship (e.g., through apology and forgiveness). Some psychological theory and research suggest that ruptures in interpersonal relationships— like getting caught in a lie—that are addressed and repaired are important to the development of interpersonal closeness.[36] So, being caught lying in a developing relationship, if addressed and repaired, can be a part of developing the sort of relational connection that is

36. See, e.g., Kohut 1984, Tronick 2006.

needed to refrain from lying. Furthermore, while tolerating the self-serving lies of children is in some sense developmentally appropriate, there can be appropriate ways to extend such toleration and relational connection to adult relationships.

In these ways, one does not have to refrain from lying in order to develop the kinds of secure interpersonal relationships that can assist one in refraining from lying. While this successful response does not show that the correlation between secure attachment and honesty is a causal one, it certainly leaves open that interpretation of the data.

8. CONCLUSION

The indirect path of virtue formation presented here proposes that persons who regularly tell the truth—even when the truth hurts—at times do so in part because they are relationally situated in such a way that the desires to lie for the purpose of self-protection, self-preservation, and self-enhancement are muted. They are relationally safe, secure, and accepted. As such, they are largely unmoved by the need to improve their lot or standing—at least, at the cost of lying to do so. This overall orientation to the world, so the argument goes, emerges from a way of life constituted by practices that cultivate certain kinds of securely attached relationships which provide needed social-emotional support. It is the social-emotional support of others and the way of being it engenders that inoculates one against temptations to lie to benefit oneself.

Of course, there are other aspects of honesty besides truth telling (e.g., respecting others' property, rule-following, forthrightness, promise-keeping, etc.).[37] Will practicing a relationally connected

---

37. For discussion of various forms of honesty, see Miller 2017 and Roberts and West (chapter 4 in this volume).

way of life, as described in this chapter, help enable one to refrain from stealing, cheating, withholding important information, promise breaking, and the like? Presumably so, at least to the extent that persons perform these actions partly in search of self-protection, self-preservation, and self-enhancement. The sort of social-emotional support envisioned in this chapter might go a long way toward meeting the relational needs that could otherwise motivate dishonest acts in these and other ways.[38]

BIBLIOGRAPHY

Aristotle. *Nicomachean Ethics*, 2nd ed. Translated by Terence Irwin. Indianapolis, IN: Hackett, 1999.

Baier, Annette C. "Why Honesty Is a Hard Virtue." In *Identity, Character, and Morality: Essays in Moral Psychology*, edited by Owen Flanagan and Amelie O. Rorty, 259–281. Cambridge, MA: MIT Press, 1993.

Bowlby, John. *A Secure Base*. London: Routledge, 1988.

Burnyeat, M. F. "Aristotle on Learning to Be Good." In *Essays on Aristotle's Ethics*, edited by Amélie Oksenberg Rorty, 69–92. Berkeley: University of California Press, 1980.

Carson, Thomas L. *Lying and Deception: Theory and Practice*. Oxford: Oxford University Press, 2010.

Cassidy, Jude. "The Nature of the Child's Ties." In *Handbook of Attachment: Theory, Research, and Clinical Applications*, edited by Jude Cassidy and Phillip R. Shaver, 3–22. New York: Guilford Press, 2008.

Cole, Tim. "Lying to the One You Love: The Use of Deception in Romantic Relationships." *Journal of Social and Personal Relationships* 18 (2001): 107–129.

Cooper, John M. *Pursuits of Wisdom: Six Ways of Life in Ancient Philosophy from Socrates to Plotinus*. Princeton, NJ: Princeton University Press, 2012.

Curzer, Howard J. "Aristotle's Painful Path to Virtue." *Journal of the History of Philosophy* 40 (2002): 141–162.

DePaulo, Bella M. "The Many Faces of Lies." In *The Social Psychology of Good and Evil*, edited by Arthur G. Miller, 303–326. New York: Guilford Press, 2004.

38. Thanks go to Nancy Snow and her staff (particularly Max Parish) for convening the workshop at the University of Oklahoma where this paper was first presented. All of the participants at the workshop provided helpful and stimulating conversation. Special thanks go to Christian Miller and Ryan West for their suggested edits.

DePaulo, Bella M. "The Gift of Dishonesty." In *Moral Psychology, Volume V: Virtue and Character*, edited by Walter Sinnott-Armstrong and Christian B. Miller, 287–294. Cambridge, MA: MIT Press, 2017.

DeSteno, David. "How America Can Finally Learn to Deal With Its Impulses." *Pacific Standard*, The Social Justice Foundation, Sept. 15, 2014, psmag.com/social-justice/feeling-control-america-can-finally-learn-deal-impulses-self-regulation-89456.

Dwiwardani, Carissa, Peter C. Hill, Richard A. Bollinger, et al., "Virtues Develop from a Secure Base: Attachment and Resilience as Predictors of Humility, Gratitude, and Forgiveness." *Journal of Psychology and Theology* 42:1 (2014): 83–90.

Ennis, Edel, Aldert Vrij, and Claire Chance. "Individual Differences and Lying in Everday Life." *Journal of Social and Personal Relationships* 25:1 (2008): 105–118.

Epictetus. *Discourses, Fragments, Handbook*. Translated by Robin Hard. Oxford: Oxford University Press, 2014.

Gill, Christopher. "Stoicism Today: An Alternative Approach to Cultivating the Virtues." In *The Theory and Practice of Virtue Education*, edited by Tom Harrison and David Ian Walker, 44–55. New York: Routledge, 2018.

Gillath, Omri, Amanda K. Sesko, Phillip R. Shaver, and David S. Chun. "Attachment, Authenticity, and Honesty: Dispositional and Experimentally Induced Security Can Reduce Self- and Other-Deception." *Journal of Personality and Social Psychology* 98:5 (2010): 841–855.

Hadot, Pierre. *Philosophy as a Way of Life: Spiritual Exercises from Socrates to Foucault*. Malden, MA: Blackwell, 1995.

Hadot, Pierre. *What is Ancient Philosophy?* Cambridge, MA: Harvard University Press, 2004.

Kashy, Deborah A. and Bella M. DePaulo. "Who Lies?" *Journal of Personality and Social Psychology* 70 (1996): 1037–1051.

Kohut, Hienz. *How Does Analysis Cure?* Chicago: University of Chicago Press, 1984.

Miller, Christian B. *Moral Character: An Empirical Theory*. Oxford: Oxford University Press, 2013.

Miller, Christian B. "Honesty." In *Moral Psychology, Volume V: Virtue and Character*, edited by Walter Sinnott-Armstrong and Christian B. Miller, 237–273. Cambridge, MA: MIT Press, 2017.

Porter, Steven L. "Contentment." In *Being Good: Christian Virtues for Everyday Life*, edited by Michael W. Austin and R. Douglas Geivett, 126–144. Grand Rapids, MI: Eerdmans, 2012.

Porter, Steven L. "A Therapeutic Approach to Intellectual Virtue Formation in the Classroom." In *Intellectual Virtues and Education: Essays in Applied Virtue Epistemology*, edited by Jason Baehr, 221–239. New York: Routledge, 2016.

Reydam-Schils, Gretchen. *The Roman Stoics: Self, Responsibility, and Affection*. Chicago: University of Chicago Press, 2006.

Robertson, Donald. *The Philosophy of Cognitive-Behavioral Therapy: Stoic Philosophy as Rational and Cognitive Psychotherapy*. London: Karnac, 2010.

Sherman, Nancy. *The Fabric of Character: Aristotle's Theory of Virtue*. Oxford: Oxford University Press, 1989.

Snow, Nancy E. "Notes Toward an Empirical Psychology of Virtue: Exploring the Personality Scaffolding of Virtue." In *Aristotelian Ethics in Contemporary Perspective*, edited by Julia Peters, 130–144. New York: Routledge, 2013.

Snow, Nancy E. "How Habits Make Us Virtuous." In *Developing the Virtues: Integrating Perspectives*, edited by Julia Annas, Darcia Narvaez, and Nancy E. Snow, 135–156. New York: Oxford University Press, 2016a.

Snow, Nancy E. "Virtue Acquisition: The Paradox of Striving." *Journal of Moral Education* 45:2 (2016b): 179–191.

Snow, Nancy E. "From 'Ordinary Virtue' to Aristotelian Virtue." In *The Theory and Practice of Virtue Education*, edited by Tom Harrison and David Walker, 67–81. New York: Routledge, 2018.

Sorenson, Roy. "Bald Face Lies! Lying Without the Intent to Deceive." *Pacific Philosophical Quarterly* 88 (2007): 251–264.

Staats, Sara, Julie M. Hupp, and Anna M. Hagley. "Honesty and Heroes: A Positive Psychology View of Heroism and Academic Honest." *The Journal of Psychology* 142:4 (2008): 357–372.

Thompson, Ross. "The Development of Virtue: A Perspective from Developmental Psychology." In *Cultivating Virtues: Perspectives from Philosophy, Theology, and Psychology*, edited by Nancy E. Snow, 279–306. Oxford: Oxford University Press, 2015.

Thompson, Ross. "The Development of Virtuous Character: Automatic and Reflective Dispositions." In *Developing the Virtues: Integrating Perspectives*, edited by Julia Annas, Darcia Narvaez, and Nancy E. Snow, 95–115. Oxford: Oxford University Press, 2016.

Tronick, E. Z. "The Inherent Stress of Normal Daily Life and Social Interaction Leads to the Development of Coping and Resilience, and Variation in Resilience in Infants and Young Children." In *Resilience in Children: Annals of the New York Academy of Sciences*, Vol. 1094, edited by M. Lester, A. Masten, and B. McEwan, 83–104. Malden, MA: Blackwell, 2006.

Vrij, A, M. Floyd, and E. Ennis. "Telling Lies to Strangers or Close Friends: Is Relationship with Attachment Style." In *Advances in Psychology Research*, Volume 20, edited by S. Shohov, 61–74. New York: Nova Science Publishers, 2003.

Winnicott, D. W. *Playing and Reality*. New York: Routledge, 2005.

PART III

TRUTH SEEKING

Chapter 8

Intellectual Temperance

*Lessons in Truth Seeking
from Augustine and Aquinas*

W. JAY WOOD

1. INTRODUCTION

Virtue epistemologists refer often to virtues such as intellectual humility and intellectual generosity, applying to habits of intellectual excellence qualities once reserved only for moral virtues. Of course, prudence—the deeply anchored, acquired habit of thinking well in order to act and live well—has been a canonical intellectual virtue from antiquity.[1] Now we see philosophers attaching the descriptor "intellectual" to other cardinal virtues, such as "intellectual justice" and "intellectual courage."[2] Less attention has been given of late to the cardinal virtue of temperance and its role in the intellectual life. That we should moderate our appetites for food, drink, and sex has ancient roots and the support of common sense. Moderating our

1. See Wood 2014.
2. See Fricker 2007, Roberts and Wood 2007.

W. Jay Wood, *Intellectual Temperance* In: *Integrity, Honesty, and Truth Seeking*. Edited by: Christian B. Miller and Ryan West. Oxford University Press (2020). © Oxford University Press.
DOI: 10.1093/oso/9780190920487.003.0008

appetite for truth, knowledge, and related epistemic goods sounds somewhat counterintuitive. Deficiency of knowledge we understand and seek to remedy through various forms of education. But how can one's appetite for knowledge be defective? In what ways do our intellectual appetites miss the mean by erring on the sides of excess or deficiency? What positive contribution does intellectual temperance make to the way we pursue, refine, purvey, and apply knowledge? I will argue that intellectual temperance deserves recognition as an intellectual virtue in its own right and that it plays an important, but largely underappreciated role in regulating our pursuit of truth and preserving our integrity as wise, morally mature intellectual agents.[3]

I begin by unpacking the concept of temperance as it has been classically understood, as an excellence of moderation with respect to our bodily appetites for food, drink, and sex. Along the way, I argue that Augustine and Aquinas, and the Christian tradition more broadly, depart from Aristotle's account of temperance, due to the ever-present likelihood of temptation. Finally, I explore how their teachings on *curiositas* and *studiositas* have relevance for intellectual temperance in our contemporary epistemic context.

2. WHAT IS TEMPERANCE?

Temperance, in the broadly Aristotelian tradition, is a feature of many virtues insofar as they achieve a path of moderation between the vices of excess and deficiency. As a standalone virtue in its own right, however, temperance is an acquired disposition of wise satisfaction of our natural appetites, especially those for food, drink, and sex, as

---

3. A notable exception is Paul Griffiths' superlative treatment of the subject in his 2009. My indebtedness to his work will be apparent.

governed by right reason and, some would add, divine law.[4] There is nothing wrong with food, drink, and sex, each being a source of pleasure connected with our sense of touch. Indeed, these goods are essential for a good life and the survival of the species. It is precisely their centrality to the good life, however, that contributes simultaneously to the strength of our appetites for these goods, as well as their need for bit and bridle. The temperate person's appetites for these goods are shaped by wise judgment about the ways they contribute to a balanced, moderate, and flourishing life. Most of our struggles with these appetites cause us to err on the side of excess and inappropriateness more broadly. A temperate person's appetites are trained to avoid excess as well as deficiency, as an anemic appetite for these essential goods also adversely affects one's overall health and well-being. Following Aristotle and Aquinas, I hold that not all bodily pleasures are the concern of temperance. A person might enjoy the smell of fragrant flowers, or a lovely tune, but these do not concern the pleasures of touch, nor do they bear so centrally on our preservation and human flourishing.

The moderation of our appetites in which temperance consists concerns more than the frequency and degree to which we indulge bodily pleasures. Tempered appetites are guided by practical wisdom drawn from a particular understanding of human nature, the conditions of our flourishing, and our *telos* or final end. Appetites must be assessed as they bear positively or negatively on the particulars of a person's health, vocation, financial means, station in life, and the needs of one's family, neighbors, and the broader community, among other concerns. Even these particulars admit of significant variation. How, for example, would illness, food rationing in wartime, or a religious fast shape one's thinking about what counts as moderate eating? A person's pursuit of the pleasures of food, drink, and sex is thus

4. Aristotle 1999: III.10–12.

motivated and shaped both by personal concerns of self-care and by other-regarding communal concerns, giving temperance its distinctive structure and orientation.

According to Paul Griffiths, "All appetites seek not only the presence of some absence, but also that presence under some understanding or description."[5] Robert Roberts explains that the required "understanding" is minimal in raw, primitive animal appetites, where the animal merely needs to be able to identify food as food and mate as mate. But human appetites are intermingled with, conditioned by, and conceptualized in terms of our concerns, which include our loves, cares, desires, attachments, and emotions.[6] Concerns are also desiring states, which pertain to the things persons care about and that have significance for them. Concerns focus our attention, making various objects and aspects of our surroundings and circumstances salient for us. Concerns are thus directed to various objects of concern—that I eat and sleep well, that justice be done, that peace prevail, that family and friends flourish, that God's will be done—which concerns are in turn shaped by a generalized understanding of the human good and the conditions for human flourishing. Concerns can also narrow in their degree of specificity. I may be concerned not simply to eat well but to eat gluten-free and kosher food. Tempered appetites are thus those that have incorporated wise understanding that reflects both general and specific concerns about the good life.

The appetites of the heart bear upon the appetites of the flesh, and vice versa. We can, for instance, have second-order desires that our physical hunger for food were weaker than it is. And when our appetites for food, drink, and sex are satisfied physically, we typically enjoy an accompanying emotional or psychological satisfaction. Consequently, satisfaction of our appetites for food, drink, and

5. Griffiths 2009: 98.
6. Roberts 2014: 104.

sex is not reducible to whether and to what degree we indulge them. Conditioned by concerns as appetites are, judgments concerning whether and how much to indulge them depend in varying degrees on the sorts of circumstantial particulars mentioned above. The virtue of temperance, says Roberts, is thus a disposition to have appetites and pleasures that are "qualified by *appropriate* concerns and *not by inappropriate* concerns, and thus are *appropriate* desires, and *appropriate* pleasures."[7] This constellation of wise judgment, concerns, and habits shapes and guides the temperate life.

Integrating temperance with the affections (our loves, cares, concerns, desires, etc.) finds antecedents in the medieval masters. "A man is conformed to whatever he loves,"[8] says Augustine. Aquinas echoes Augustine saying, "man's mind is drawn on account of his affections, toward the things for which he has an affection."[9] Augustine was acutely sensitive to the interactions of appetite between body and heart, investing temperance with the task of integrating and harmonizing the two. "Temperance is love giving itself entirely to that which is loved,"[10] which, for Augustine, is God, the chief and highest good. "Temperance," says Augustine, "promises us a kind of integrity and incorruption in the love by which we are united to God."[11] Note that Augustine goes on to assign to temperance the tasks of "restraining and quieting the passions," which tasks are traditionally assigned to self-control.[12] This Augustinian move marks an important divide between classical (Aristotelian) and Christian understandings of temperance.

7. Roberts 2014: 104, italics in original.
8. Augustine 1948: 338
9. Aquinas *ST* II–II.166.1 ad. 2.
10. Augustine 1948: 331.
11. Ibid., 336.
12. Ibid.

Neither Aristotle nor significant medieval accounts of temperance see it as grim, cramped, asceticism solely for the sake of self-denial, or abasement of the flesh. Just the opposite; they regarded pleasure as essential for the good life, despite our tendency toward excess. Pleasures are enjoyed more, however, when we are not mastered by them. "Excess," writes Montaigne, "is the pest of pleasure, and self-restraint is not its scourge but its spice."[13] The effects of temperance go deeper than the pleasure of sex, food, and drink; it orders our appetites to achieve what Aquinas calls an inner "tranquility of the soul."[14] The integrity of body and soul of which Augustine speaks likewise underscores that our appetites are intertwined with the concerns of our hearts and the orientation of our thoughts. Temperance is the integration of right reason and appetite that serves and does not stray from the overriding goods of justice, healing, aesthetic delight, intellectual understanding, and other worthy goods.

To lack temperance disposes one to internal discord: a lack of a cohesive inner soul. To eat, drink, and copulate indiscriminately is to court ill health, thus pitting appetite against proper self-care. Disease aside, the vice of intemperance contributes to a loss of integrity, the inner tranquility and harmony of the soul, of which Aquinas speaks. To struggle with temptation toward the ill use of food, drink, and sex is at once to see them as attractive, yet wrong, thus creating an opposition—an internal tension—between right reason and our bodily appetites. Intemperance opposes the integrated, tranquil life that is the goal of true temperance. For this reason, the virtue of caution is a supporting ally to temperance. It is a disposition to show proper, circumstantially appropriate regard for potential harms posed by inappropriate indulgence of pleasure. The reckless court danger; the cautious listen to their fears. Caution prompts us

13. Comte-Sponville 2002: 41.
14. Aquinas *ST* II–II.141.2 ad. 2.

to attend to the better part of practical wisdom when it advises that it is sometimes better to avoid danger than to charge headlong into it. Caution thus aids the development of temperance. For caution's sensitivity to potential pitfalls supplies the less-than-temperate with reasons to avoid the harms of intemperance.

Johann Sebastian Bach is famous for his compositions of preludes and fugues in all the major and minor keys for which he employed a well-tempered or equal tempered tuning system. This tuning system avoided the problem of music with many accidentals from sounding out of tune. Bach arranged the intervals between notes to prevent discordant sounds. In an analogous way, a temperate person's appetites are tuned and suitably adjusted to avoid "discordant pleasures." Temperate appetites suitably tuned to one's circumstances, promote a balanced, tranquil interior life, one not rocked by passions at war with each other, leading to a disintegrated self. Ironically, persons in the grip of the vice of intemperance possess a sort of perverse, "upside-down integrity": mind, will, and action are together coordinated so as to miss the requirements of virtue on all fronts. They fail to understand and to do what temperance requires, and they take pleasure in their vices.

Temperance (*sophrosyne*) isn't simply the power to resist temptation to immoderate indulgence of our appetites. Aristotle calls that "continence" or "self-control" (*enkratia*). Aristotle is quite plain about the difference between temperance and self-control.

> For the continent and the temperate person are both the sort to do nothing against reason because of bodily pleasures, but the continent person has base appetites, whereas the temperate person lacks them. The temperate person is the sort to find nothing pleasant against reason, but the continent is the sort to find such things pleasant, but not be led by them.[15]

15. Aristotle 1999: VII.9.6.

Aristotle thinks temperate people never act contrary to right reason. They are in perfect possession of their appetites and thus have no contrary impulses to overcome.

Take, for example, a young college student, alive with a full measure of hormones typical of the age, torn between the offer of a hookup and the conviction that it is wrong to use and discard another person for one's own gratification. After an interior tug of war, the student declines the offer. Yet, as the young man drives home, he fantasizes about what might have been. While the young man activated his power of self-control, he nevertheless lacks the virtue of temperance, that habitual inner attunement of the appetites that would have found the offer repugnant and would never have been tempted in the first place. Our student has demonstrated moral strength by successfully resisting his lustful leanings, but he still lacks the tempered passions that contribute to a harmonious and tranquil interior life. He is still at war within himself. Temperance, says Roberts, "integrates a concerned understanding into the appetites, and it has a habitual character so that, unlike self-control, it does not require active application, but automatically applies itself by being a feature of the appetite."[16] On the Aristotelian view, the temperate person does not so much yank at the reins of unruly horses, as allow them to take their habitual, well-trodden path to the barn.

While our young man doesn't rise to the virtue of temperance, neither does he sink to the level of incontinence or the vice of intemperance. Were he incontinent, he would through weakness of will have succumbed to temptation, the desire for sex overpowering the counsel of his own better judgment. Were he intemperate, his disposition would have been to misfire morally on all fronts. Lacking practical wisdom, his defective reason would have offered as a genuine good what is in fact only an apparent good. His untutored and

16. Roberts 2014: 106.

wayward sexual appetites would then incline him to pursue and to partake of the sexual activity on offer.

Consider a virtuously temperate Aristotelean as she moves down the line of a sumptuous buffet, overflowing with sweet and savory delights. She moves effortlessly and unimpeded down the line selecting only the right kinds and amounts of food that contribute to her health and other situational concerns. She does not linger, even momentarily, at the supersized desserts, as they hold no appeal for her. "A temperate person, unlike a person with self-control, does not resist temptation as she has no temptation to resist. Her desire is not contrary to reason, because reason has been incorporated into her desire."[17] Yet the temperate person is no automaton; her agency is active insofar as she is cognizant of what she is doing and takes pleasure in acting out of her virtue. She sees and appreciates how her concerns and reasoned assessment of her circumstances combine to direct her toward wise temperance.

But who among us is perfectly temperate, beyond even a twinge of temptation, with appetites perfectly and unfailingly adjusted to right reason? The Christian view of temperance as taught by Augustine and Aquinas would answer, "no one." Notice Augustine's description of temperance above: "The office of temperance lies in restraining and quieting the passions." Elsewhere he describes temperance as "a disposition that restrains our desires for things which it is base to desire."[18] Aquinas echoes Augustine saying, "Temperance is called a cardinal virtue because it restrains the desire for tactile pleasures."[19] Neither Augustine nor Aquinas embraces temperance as a perfected state whereby one is immune to temptation and moral

---

17. Ibid., 94.
18. Augustine 1953a: 128.
19. Aquinas 1999: 109.

backsliding. Rather, the virtue of temperance sometimes requires active application.

The Christian tradition teaches that no one is above temptation that includes a felt attraction to an inappropriate desire. So St. Paul laments, "I do not understand my own actions. For I do not do what I want, but I do the very thing I hate."[20] For this reason, Christians are taught to pray, "lead us not unto temptation," for we are never entirely free of a concupiscible power, wounded by the fall, that makes us susceptible to the disordered pleasures for food, drink, and sex. The dominant Christian tradition has never insisted, as Aristotle does, that to possess a virtue is to be impervious to all temptations associated with the flesh.[21] In the *City of God* Augustine asks of virtue:

> What is its activity in this world but unceasing warfare against the vices, and those not external vices but internal, not other people's vices but quite clearly our own, our very own? And this is the particular struggle of that virtue called in Greek *sophrosyne*, which is translated 'temperance,' the virtue which bridles the lusts of the flesh to prevent their gaining the consent of the mind and dragging it into every kind of immorality. . . . But what in fact, do we want to achieve, when we desire to be made perfect by the Highest Good? It can, surely, only be a situation where the desires of the flesh do not oppose the spirit, and where there is in us no vice for the spirit to oppose with its desires. Now we cannot achieve this in our present lifetime, for all our wishing.[22]

20. Romans 7:15, Revised Standard Version.
21. All virtue, says Aristotle, must be held from a "firm and unchangeable character." The temperate person therefore "finds no pleasure in what pleases the intemperate person, but finds it disagreeable; he finds no pleasure at all in the wrong things—he has no appetite for them" (1999: III.8). One can't be tempted by what one finds no pleasure in whatsoever, but finds disagreeable.
22. Augustine 2003: 854.

From Augustine's perspective, ancient philosophers were mistaken in thinking that any human being can be morally flawless.[23] Aquinas agrees, putting the point succinctly: "Sensuality cannot be cured in this life except by a miracle."[24] Indeed, not only are we not immune to temptation, says Aquinas, but we can actually lose virtues once gained through corrupted judgments of reason owing to ignorance, passion, or deliberate reason.[25] Bonnie Kent says "Aquinas refuses to make virtue a lofty idea that very few, if any, real people can attain. He accordingly warns virtuous people about the risk of moral backsliding."[26]

So what is the difference between temperance and self-control on this Christian reading? Temperance is not an all or nothing affair according to Augustine and Aquinas; like self-control, it comes in degrees. Perfect temperance is an ideal, something we approach "asymptotically," as it were, but never perfectly achieve in this life. Persons with virtuous temperance display a mature, intelligent, and highly reliable—though not impeccably perfect—resistance to rare temptations pertaining to the pleasures of food, drink, and sex. Virtuous temperance might be best understood as a threshold term, the exact point at which it is achieved is difficult to say. Still, we have little difficulty contrasting someone whose appetites, shaped by prudence, make one highly resistant to temptation, with the person whose life is marked by frequent temptations resisted only after great struggle. The former, but not the latter, has appetites attuned to right reason and deserves to be called temperate.

Since Augustine and Aquinas reject Aristotle's view that the temperate are beyond temptation, it follows that all persons will face

23. Kent 2001: 228.
24. Aquinas 1952: 237.
25. Aquinas ST I–II.53.1.
26. Kent 2013: 105.

temptation at some time. And to resist temptation, we need on occasion to activate strategies of self-control which, among other ways, can be recruited simply by recalling the good reasons and concerns that are ingredients in being temperate. I forgo that beer by turning my mind to the fact that I'm dining in the company of a friend who is a recovering alcoholic. I skip the rich dessert because I remind myself that I'm fasting from sugar during Lent. We would not exercise self-control if we did not believe there were prior rational reasons for doing so. Such good reasons, ones that are constitutive of temperance and automatically active in regulating the appetites of the temperate person, are the very reasons we rehearse inwardly when exercising self-control. Ideally temperate persons act spontaneously and effortlessly out of virtue, fully manifesting the harmonious interplay between their deep concerns, desire, and practical wisdom. For them, the guidance of good judgment is in play but not always occurrently at the forefront of their consciousness. At other times we must consciously rehearse these very same reasons and concerns when exercising temperance. The line between temperance and self-control is a thin one, and where exactly temperance shades into self-control, and self-control matures into temperance, is admittedly difficult to say.

3. INTELLECTUAL TEMPERANCE IN AUGUSTINE AND AQUINAS

The intellectual life encompasses more than seeking truth as propositional knowledge and defining epistemological terms. There are other intellectual goods to be gained: wisdom, understanding, and experiential acquaintance among them. Knowledge once gained must be revised and refined in the light of new learning, criticism, and deepened understanding. We also deem it a great good to share knowledge, to which end we found schools, write books, and attend conferences; and we find most unfortunate those who lack access to formal schooling. Finally, the ways we apply our knowledge are also subject to moral appraisal. In all of these areas of the intellectual life, our appetites need tempering.

Throughout his *Confessions* Augustine catalogues the many ways our appetites are excessive or in various ways disordered. He admits that his appetites for food and sex were matters of prolonged personal struggle, vices to which we moderns can easily relate. In book X, Augustine confesses to a sin unfamiliar to our modern ears: "*curiositas*," or vicious curiosity, a disordered appetite for knowledge that he also dubs "vain inquisitiveness," "the lust of the eyes," and "the empty desire to possess." *Curiositas* is the disposition to desire knowledge of the wrong things, or to pursue knowledge, even of good things, from wrong motives, in wrong ways, or for wrong ends.

Studiositas, its virtuous counterpart and a part of temperance, is the habit of rightly directing our intellectual powers and appetites, exercising due restraint over our desires for knowledge so that it stems from the right motives, toward the right objects, in the right way, and directed to appropriate ends. Aquinas expands on Augustine's treatment of *studiositas* and *curiositas* in questions 166 and 167 of *ST IIa-IIae*. While both affirm that "all humans desire to know," they nevertheless agree that this natural appetite we so often praise and encourage in children and students can nevertheless take a defective form when it lacks the boundaries set by prudence and temperance.

Warnings about vicious curiosity antedate Augustine. Cicero recognized curiosity's importance in motivating the search for knowledge but also warned against an intemperate and excessive desire for inappropriate knowledge. In his *Confessions* Augustine recalls Cicero's effect on his own thinking regarding intellectual appetite: "the one thing that delighted me in Cicero's exhortation was the advice 'not to study one particular sect but to love and seek and pursue and hold fast and strongly embrace wisdom itself, wherever found.' "[27] And Cicero is not unique. Seneca puts the concern succinctly: "The desire to know more than enough is a form of intemperance."[28] The story of Pandora is older still. Many Fathers of the patristic period saw *curiositas* as morally suspect in its motivation. Following St. Paul, they deemed the concern to gain certain sorts of knowledge as motivated by a desire to lord one's knowledge over others, leading one to become "puffed up" and swelled with pride.[29] They worried too that *curiositas* might lead to "heresy" and so-called "worldly wisdom." Such was the charge Augustine leveled against the Manicheans, with whom he associated for nearly a decade.[30] Following a pattern common to gnostic sects, they regarded themselves as the exclusive possessors of a saving knowledge reserved solely for the spiritually and intellectually elite, thereby compounding their pride with a form of possessiveness.[31]

Augustine and Aquinas develop the importance of temperance to the excellent intellectual life through their own analyses of *curiositas* and *studiositas*. Their views about human flourishing and the contribution knowledge makes to it obviously reflect the Christian worldview they both embraced. Even so, many of the points they make have ready application to our contemporary, largely secular, intellectual context.

In the first section, I noted how the structure of our concerns shapes our appetites for food, drink, and sex. Augustine and Aquinas argue that our deep-seated concerns shape our intellectual appetites

---

27. Augustine 2008: III.4.8.
28. Quoted in Harrison 2001: 265.
29. I Corinthians 8:12, 13:2.
30. See Augustine 2008: IV.
31. In his book, *Intellectual Appetite,* Paul Griffiths elegantly and forcefully argues that there is something defective about knowledge gained and unshared, secreted away as a private possession. See Griffiths 2009: chapter 9, on "Owning."

in a similar way. What we care about, what matters to us, what we love and desire, bear on what aspects of our environment we notice, attend to, remain captivated by, and seek to know and understand. These concerns can be more or less virtuous, and serve to shape intellectual appetites that are more or less temperate. It is a perverse concern, for example, that impels a person to pursue the latest gossip around the water cooler, as it often traffics in misinformation and partial truths lacking important context, and typically bears unfavorably on the subject of the gossip. It is knowledge sought not for another's well-being, but to their detraction, and is thus vicious. By contrast, the concern of a teacher to impart significant academic content to her students is admirable.

In the following I sketch a number of ways Augustine and Aquinas thought the intellectual life goes awry for lack of intellectual temperance. Defective forms of intellectual appetite include inordinate desire for knowledge that is forbidden or utterly mundane, knowledge that is harmful to oneself or others, knowledge that is vain or fruitless, knowledge that is too high or too low, knowledge sought and applied wrongly, as well as knowledge that can frustrate various intellectual goals. A brief discussion of pusillanimity reveals ways an anemic, underdeveloped appetite for knowledge frustrates the pursuit of truth. I then consider what relevance their warnings may have for our contemporary context. We will see a pattern of perverse and admirable concerns leading to malformed and well-formed intellectual appetites as they bear on the motive, content, means, and application of the types of knowledge we desire.

3.1 Forbidden Knowledge

Aquinas quotes Aristotle's famous beginning to his *Metaphysics* that "all men by nature have a desire to know."[32] The moderation of this

---

32. Aristotle 1948: A.1.

desire is the work of studiousness, and for this reason reckoned a part of temperance. "But as regards knowledge, man has contrary inclinations. For on the part of the soul, he is inclined to desire knowledge of things; and so it behooves him to exercise a praiseworthy restraint on this desire, lest he seek knowledge immoderately."[33]

One obvious way to fail in temperance, according to Augustine and Aquinas, is to seek knowledge and use means to knowledge that God expressly forbids. Their examples include the practice of astrology, magical arts, and divination.[34] Arguably the most famous case of knowledge marked as forbidden was the experiential acquaintance with evil our primordial parents acquired by eating the forbidden fruit. According to Augustine and Aquinas, and the Christian tradition generally, this was knowledge forbidden precisely because seeking it would constitute an act of blatant disobedience resulting in alienation from God. Augustine adds to the list of things forbidden scripture's prohibition against tempting God for signs and wonders for the purpose of spiritual "thrill-seeking."[35] Here defective motive looms large, as such persons presumptuously believe God is "on call" to perform signs and wonders at their bidding. They are more keen to see a spectacle than to receive the message (knowledge) such miracles were meant to convey.

Knowledge can be declared "forbidden" for political as well as religious and moral reasons, whereupon a person is guilty of *curiositas* for trafficking in the ideas of socially unacceptable or "outlawed groups."[36] Academic and corporate cultures erect their own intellectual "no-fly zones," for reasons very similar to those invoked by

33. Aquinas *ST* II–II.166.2 ad. 3.
34. See Aquinas *ST* II–II.167.2 *sed contra*, and Augustine 2008: XXXV.55.
35. Augustine 2008: 212.
36. Which groups are deemed outlawed will typically reflect one's own group membership. Sometimes an outlawed group may be the truly virtuous group to be with. From a Christian point of view, distributing Bibles into the USSR was outlawed, though virtuous.

ecclesial authorities. Some research programs are deemed off limits because they are believed to cause harm to others as well as to those who undertake such studies. (For more on harmful knowledge, see section 3.2.) They might be forbidden because they are thought to reinforce intellectual appetites that perpetuate harmful stereotypes and habits of prejudicial thinking. These bad habits have the further ill consequence of making those who have contracted them resistant to criticism and correction, all of which frustrate the goal of gaining truth and related intellectual goods.

Consider, for example, the firing of James Damore, who, after attending a diversity training session at Google Inc., wrote a ten-page memo suggesting that "differences in distributions of traits between men and women may in part explain why we don't have 50% representation of women in tech and leadership," and that "not all differences are socially constructed or due to discrimination."[37] Critics were quick to denounce Mr. Damore's speculations, measured though they were. One recently departed senior engineer at Google scolded Mr. Damore for having "caused significant harm to people across this company," adding that "not all conversations about ideas even have basic *legitimacy*."[38] Mr. Damore was subsequently fired, the same fate that befell Laurence Summers, former president of Harvard University, who speculated that the lack of female faculty in the math department may be due to unequal distribution of high-level mathematical abilities. Persons whose intellectual appetites closely align with those of many Harvard faculty members may believe that Mr. Damore's and Mr. Summer's speculations were harmful and a form of vain inquisitiveness, unworthy of serious intellectual inquiry. They are forbidden because they upset the reigning social and academic standards. (Of course, by the lights of Damore and his supporters,

37. MacDonald 2017.
38. Ibid.

the critics' unwillingness to consider Damore's hypothesis itself exhibits a deficient intellectual appetite—a kind of politically correct closed-mindedness.)

Defective appetite for forbidden knowledge is further fueled by modern technology that enables corporate spying, electronic eavesdropping, computer hacking, and other types of technological intrusion. There is a truth about how one could use these means to steal state secrets or embezzle money entrusted to one's care undetected. It would be malicious to seek it. Augustine and Aquinas realized that there is knowledge we have the power but not the permission to pursue, no matter how strong the desire to obtain it.

3.2 Harmful Knowledge

Aquinas makes an important distinction between knowledge itself and the desire for knowledge that helps to explain how our intellectual appetites, even appetites for the truth, can go wrong. "We must judge differently of the knowledge itself of truth, and of the desire and study in the pursuit of knowledge and truth. For knowledge of truth, strictly speaking is good, but it may be evil accidentally, by reason of some result."[39] To pursue pharmacological knowledge of a chemical's potential medicinal benefits is commendable. To do so on prisoners without their consent is to deprive them of their rights and to expose them to possible harms. Such treatment is rightly viewed as an instance of *curiositas*. While all truth is God's truth, as the saying goes, some truths, while good in themselves, may not be good *for us*, because they are likely to harm others and ourselves. (God, of course, faces no such difficulties, as all divine knowledge is united within a perfectly integrated, morally impeccable nature.)

39. Aquinas ST II–II.167.1.

Our appetites go wrong, says Aquinas, "when the knowledge of sensible things is directed to something harmful."[40] It is virtuous studiousness to attend to the sense experiential world for the sake of safety, survival, and intelligible truth, says Aquinas. It likewise may be virtuous to inquire into your neighbor's affairs if it redounds to your good or your neighbor's edification. Such inquiry is disordered when directed to things that are harmful, such as when looking lustfully at another, or inquiring into other people's affairs to detraction. Nosy, prying people may acquire information about friends and co-workers, but it will likely come at the expense of good relationships and is unlikely to be motivated by the other's edification. Even if the nosy are clever enough to snoop undetected, their appetite for knowledge is deformed, ungoverned by prudence, disrespectful of the persons snooped upon, and thus an example of *curiositas*.[41]

Of course knowledge of the sensible world around us can lead to harm far surpassing that of poking our nose into other people's affairs. The notorious Nazi and Tuskegee experiments yielded knowledge defective in mode of motivation, acquisition, and application. To one whose appetites are tempered by justice this knowledge came at appalling cost. After seeing the terrible use to which the atomic bomb was put, J. Robert Oppenheimer, the famous physicist in charge of the Manhattan Project, came personally to regret ever having been a part of the project. "In some crude sense which no vulgarity, no humor, no overstatement can quite extinguish," said Oppenheimer, "the physicists have known sin; and this is a knowledge they cannot

---

40. Aquinas *ST* II–II.167.2.
41. Augustine and Aquinas use the term *curiositas* to refer to all instances of malformed intellectual appetite. For instance, neither uses separate terms to refer to malformed appetite leading to harm and appetites for knowledge that is beneath us. Contemporary virtue epistemologists, by contrast, differentiate many intellectual vices.

lose."[42] Eve couldn't have said it better. It doesn't follow, however, that because some quest for knowledge is well motivated by the desire to help rather than hurt that it lacks moral boundaries. Current medical research in gene editing and cloning techniques are controversial cases in which the inquiry itself requires moral scrutiny. The temperate person, attentive to reason's appropriate cautions, will not allow the desire for research results to run ahead of what is good for those affected by it. The Nazi and Tuskegee experiments were defective on multiple grounds: in their means (they obviously lacked informed consent), in the harm done to those experimented on, and in the deceptions perpetrated on the subjects of the experiment by the scientists.

Contemporary psychology and neuroscience reinforce Aquinas's claim that some knowledge may be good in and of itself, but not good *for us*. As with bodily appetites, some intellectual appetites disrupt the "inner tranquility of the soul" that is a condition of tempered appetites. Habitués of Facebook and other social media sites, for instance, experience well-documented, above-average incidence of envy, depression, and loneliness, as well as cognitive impairments such as weakened powers of discrimination, memory, and attentiveness. The call for temperance against the adverse effects of extensive use of social media has been widely sounded.[43]

C. S. Lewis's comments about writing the *Screwtape Letters* reveal his own admirable temperance characteristic of *studiositas*. Lewis comments autobiographically about the strain he experienced from duplicating in imagination the diabolical attitude the text expresses.

> Though I had never written anything more easily, I never wrote with less enjoyment. . . .Though it was easy to twist one's mind

42. Oppenheimer 1947.
43. Typical of such warnings are O'Keeffe and Clarke-Pearson 2011, and the Council on Communications and Media.

into the diabolical attitude, it was not fun, or not for long. The strain produced a sort of spiritual cramp. The world into which I had to project myself while I spoke through Screwtape was all dust, grit, thirst and itch. Every trace of beauty, freshness and geniality had to be excluded. It almost smothered me before I was done.[44]

For this reason, and despite numerous requests, Lewis refused to write another volume to his highly popular *Screwtape* book. His comment shows him to be no stranger to the intellectual caution characteristic of *studiositas*. He was sufficiently aware of himself to see early on the psychic toll the book exacted, but he persisted so that his readers might benefit from his work. Yet he also knew that he should not do so again. It is interesting to note that what is harmful here is not propositional knowledge. The propositional knowledge is, in fact, very helpful! Rather, it's the process, the effect on the inquirer, and the acquaintance with darkness that posed a harm to Lewis.

Lewis's restraint regarding the sequel to *Screwtape* suggests that the appropriate mean with respect to our appetite for knowledge, like our appetite for the pleasures of touch, is person-relative. Other Christian authors (including Lewis's fellow Inkling, Charles Williams) delved deeply into occult literature with no obvious ill effects. Lewis was sufficiently self-aware to know he should not. There are truths to be gained in the dark places of human depravity, and society may benefit from some persons—the police, psychotherapists, and priests, for example—having intellectual appetites that can stomach such fare. Such knowledge, however, is not only irrelevant to the particular vocations and callings of most persons but also is potentially harmful.

44. Lewis 1986: 9.

As these examples attest, untempered appetite for knowledge can bring about harms to ourselves and to others, harms ranging in severity from mild to catastrophic. Knowledge motivated by *curiositas* alienates us from God, our neighbor's good, and from our true selves—the selves God created us to be.

3.3 *Knowledge That Is Beneath Us*

Augustine and Aquinas agree that not all knowledge is of equal value. Given their religious perspective, a person's appetites for knowledge can be aimed too low or too high given one's personal obligations to God, vocation, social roles and responsibilities, and abilities. Clearly, one's hierarchy of knowledge most and least worth seeking will reflect background beliefs and concerns, connected to one's beliefs about human nature and the conditions for human flourishing. Even so, it is difficult to imagine any hierarchy deeming it a matter of first importance to know how many grains of sand are in a cubic meter of the Sahara, or that such a trivial truth should outrank in importance knowledge of medicine or engineering. *Curiositas* thus comes in degrees, depending on the importance of the knowledge we are distracted from, and what does the distracting. It is worse to be distracted from knowledge necessary to do one's job than from efforts to memorize sports trivia, and worse still to have our attention diverted by pornographic violence than, say, by tabloid "news."

Knowledge can be beneath us (in the person-relative sense noted in the previous paragraph) in at least two respects: when it stems from intellectual appetite that fails to call forth our best intellectual efforts, and worse, when the knowledge, especially in the form of experiential acquaintance, makes us base or unbecoming as persons. Sometimes we err by satisfying our appetite for knowledge with "intellectual junk food," with trivia that detract from matters more worthy of our attention. To be sure, we need rest from the rigors of our intellectual labors, academic and otherwise. Aquinas admits that the mind grows weary with much study, for which he prescribes some pleasure as a remedy. As a bow put to nonstop use will break, so, says Aquinas, a "man's mind would break if the tension were never relaxed."[45] We may discover on reflection, though, that we stray too often from the intellectual work our vocations require of us toward a variety of distractions. Augustine himself laments that his intellectual appetites and attention were too easily satisfied by games in the circus or the sight of dogs chasing hares, as they allowed frivolous thoughts to "distract me perhaps indeed from thinking out some weighty matter."[46] To yield to the entertainments of the circus risks undermining good habits of attentiveness. It also, says Augustine, runs the risk of our missing out on knowledge we deem to be of "deepest importance."[47]

Aquinas agrees with Augustine, noting how someone's appetites for knowledge can be "withdrawn by a less profitable study from a study that is an obligation incumbent upon him."[48] Aquinas quotes Jerome, who laments "priests forsaking the gospel and the prophets, reading stage-plays and singing the love songs of pastoral idylls"[49] Aquinas isn't criticizing the arts so much as underscoring that for each of us, given our particular vocations and the responsibilities that accompany them, some knowledge trumps other knowledge in its level of importance. Maybe he would have been equally critical of a professional actor who neglected to learn his lines for opening night because he spent too much time reading Bible stories of Israelite battles won and lost. The intellectually temperate person's appetites are moderated by right reason in full consideration of the responsibilities we bear.

45. Aquinas *ST* II–II.168.2.
46. Augustine 2008: 212.
47. Ibid.
48. Aquinas *ST* II–II.167.1.
49. Ibid.

Augustine thinks that humans are susceptible to a powerful and sometimes perverse "itch to experience and find out." He poses the case of people like Leontius,[50] who go out of their way to see a mangled corpse along the roadside, knowing in advance that such disturbing experiential acquaintance will upset their sleep.[51] In our own day consider the sort of rubbernecking that prompts motorists to slow down to look at an automobile accident, or the impulse to watch gory horror movies that plant gruesome images in our minds we later regret having seen. If asked, "why did you seek an experience you knew would haunt you later?" Augustine thinks your answer might be, "I just wanted to see what it was like. It was an intellectual itch I had to scratch." This lack of restraint against what is base and beneath us betrays the lack of temperance characteristic of *curiositas*. Appreciation of this human itch is the sort of thing the self-controlled person will be cautious to guard against.

Augustine's Neoplatonism inclined him strongly toward knowledge that is eternal and immutable, most importantly, to knowledge of God. Add to this his concern to escape the materialist errors of the Manicheans, and we see the seeds of Augustine's suspicion of empirical inquiry. Augustine's account of *curiositas* stresses "the lust of the eyes" for sensory input: "a worship of phantasms," a "vain inquisitiveness dignified with the title of knowledge and science."[52] He sees *curiositas* as leading us away from contemplation of higher goods, to goods of lesser worth. Aquinas, steeped in Aristotle, showed a greater appreciation of the fledgling empirical sciences of his day, as they treated the subjects of biology, zoology, and optics. While Aquinas validates such knowledge as good, he too claims it is inferior to knowledge of God. To the extent that the world's showy spectacle

50. Plato 1959: XIII.4.439e.
51. Augustine 2008: 211.
52. Augustine 1953b: xxxvii.69, 2008: 211.

distracts us from setting our minds on "the sovereign truth about God, wherein supreme happiness consists," we succumb to *curiositas*.[53] In his estimation, it's a bad bargain to acquire encyclopedic knowledge of the world while remaining ignorant of God.

Intellectually tempered appetites are tuned to prefer and pursue knowledge that is well-grounded, relevant, epistemically significant, and worthy. Well-grounded knowledge is supported by good reasons that show the target belief likely to be true. But even if everyone should desire well-grounded knowledge, it doesn't follow that each person's intellectual appetite should be directed to the same things. Often, the truths we are most in need of pursuing are those most relevant to our immediate needs and current circumstances. If my wife is in the advanced stages of labor, what I need to know most is where I left my car keys and what the fastest route to the hospital is. What beliefs are relevant for a person to desire and pursue will be a person-relative affair, as the circumstances of a particular person are so variable as to make it unlikely they are shared by others in every respect. We also want beliefs that are significant—beliefs that bear a central epistemic load by supporting and being supported by other beliefs in an integrated, comprehensive web of beliefs. The truth about grains of sand in the Sahara is an isolated and trivial fact, apropos of nothing beyond itself. To seek less when one is capable of seeking what is preferable from an epistemic point of view, is to seek knowledge that is beneath our ability. (See section 3.4 on pusillanimity.)

A fourth criterion of intellectual desirability, worthiness, does have more interpersonal bearing as it directs us to seek knowledge that is intrinsically important or that bears on human eudaimonia. It is hard to imagine lives that are not better for knowing how to preserve health, nurture friendships, raise happy, well-adjusted children, participate in meaningful work, and so on. But it is also unlikely

53. Aquinas *ST* II–II.167.1 ad. 1.

that anyone has a comprehensive grasp of all knowledge worth loving. For this reason, intellectual temperance doesn't require strict, regimented adherence to these criteria but makes room for a bit of experimentation and epistemic playfulness. Most likely, the path to temperance grounded in practical wisdom is strewn with missteps and occasional failure.

3.4 Pusillanimity

Curiositas is the vice of disordered intellectual appetites, prompting the viciously curious to apply their intellectual powers either to knowledge of the world from corrupt motives, to inappropriate objects, by malicious means, or to wrongful ends. But what about a lack of that inquisitiveness we find admirable and stage appropriate in school children, in scholars, and in senior citizens who remain intellectually alive and interested in the world around them? While intellectual intemperance is most frequently expressed as an inordinate (excessive) appetite for knowledge, there is also a vice of deficiency associated with having an anemic intellectual appetite.

Thomas classifies *studiositas* as a species of temperance, the virtuous state made possible by exercising the power to rein in and appropriately direct our intellectual appetites. Consequently, Aquinas doesn't address under the heading of temperance a puny appetite for knowledge and other intellectual goods. Aquinas realizes that some persons have an anemic appetite or even an aversion to some kinds of knowledge and other intellectual goods. This might be thought of as the intellectual counterpart to sloth, the lack of zeal, the utter lassitude we display toward spiritual concerns. To this deficiency of appetite for intellectual and other goods Aquinas gives the name "pusillanimity."[54]

---

54. Aquinas *ST* II–II.133.

He writes:

> Whatever is contrary to a natural inclination is a sin, because
> it is contrary to a law of nature. Now everything has a natural
> inclination to accomplish an action that is commensurate with
> its power. Pusillanimity makes a man fall short of what is pro-
> portionate to his power, by refusing to tend to that which is com-
> mensurate thereto.[55]

The evidentialist W. K. Clifford melodramatically declared that
we risk "sin," "a stain that can never be wiped away," if we ever allow
ourselves to believe anything on insufficient evidence.[56] The ship
owner in Clifford's famous essay yielded to the temptation to comfort himself with the belief that his ship was seaworthy and did so in
"defiance of his duties to mankind."[57] The ship owner has an underdeveloped concern for well-grounded beliefs resulting from too high
a regard for profit.

A higher regard for the truth and greater resources of intellectual
temperance might have allowed the ship owner to resist believing
what was comfortable rather than what was true.

3.5 Knowledge That Is Too High for Us

What about *curiositas* directed to matters that are too high for us?
Augustine thinks our intellectual appetites are misdirected when we
desire to study "the operations of nature which lie beyond our grasp,
when there is no advantage in knowing and the investigators simply
desire knowledge for its own sake."[58] Aquinas warns against studying

55. Aquinas *ST* II–II.133.1.
56. Clifford 2017: 124.
57. Ibid., 125.
58. Augustine 2008: 211.

"to know the truth above the capacity of [our] own intelligence, since by doing so men easily fall into error."[59] He cites the book of *Sirach* in support: "Seek not what is too difficult for you nor investigate what is beyond your power. Reflect upon what has been assigned to you, for you do not need what is hidden. Do not meddle in what is beyond your tasks."[60] Here the warning is less about incurring harms and more about presumption and spinning one's intellectual wheels in vain.

Viewed from our contemporary liberal democratic point of view, Augustine and Aquinas might come off as retrograde, as opposing the liberal arts ideal of knowledge for knowledge's sake, available to as many as have ability and opportunity to pursue it. A charitable reading of Aquinas's text is nevertheless possible. Aquinas is especially concerned to check any conceit concerning reason's access to knowledge of God and the malformed intellectual appetite it embodies. Natural theology knows no greater advocate than Thomas Aquinas, yet he acknowledges that most persons lack the time, training, and talent for such work, and even those who are suitably equipped are liable to error. The author of the five ways also wrote, "If the only way open to us for knowledge of God were solely that of reason, the human race would remain in the blackest shadows of ignorance."[61] Even if natural theology succeeds in showing that God exists, Aquinas denied that it discloses God's essence, or that by it we can comprehend God. As regards knowledge of God's essence we are, as he is fond of saying, "owls in the daytime," utterly blinded by light too intense to take in, making any efforts to do so vain.[62] An intellectual appetite oriented to such a task aims too high. Aquinas thus counsels a measure of modesty regarding the reach of our creaturely intellects. In so doing he joins an illustrious history of philosophers

59. Aquinas *ST* II–II.167.1.
60. *Sirach* 3:21–23, Revised Standard Version.
61. Aquinas 1975: I.4.4.
62. Aquinas *ST* I–II.102.6.

who likewise warn against the appetite for knowledge beyond what they took to be our human limitations: Hume (metaphysics), Kant (noumenal knowledge), Pascal and Kierkegaard (proofs for God's existence), Nietzsche (objective truth), Wittgenstein (Cartesian certainty), and Plantinga (Gettier-proof definitions of knowledge). Put in this light, Aquinas finds himself in good company.[63]

Aquinas points to knowledge that is too high for humans in general. The passage from Sirach, however, also warns against seeking knowledge that exceeds one's personal competence. Edward Casaubon, from George Eliot's *Middlemarch*, is a scholar stuck in the quest for the "key to all mythologies," an Ur source from which all mythologies allegedly derive.[64] Casaubon spends thirty years fruitlessly compiling notes from which no foundation or unifying themes emerge. Eliot's portrayal makes clear that Casaubon derives a certain amount of pleasure from his task. He is also motivated by vanity as he anticipates the esteem his work will receive from the broader scholarly community should it ever come to completion. But it is clear to his wife and acquaintances that he lacks the intelligence for such an academic undertaking, even if there is a key to all mythologies. His powers of imagination, intellectual synthesis, and hermeneutic insight are insufficient for the task he has set for himself, despite the pleasure he derives from the project. Casaubon manifests multiple character flaws, vanity and irrational persistence among them. Had he not derived a level of pleasure from his academic endeavors, it's reasonable to think he would have abandoned his project. Intellectual temperance, modesty, and a greater concern for knowledge that is significant and relevant would have provided Casaubon the needed check against knowledge that was for him, at any rate, too high.

63. Whether or not an intellectual inquiry is vain may not be self-evident but may come to light only after repeated unsuccessful efforts resulting in general consensus. For an argument that certain historical truths are beyond the ken of historians, see Martin Jay's essay in chapter 9 of this volume.

64. This example appears in Roberts and Wood 2007: 199–201.

Our appetites for knowledge, as we have seen, can be defective by reason of being harmful, trivial, or vain. One might ask: are there distinctively epistemic reasons, as opposed to practical reasons, for fostering intellectual temperance? Consider a graduate student aspiring to a PhD in philosophy, about to begin work on her dissertation. She is sufficiently self-aware to know that she is highly attracted to (and susceptible to deferring to) the ideas of various philosophical luminaries, one of whom has just published a book in the area in which she wishes to work. She recognizes that she needs to foster within herself the virtue of intellectual autonomy, in order to cultivate her own "philosophical voice," so to speak. So she sets the book aside, deferring exposure to its ideas and arguments until her own thinking has reached a more mature and settled state. She avoids acquiring knowledge—at least for a time—for the sake of an epistemic end: the virtue of intellectual autonomy.

Another distinctively epistemic reason to foster *studiositas* comes from Alvin Plantinga, who notes how acquiring knowledge can sometimes actually result in a net loss of knowledge. Consider a philosophical novice venturing into the subject of religious pluralism. Our budding philosopher learns of practitioners of other religions who testify to experiences of the divine incompatible with his own. The beginning student lacks any arguments that shows his own views to be superior to those held by practitioners of another religion. Plantinga concedes that the problem of pluralism may reduce the student's level of confidence to such a degree that one loses the degree of warrant one has in one's own religious convictions. If the degree of confidence were to fall low enough, it could deprive him of warrant, and thus knowledge. "In this way he may come to know less by knowing more."[65] This possibility counsels a measure of caution

65. Plantinga 2015: 113.

in our pedagogy, that we exercise care when exposing students to attacks of their views they can understand, but not process.[66]

Practical wisdom counsels that our truth seeking will be most productive and profitable if done in full recognition of our intellectual gifts and limitations. If one has done dismally in elementary math, the pursuit of a PhD in math's upper reaches will likely prove a vain endeavor. Equally vain is the quest for knowledge one's philosophical views commit one to saying doesn't exist. Of course, these philosophical views are highly contentious and vary in what domains of knowledge they rule out as beyond our ken. These limitations aside, there remains much knowledge worth seeking that is worthy, significant, and relevant that satisfies the conditions of *studiositas*.

4. CONCLUSION

Intellectually virtuous persons are alive to the ways our pursuit of knowledge is subject to moral appraisal. Virtuous truth seekers have a finely tuned appetite for the right kinds of knowledge, shunning knowledge that is forbidden, trivial, base, vain, or harmful, among other ways our appetite for knowledge can be defective. They strive to shape their appetites to right reason and the structure of their deeply held concerns. This chapter is an attempt to articulate the shape of the virtuous intellectual appetite. I have focused on the contributions of Augustine and Aquinas, both for their role in articulating a distinctively Christian account of temperance and for their rigorous application of temperance to the intellectual life. Each offers an account of *studiositas*, of knowledge rightly sought, and of *curiositas*, its vicious

---

66. Richard Rorty casts all cautions aside in his treatment of his "fundamentalist" students, as he admits to trying to "strip [the] fundamentalist religious community of dignity, trying to make your views seem silly rather than discussable." See Rorty 2000: 21.

counterpart. Each acknowledges the role that the structure of our affections has in shaping our intellectual appetite.[67]

BIBLIOGRAPHY

Aquinas, Thomas. *Disputed Questions on Truth*. Translated by Robert W. Mulligan. Chicago: Henry Regnery Company, 1952.

Aquinas, Thomas. *Summa Contra Gentiles*. Translated by Anton Pegis. South Bend: University of Notre Dame Press, 1975.

Aquinas, Thomas. *Summa Theologiae*. Translated by Fathers of the Dominican Province. Westminster, MD: Christian Classics, 1981.

Aquinas, Thomas. *Disputed Questions on Virtue*. Translated by Ralph McInerny. South Bend: St. Augustine's Press, 1999.

Aristotle. *Metaphysics*. In *The Basic Works of Aristotle*, translated by W. D. Ross, edited by Richard McKeon, 689–926. New York: Random House, 1948.

Aristotle. *The Nichomachean Ethics*, 2nd ed. Translated by Terence Irwin. Indiana: Hackett Publishing Company, 1999.

Augustine. *The Morals of the Catholic Church*. In *The Basic Writings of Saint Augustine*, Vol. 1, edited by Whitney J. Oates, 329–357. Grand Rapids: Baker Book House, 1948.

Augustine. *On Free Will*. In *Augustine: Earlier Writings*, edited by J. H. S. Burleigh, 102–217. Philadelphia: Westminster Press, 1953a.

Augustine. *On True Religion*. In *Augustine: Earlier Writings*, edited by J. H. S. Burleigh, 225–283. Philadelphia: Westminster Press, 1953b.

Augustine. *City of God*. Translated by Henry Bettenson. London: Penguin Books, 2003.

Augustine. *Confessions*. Translated by Henry Chadwick. Oxford: Oxford University Press, 2008.

Clifford, W. K. "The Ethics of Belief." In *Readings in the Philosophy of Religion*, 3rd ed., edited by Kelly James Clark, 123–126. Peterborough, ON: Broadview Press, 2017.

Comte-Sponville, Andre. *A Small Treatise on Great Virtues: The Uses of Philosophy in Everyday Life*. New York: Metropolitan Books, 2002.

Council on Communications and Media. https://services.aap.org/en/community/aap-councils/council-on-communications-and-media/

Fricker, Miranda. *Epistemic Injustice*. Oxford: Oxford University Press, 2007.

---

67. I am deeply grateful to the excellent advice I received from Christian Miller, Ryan West, and Robert Roberts on multiple drafts of this paper.

Griffiths, Paul. *Intellectual Appetite.* Washington DC: Catholic University Press, 2009.

Harrison, Peter. "Curiosity, Forbidden Knowledge, and the Reformation of Natural Philosophy in Early Modern England." *Isis: A Journal of the History of Science Society* 92:2 (2001): 265–290.

Kent, Bonnie. "Augustine's Ethics." In *The Cambridge Companion to Augustine,* edited by Eleonore Stump and Norman Kretzmann, 205–233. Cambridge, UK: Cambridge University Press, 2001.

Kent, Bonnie. "Losable Virtue: Aquinas on Character and Will." In *Aquinas and the Nichomachean Ethics,* edited by Tobias Hoffman, Jorn Muller, and Mathias Perkams, 91–109. Cambridge, UK: Cambridge University Press, 2013.

Lewis, C. S. *Screwtape Proposes a Toast And Other Pieces.* Glasgow: William Collins Sons, 1986.

MacDonald, Heather. "Don't Even Think About Being Evil." *Wall Street Journal,* August 15, 2017. https://www.wsj.com/articles/dont-even-think-about-being-evil-1502750235.

O'Keeffe, Gwen Schurgin, and Kathleen Clarke-Pearson. "The Impact of Social Media on Children, Adolescents, and Families." *Pediatrics* 127:4 (2011): 800–804.

Openheimer, J. Robert. "Physics in the Contemporary World." Lecture delivered at Massachusetts Institute of Technology, November 25, 1947.

Plantinga, Alvin. *Knowledge and Christian Belief.* Grand Rapids: Eerdmans, 2015.

Plato. *The Republic.* In *Plato: The Collected Dialogues.* Translated by Francis MacDonald Cornford, 845–919. Princeton: Princeton University Press, 1959.

Reichberg, Gregory M. "The Intellectual Virtues." In *The Ethics of Aquinas,* edited by Stephen J. Pope, 131–150. Washington DC: Georgetown University Press, 2002.

Roberts, Robert C. "Temperance." In *Virtues and Their Vices,* edited by Kevin Timpe and Craig A. Boyd, 93–111. Oxford: Oxford University Press, 2014.

Roberts, Robert C., and W. Jay Wood. *Intellectual Virtues: An Essay in Regulative Epistemology.* Oxford: Oxford University Press, 2007.

Rorty, Richard. "Universality and Truth." In *Rorty and his Critics,* edited by Robert B. Brandom, 1–30. Oxford: Basil Blackwell, 2000.

Wood, W. Jay. "Prudence." In *Virtue and Their Vices,* edited by Kevin Timpe and Craig A. Boyd, 37–58. Oxford: Oxford University Press, 2014.

Zagzebski, Linda. *Virtues of the Mind.* Cambridge, UK: Cambridge University Press, 1996.

Chapter 9

Historical Truth and
the Truthfulness of Historians

MARTIN JAY

The question of history's relationship to truth, always a challenge to answer, seems especially fraught in this era of "fake news,"
"alternative facts," and the erosion of established media gatekeep-
ers. Traditionally, it has been addressed either ontologically—
the possibility of eternal verities appearing amidst the flux of
historical change—or epistemologically—the veracity of our
accounts of the past. Whereas some philosophers and theologians
still ponder the former, few working historians have been concerned with the alleged relationship between ontological truth,
however it might be construed, and historical occurrence.[1] They
have remained content instead with understanding their subject matter, to cite the subtitle of Siegfried Kracauer's insightful
ruminations on history, as merely "the last things before the last,"[2]

---

1. See Roberts 1995a. It should be noted that professional philosophers in the recent past, especially in the Anglo-American tradition, have also been loath to spin out speculative philosophies of history. See Klein 2011.
2. Kracauer 1969.

Martin Jay, *Historical Truth and the Truthfulness of Historians* In: *Integrity, Honesty, and Truth Seeking.* Edited
by: Christian B. Miller and Ryan West. Oxford University Press (2020). © Oxford University Press.
DOI: 10.1093/oso/9780190920487.003.0009

at least one step removed from anything pretending to be absolute in metaphysical terms.[3]

Ever since what has been called the "scientific revolution" in the practice of writing about the past, a slow and uneven process of professionalization that made of history a proper scholarly "discipline," working historians have focused on truth as an effect of valid cognition, plausible inference, logical reasoning, or warranted assertion, rather than speculative metaphysics.[4] History, they insist, cannot depend on authority or memory, but must instead be a critical, always open-ended process of discovery. Using the methodological tools developed by archaeologists, paleographers, diplomatists, archivists, and statisticians, practicing historians have sought to separate historical knowledge from myths, legends, and fables by refining their techniques of retrieval and subjecting the results to various tests of plausibility and authenticity.[5] Anachronisms—the term itself was invented in the seventeenth century[6] —were challenged, and residues of material culture, such as inscriptions, coins, or architectural ruins, were examined to supplement the written word. What are sometimes called the "disciplines of erudition,"[7] devoted to the rigorous examination of the formal properties of texts or images beyond the content

---

3. A characteristic expression of this reluctance can be found in Quentin Skinner's declaration: "I am not in general talking about truth; I am talking about what people at different times may have had good reasons by their light for holding true, regardless of whether we ourselves believe that what they held true was in fact the truth .... I am convinced, in short, that the importance of truth for the kind of historical enquiries I am considering has been exaggerated." Skinner 1988: 256.

4. For accounts of the emergence of "scientific" history, see Appleby, Hunt, and Jacob 1994: Part One, and Howell and Prevenir 2001.

5. For a discussion of these different sub-disciplines, see Howell and Prevenier 2001: chapter 2. Rather, however, than dismissing myth, legend, and fables as merely fallacious, many historians, perhaps beginning with Giambattista Vico, began to read them as symptomatic of cultural mentalities—that is, as hermeneutically legible evidence of past beliefs.

6. Burke 1994: 172.

7. Chartier 1997: 6.

they convey, enrich the repertoire of forensic instruments in the toolbox of professional scholars of the past.[8]

History's "scientific revolution" has, however, been dogged by increased concern about the truth claims—often expressed in terms of "objectivity"—it has generated.[9] What allows us to claim our knowledge about the past is both plausible and reliable? How do we ascertain the convincing evidence on which to justify our accounts? By what criteria do we deem some documents more accurate, some artifacts more authentic, and some accounts more persuasive than others, and who has the authority to judge? Can accounts of the past be verified, or only falsified, and what counts as conclusive for either outcome? How do we build compelling narrative reconstructions from the evidence deemed reliable and authentic?

All of these questions assume an inherent distinction between the two dominant meanings, at least in English, of the word "history": first, as the events, occurrences, or actions that happened in the past (*res gestae* or "things done"), and second, as the representation, narrative, or account of those happenings (*historia rerum gestarum* or "the story of things done") in the present. "History" thus signifies, for epistemologists of historical knowledge, both an object of inquiry and a subjective discourse or narrative about that object. As such, it raises issues similar to those raised by other self-described scientific methods based on the binary distinction between subjects and objects. But it differs from them in the inevitable absence,

---

8. A salient example, recently revived by Carlo Ginzburg, is the method of the nineteenth-century Italian art historian Giovanni Morelli to identify involuntary, symptomatic clues, such as the way ears were typically rendered, to settle questions of attribution for paintings. Ginzburg 1989.

9. The unevenness of the relationship between professionalization and the struggle for objectivity in historical accounts, at least in the American context, is made clear in Novick 1988. Doubts about the truth claims of historical narratives are, of course, almost as old as the practice of writing them. Peter Burke notes that Lucian already parodied Herodotus and Thucydides in the second century CE. See Burke 1994: 169.

indeed irretrievable loss, of the past object it seeks to "re-present" in the present.[10]

1. TWO EXTREME ALTERNATIVES

1.1 *The Positivist or Hyperrealist Fallacy*

At each end of the spectrum of possible answers to the epistemological questions raised by the distinction between the dual meanings of "history" are two extreme positions that are equally untenable. The first, which can be called "naïve positivism" or "hyperrealism", claims that history, understood as a narrative or a discourse, can accurately and adequately represent history, understood as significant past occurrences, events, and actions. It is often emblematized, with little regard for the complexities of his actual practice, by the great nineteenth-century German historian Leopold von Ranke's imperative to write history *"wie es eigentlich gewesen"* ("as it actually happened").[11] Here the historian's craft, based on what Ranke called his "pure love of truth,"[12] is understood essentially as a "science"— or at least *"Wissenschaft"* in the German sense of a rigorous scholarly discipline—which can skillfully sift through reliable evidence to present an accurate, unbiased, and complete representation of the past, or at least of those aspects of it deemed significant. Aping the visual model of cognitive distance favored by modern science and

10. This difference has long been noted, for example, by R. G. Collingwood, who claimed it defeated positivist attempts to write accurately about the past as if it were an object analyzable from the outside. For an attempt to answer him, see William Dray 1995): 269–270. There is, however, a parallel between history and one scientific subject: stellar astronomy, whose objects of inquiry are long past. For a discussion, see Jay 2003.

11. For a history of the adoption of that phrase in American historiography, see Iggers 1962.

12. Ranke 1973: 39.

drawing on the metaphor of a non-distorting mirror,[13] it privileges an ideal observer identified with "posterity," which extends beyond any concrete subject situated at a particular vantage point at a particular moment in time. It elevates disinterested observing over evaluative judging, which it rhetorically signals by the adoption of an impersonal and omniscient narrative voice, in which the historian's deictic particulars—his or her temporal and spatial locations—are suppressed. Honoring the alleged authority of "primary sources" often gathered as "documents" in institutional "archives," it understands historical research as an essentially empirical enterprise based on uncovering "facts" or describing "events" unfiltered through a theoretical or ideological lens.[14] Historical truth for those who hold this position is essentially the same as it is for those who believe with Thomas Aquinas that *"veritas est adaequatio intellectus et rei,"* truth is a correspondence between the object of inquiry and a mental representation of or linguistic statement about it.[15]

Correspondence theories of truth may be defended in sophisticated ways by contemporary philosophers like Rasmussen.[16] But they rarely inform serious discussions of historical epistemology. Although the advances made since the historical "scientific revolution" in evaluating the reliability of sources are widely appreciated, little, if any, confidence remains in the ability of even the most rigorous methods to produce an objective and accurate representation of the past "as it actually was," even on the level of seemingly granular

---

13. The primacy of the visual model has been detected as far back as the Greek historian Herodotus, who dismissed the value of hearsay. See Hartog 1992. The undistorted mirror can be found in Lucian and was still in use in the seventeenth century. See Koselleck 1985: 133.

14. All of these key terms warrant scare quotes because each has been shown to be the result of a process of historical definition and clarification. See, for example, in the case of "facts," Poovey 1998 and Shapiro 2003, and for "event," Jay 2011, 2014.

15. See Roberts and West, chapter 4 in this volume.

16. See Rasmussen 2014.

events. The majority of historians and philosophers of history alike have awakened from the "noble dream" of objectivity, the motto ironically adopted by Peter Novick to characterize the American historical profession's quest for disinterested and accurate representations of the past.[17]

There are many reasons the quest was abandoned, but I want to foreground only three. The first is the radical asymmetry between history as the totality of all that happened in "the past" and history as an inevitably finite and selective representation of "what happened." Even if totality as a goal is abandoned, the assumption that "significance" can replace it as a norm is problematic because of the inevitable quarrel over what is meaningful, both for those who lived through it and those who attempt to recount it. Although in many other respects unlike individual or collective memory, history as post-facto representation shares with them an inevitable and, I would argue, salutary dependence on the involuntary forgetting of the vast majority of past actions, events, experiences, and occurrences that might serve as grist for its mill.[18] Rather than full anamnestic recall, in which everything of possible significance in the past is available for later recapitulation, history as a representative discourse ironically depends on the limits of memory and the fickleness of preservation. For without the drastic selection and condensation of what is worthy of being recalled and recorded, as well as the limited, often chance survival of a small portion of possible remnants of the past, no finite

---

17. Novick 1988. The phrase was coined by Theodore Clark Smith and then mocked by Charles Beard in the 1930's. See also Natter, Schatzki, and Jones III 1995.

18. See Gross 2000, Ricoeur 2004, and Ankersmit 2005: 319–325, for discussions of the dialectic of forgetting and remembering. Not only is this limitation acknowledged by working historians, who depend on the scattered shards of a past that escaped time's ravages and choose only some of them to build their reconstructions, but it is also part of our everyday understanding of the distinction between normal quotidian existence, which falls into condign oblivion, and those highly unusual exceptions that are recognized as "memorable" or a fortiori "historical."

historical narrative could be fashioned. Although historians do, of course, often seek to reverse the malign effects that can also flow from undeserved oblivion, seeking to hear the voices of those previously silenced, they concede that the vast majority of past occurrences remain shrouded in the proverbial mists of time.

As a result of this radical asymmetry, no plausible notion of historical truth can aspire to what is demanded of witnesses in a court of law sworn to tell "the truth, the whole truth, and nothing but the truth."[19] For there can be no simple adequation between subjective knowledge—even understood as the cumulative knowledge contained in all the history books ever written—and an impossible object which is the entire "past as such."[20] Put differently, there can never be a satisfactorily replete, fully saturated "context" in which to situate "texts" or "documents," the latter understood in the broadest sense as evidentiary traces left by the past, because the boundary of such a context would ultimately have to encompass all of the past at any one moment as well as an infinite temporal regress with no access to an ultimate ur-cause (cosmogenic theories of the "Big Bang" notwithstanding). The historian's frames are always limiting devices, necessarily if sometimes arbitrarily employed to blunt the threat of infinite explanatory or narrative regression. What was once present and its post-facto re-presentation are thus inherently distinct in terms of scale and plenitude, making any simplistic notion of accuracy as a perfect isomorphic fit between the two nonsensical.

There is, moreover, no inductive transfer from micro-history, focusing on the atomic level of past occurrences that may seem less

---

19. In one of the few missteps in *That Noble Dream*, Novick claims that "in their academic writings scholars strive to present 'the whole truth and nothing but the truth' for a variety of reasons, not least among them fear of the embarrassment which followed being caught doing otherwise" (Novick 1988: 471).

20. As Frank Ankersmit has noted, representations of the past are never of objects per se, but only of finite aspects of them. Ankersmit 2010: 40.

open to contestation, to macro-history, seeking large-scale patterns. No cumulative aggregation of isolated facts, even assuming their reliability, can produce synthetic generalizations. There is a leap in kind, not merely in degree, from a chronicle or annal, which records events or actions that occur in a periodically ordered timeline, and a more ambitious history, which imbues them with meaning, seeks their causes and effects, and presents them in stories with beginnings, middles, and ends. The universe of historical narrative is inherently heterogeneous, with multiple levels that defy easy passage from one to another.[21] There is no smooth transition from a discrete event to, say, the precise dating of an historical period, which is only a matter of retrospective interpretation. Nor can there be, *pace* advocates of "world history," a coherent synthesis of local histories, however we define their boundaries, and the general narrative of universal history, the totalized story of the species as a whole.[22] However much we may try to fill in the gaps, search for uncovered records, or listen to hitherto unheard voices, the overwhelming majority of "what happened," history as *res gestae*, is lost forever. And thankfully so, as Tristram Shandy realized when he tried in vain to write his autobiography as fully and faithfully as possible in Lawrence Sterne's famous eighteenth-century novel.[23]

A second salient reason for the implausibility of naïve positivist historiography is, paradoxically, the opposite asymmetry. That is, rather than the vastness and infinite complexity of a past that exceeds our capacity to recall or record it, we who are doing the recording have a much richer sense of the later outcomes of events and actions than those who experienced them directly in their own lives. The

21. See Kracauer 1969: chapter 5.
22. For a discussion of the rise and fall of the ideal of universal history, see Koselleck 1985.
23. Bertrand Russell addressed the paradox as a mathematical problem and claimed that Shandy could have solved it if he had lived forever; but historians, alas, don't have that luxury. For one account of Russell's attempt, see Diamond 1964.

benefit of hindsight means that our histories are written not by recovering "what actually happened" *when* it was happening but inevitably draw on the additional knowledge of what happened next, a knowledge that was impossible at the time. Although historians are often implored to avoid presentism and block out the intervening history in assessing the past, it is impossible to suspend entirely our own situation and restore the innocence of outcomes enjoyed by those from that past. We know the unintended consequences unavailable to the actors themselves and can experience an ironic distance from intentions gone astray that they could not.[24] We can periodize the past in terms of epochs, whose outlines are never known by those whose lives fall within them (think, for example, of the absurdity of a twelfth-century serf aware that he was living in "the Middle Ages"). However much historians are exhorted to be sensitive to the multiple possibilities in a still unfolding story—"side-shadowing," in the current jargon, rather than "fore-shadowing" the future[25]—we cannot willfully bracket the knowledge of which possibilities were actualized and which were not, which became factual and which remained counter-factual.

A final reason the naïve positivist or hyperrealist position is unconvincing emerges from a consideration of the subject who composes the stories of *historia rerum gestarum*. The putative "object" construed by defenders of objectivity is the mirror image of the putative "subject" of knowledge, whose certainty is assured by assigning it a transcendental position "thrown under" (the etymological Latin origin of the word "subject") all acts of cognition.[26] But not only are no narrators really omniscient, they are also never perfectly neutral, objective, and disinterested, never entirely unaffected by what Freud

24. For a discussion, see Jay 2013.
25. For a defense of the importance of "side-shadowing," see Morson 1994 and Bernstein 1994.
26. See Weber 1995.

would have called their emotionally driven "transferential" invest-ments in the past.[27] "Posterity" is a fictional, disembedded, tacitly singular placeholder for an always contested, always dynamic field of different perspectives, which defy integration into a singular tran-scendental point of view.[28] Although they may not map neatly on to discrete "subject positions" in a social or cultural field, they are also never entirely above them, able to observe with the proverbial eye of a bird, such as Minerva's famous owl, let alone that of an omniscient God-like posterity able to render a last judgment.

To complicate matters still further, if we historicize the actual subjects who write historical narrations, taking into account the ways in which the endpoints of their narratives inexorably extend into an uncertain future, it is highly unlikely that any one representation, however definitive it may now seem, will survive the new evidence or interpretative tools that are still to be discovered. We are, in short, always in the middle of a story whose conclusion is yet to come, for as Zhou En-Lai allegedly said when asked his opinion of the impact of the French Revolution, "it is too early to tell."[29] Because of all these reasons, and others that might be adduced, there can never be a fully adequate correspondence between "history" in its two distinct meanings, as what happened and our representations of it.

27. See LaCapra 1985: chapter 3. He argues that "transference causes fear of possession by the past and loss of control over both it and oneself. It simultaneously brings the temptation to assert full control over the 'object' of study through ideologically suspect procedures that may be related to the phenomenon Freud discussed as 'narcissism'" (72).
28. It was understood as early as J. C. Chladenius in the eighteenth century that not only did historical actors often have different points of view or perspectives, but that historical nar-rators did as well. See Koselleck 1985: 137–140.
29. It turns out that this now famous remark from a conversation during Richard Nixon's trip to China in 1972 may have referred to the events of 1968 rather than the Revolution of 1789. See Nicolas 2011.

1.2 The Constructivist Fallacy

Because the naïve positivist and hyperrealist faith in objective, scientific history has been undermined by these and other qualms, some commentators have been led to deny any veridical relationship between the past and its subsequent representations. Recalling Cicero's claim that written history is an *"opus oratorium"*[30] (rhetorical work), "constructivists"—or "hyperrelativists," as their critics sometimes call them[31]—question the very distinction between fact and fiction. Having come to prominence in the heyday of "post-modernism," they apply the lessons of the "linguistic turn" in the humanities during the last third of the twentieth century.[32] Constructivists argue it is representations all the way down, for there is no access to the past unmediated through present interpretive reconstructions and implicit criteria of value.[33] If Ranke's *"wie es eigentlich gewesen"* became the emblem of the naïve realist position, the Italian Idealist philosopher Benedetto Croce's assertion that "all history is contemporary history" often plays a comparable role for radical constructivists, who tip the balance between "history" as what happened in the past and "history" as the representation of those happenings in the present entirely in the latter direction.[34] Even isolated "facts," they contend, should be understood as "events under description," which like truth claims in general, are linguistic through and through.[35]

---

30. Cited in Bowersock 1994: 12.
31. See, e.g., Pihlainen 2014, for the former, Novick 1988 for the latter. One stresses the cognitive, the other the moral implications of the debunking of an emphatic concept of historical truth.
32. See Vann 1995.
33. An extreme version of this argument, occasionally ventured by philosophers, would deny the ontological status of the past as such, arguing instead that all we have are remnants of previous "present" moments in our "present." For a consideration and refutation of this argument, see Dummett 2004.
34. As in the case of Ranke, Croce's own position was often simplified by those who cited this slogan. See Roberts 1995b, 2002.
35. For a recent discussion of this issue, see Stepantsov 2013.

If there is any "truth" in historical reconstructions, constructivists argued, it is thus more "made" than "matched," "discovered," or "found." Historical narratives are always dependent on what Roland Barthes called "reality effects," creating an illusion of objectivity based on various rhetorical devices working to conceal the subjective intervention of the author. "Historical discourse," so Barthes charged, "is a fake performative discourse in which the apparent constative (descriptive) is in fact only the signifier of the speech-act as an act of authority."[36] The narratives fashioned by historians, Hayden White added, always follow latent conventional patterns or "tropes," with tragedy, comedy, satire, romance, and irony as the most frequent exemplars. Beneath the temporal flow of the storytelling are always structural regularities that endure no matter how unique the recounted events may seem. Also drawing on such standard figural devices as metaphor, metonymy, and synecdoche, historical narratives can never mimetically correspond to their putatively real object, even when the latter is not understood as the infinite past, but as any finite fragment of it. All history (as *historia rerum gestarum*) is thus really what White calls "meta-history," dependent on linguistic conventions that shape every post facto narrative, intentionally or not.[37]

There are, constructivists also insist, radical incommensurabilities between time as it is experienced and time as it is narratively recounted, as we say, "after the fact." The time of the told is never the time of the telling. The former is lived essentially in the present tense, even while including what phenomenologists like Edmund Husserl called the retention of the past and protention of the future,[38] while the latter is written in the preterite (or as it is sometimes called, aorist) tense, which signifies a completed action, no longer open to an

36. See Barthes 1989: 139.
37. See White 1973, 1978, 1999.
38. For a discussion, see Carr 2014: chapter 7.

indefinite future. Whereas life moves forward in chronological order, narration is often far less linear, with regressions and anticipations shaping the story as it is told. Rather than emulating the inexorable march of time, historians often flash forward or backward, leaping ahead proleptically to foreshadow outcomes or circling back to recount origins. Every written reconstruction, moreover, also contains significant differences in the pace of storytelling, so that fifty pages can be spent on one day followed by only two on the next ten years.

In addition, what narratologists following Gerard Genette call "focalization" means that all stories are necessarily told from a specific perspective.[39] A narrative where all the information presented reflects the subjectivity of a particular character is "internally focalized." "External focalization," in contrast, is more like a camera eye, which sees the action from a discrete position outside the subjective views of any of the actors. The point of view assumed by an omniscient narrator is called "zero focalization." Whichever focalization is chosen, other points of view are necessarily excluded or at least marginalized; even attempts to include different voices—for example, Saul Friedlander's acclaimed history of the Holocaust, which allows us to hear from both victims and perpetrators[40]—necessarily selects some and excludes others. The result is thus additive, not synthetic. Nor does the use of free indirect style or "the middle voice" conflating the narrator's perspective with that of a character, as in many realist novels, produce a genuinely totalized account.[41] The putative point of view of "posterity" should therefore be understood only as an imaginary overcoming of the concrete particularization of focalized

39. See Genette 1980.
40. Friedlander 1998, 2008. It should be noted that as early as the "antilogies" or opposing speeches introduced in Thucydides, historians have ventriloquized different viewpoints in a similar way.
41. For a consideration of this argument, see White 1992.

narration, or more precisely, a displacement forward of zero focalization. The historian's active imagination—whose importance had already been stressed by philosophers like R. G. Collingwood even before the "linguistic turn"[42]—always plays a key role in any story told about the past. The implied meaning of the word "source" suggests it serves as a stimulus to a post facto representation, rather than as an inert trace of a past occurrence. Instead of an objective "science," history as a discourse may well be better understood as an "art."[43]

As in the case of the un-nuanced realist pole of the spectrum, however, the constructivist alternative has also been vigorously disputed. Its critics worry that, absent a strong referential imperative, the unfettered imagination can become a bit too active and sanction a dangerous attitude of "anything goes." A slippery slope, they fear, leads to the utter conflation of fictional narratives, peopled by invented characters engaging in invented acts, with the recorded deeds of their historical counterparts, who really existed and left traces of their actions that cannot be ignored. The most compelling test case, on which much of the debate has focused, has been the Holocaust, whose outrageous denial by latter-day anti-Semites shows the dangers of effacing that distinction.[44]

While conceding that all representational narratives depend to some extent on rhetorical techniques, the critics of constructivism distinguish between those that draw on the evidentiary fruits of "scientific" retrieval and those that are free to create *ex nihilo*. Disdaining the "linguistic transcendentalism" of anti-correspondence theorists

---

42. Collingwood 1994: 231–249.
43. For one consideration of this dichotomy, see Hughes 1964. It should be noted that for all of his stress on scientificity, Ranke 1973: 33 acknowledged that "history is distinguished from all other sciences in that it is also an art. History is a science in collecting, finding, penetrating; it is an art because it recreates and portrays that which it has found and recognized.... The difference is that ... philosophy and poetry move within the realm of the ideal while history has to rely on reality."
44. See Friedlander 1992.

who bracket the world outside of language as entirely unknowable, they claim that however much language may mediate our interaction with a world beyond our consciousness, it does not spin it entirely out of whole cloth. Infants, after all, interact with the world prior to the acquisition of language, and we never entirely lose our ability to respond directly to sensual stimuli (feeling pain, for example, without having to say "ouch"). Constructivists, they charge, have succumbed to a pan-fictionalist fantasy that forgets the critical distinction, made at least since Sir Philip Sidney's sixteenth-century "Defense of Poesy," between a narrator, such as an historian, who asserts truth-claims that can be validated, and a poet—or fiction writer in general—who "nothing affirms, and therefore never lieth."[45] Although realist fiction, *pace* Barthes, may draw heavily on "reality effects" in its use of thick descriptions and references to conventionally accepted "real historical events," it does so with an explicit acknowledgement that the language game it plays is not that of referential assertion.[46] In historical narratives, in contrast, the world, including residues of the world of the past, pushes back against our fantasies about it. Although "facts" are always linguistically mediated—"events under description"— they are also derived from the disclosure of the world to our experience, which can be what Husserl called "pre-predicative," prior to language.[47]

Critics of radical constructivism also revisit the familiar contrast between chronicle or annal and history, but now in order to stress the importance of the former. That is, without an uninflected, banal, routine recording of events when they occurred arranged on a mechanically articulated timeline, there can be no later imaginative

---

45. Sidney 1974: 152–153.
46. For a discussion of the emergence of fictionality in the modern novel, see Gallagher 1994. The intertwining of history and fiction is especially fraught in the case of self-consciously historical novels and counterfactual, alternate history novels.
47. Husserl 1975. For a discussion, see, Zuidervaart 2017: 117.

emplotment of the past as a meaningful story. There is, they also point out, an important parallel between historical knowledge of the distant past and that of our own personal pasts whose practical effects cannot be ignored in our present lives. As the philosopher of history David Carr has put it,

> Just as I cannot pretend to have added salt and expect the souf-flé to turn out well, so I cannot pretend to a talent or capacity I never had and then expect to put it to use. Many of our plans go awry (and stories have to be rewritten) because we make mistakes about the past, about what happened and what we have done. The past *does* constrain us; it does have a fixedness that allows reinterpretation only up to certain limits.[48]

If, moreover, there are levels in a heterogeneous historical universe and the historian cannot move in an upward direction by inductively generalizing from micro- to macro-history, it is also wrong to move effortlessly down the ladder and conclude that the active narrative imagination that "makes" the most synthetic level also guides the primary researcher's encounter with the evidentiary record. Some of the resistance of isolated "facts" to the imposition of more general narrative meaning is expressed rhetorically in what has been called the "laminated" character of historical prose itself when it includes direct citations from original sources in its narrative reconstructions, which are unmediated residues of the past that stubbornly check the historian's full imaginative sovereignty over the story he or she is telling.[49]

48. Carr 1986: 99; italics in original.
49. Chartier 1997: 17. He attributes the term "laminated" to Michel de Certeau. White, it might be noted, concedes that there is a difference between established "facts" and the narratives woven from them. See White 1992: 38.

It is this tension between levels and voices that allows the writing of history to become a "learning process" rather than a mere chaos of different narratives, randomly replacing one another with no advance in knowledge. While such learning is never perfectly linear and there are often regressions, the telos of the advancement of knowledge is hardwired into the modern historical enterprise. Although not as inexorably cumulative as normal science (Thomas Kuhn's paradigm shifts aside), the expansion and refinement of historical knowledge can benefit from the discovery of new evidence, greater temporal perspective, and the collective vetting of competing accounts.

2. THREE PLAUSIBLE ALTERNATIVES

As a result, rather than the two untenable extremes of radical positivism and radical constructivism, the most interesting epistemological questions involve the intertwining of residues of the past with its present reconstruction, which allow us, despite everything, to retain a heuristic model or regulative ideal of historical truth asymptotically approached over time. Three suggestive responses to those questions can be characterized as falsificationism, the new experientialism, and institutional justificationism. Each helps us navigate the treacherous waters between the Scylla of naïve realism and the Charybdis of radical constructivism, without, however, allowing us to reach the dry land of certitude at the end of the voyage.

2.1 Falsificationism

Wary of ever establishing a single, verifiable version of historical truth, but reluctant to efface the distinction between history and fiction, falsificationists have stressed the value of exposing and rejecting untrue accounts, dubious facts, inauthentic documents, and the like. As the French historian and philosopher Michel de Certeau put it,

> Western historiography struggles against fiction . . . . Not that it appeals to the truth; never has the historian pretended to do that! Rather, with his apparatus for the critical reading of documents, the scholar effaces errors from the "fables" of the past. The territory that he occupies is acquired through a diagnosis of the false.[50]

The procedures of falsification are most effective in combating deliberate fabrications, such as forged documents or doctored photographs, often introduced for ideological reasons, which are very different from honest errors or fictions that explicitly identify themselves as such. Like forensic investigators in criminal cases, falsificationists employ the methodological tools honed by the scientific revolution in historical research and the "disciplines of erudition" devoted to the authentication of sources, textual or otherwise.[51]

Deliberate fabrications or forgeries are, to be sure, relatively rare, and so the more pressing issue is how honorably fashioned accounts can also be falsified. In the philosophy of scientific reasoning, the criterion of falsifiability is most often identified with the attempts of Karl Popper, a critic of the positivist faith in inductive verification, to demarcate legitimate science from pseudo-science in terms of the former's ability to be falsified experimentally.[52] Even before being

---

50. De Certeau 1986: 200. For a discussion of the ambivalences in de Certeau's use of falsifiability, see Ahearne 1995: 35. See also Weymans 2004 for a discussion of the scientific historical impulse in his idiosyncratic method.

51. According to the historian Alan Spitzer, "although the 'whole concept of historical truth' has been called into question, almost everyone claims to know what a lie about the past looks like. In historical debate, lying falls at the near end of a spectrum ranging from willful to unwitting misrepresentation, from the falsification to the misinterpretation of evidence, from arguments in manifest bad faith to well-intentioned incoherence." Spitzer 1996: 1.

52. Popper 1959, 1963.

evaluated, claims to scientific authenticity must be formulated so that every conjecture made in the context of discovery is open to refutation in the context of justification. Every hypothesis in a theory must be refutable to warrant the honorific title of "science." To avoid the threat of both relativism and dogmatism—Popper's favorite examples of the latter were Marxism and psychoanalysis—it is necessary to formulate statements about the world that can be discredited by counterexamples (e.g., the generalization "all swans are white" by the discovery of a black swan). In such a way, the desired end of objective truth, which Popper never denied was the telos of science, could be more and more closely approximated, if never fully reached.

Although Popper's anti-verificationist model of scientific method helped undermine naïve positivism, his own demarcation criteria, based on the power of observation to contradict a false scientific claim, were subjected to widespread criticism by rival philosophers of science such as Imre Lakatos, Thomas Kuhn, and Paul Feyerabend. Whether his criteria were ever applicable to the discipline of history is even more problematic, as Popper himself targeted only what he called, in an idiosyncratic defiance of normal usage, "historicism."[53] By this he meant the assertion of dubious historical laws that would allow the prediction of the future. Despite a vain search for so-called covering laws in history by philosophers like Carl Hempel in the 1940s and 1950s,[54] actual historical accounts have rarely been vulnerable to Popper's falsification criteria. The singularity of narratives and the centrality of meaning in them—meaning being a category Popper, in a polemic with Wittgenstein, had banished from scientific epistemology[55]—makes it difficult to subsume them under even a non-verificationist scientific model. Moreover, if one takes seriously

53. Popper 1957.
54. Hempel 1942.
55. For an account, see Hacohen 2000: 207.

the discontinuity between the heterogeneous levels of the historical universe, an anomalous "fact" on a micro-historical level cannot easily refute a macro-historical generalization. There is nothing comparable to the *experimentum crucis* of natural science, at least as Popper understood it, that would definitively falsify a large-scale historical narrative or complicated causal explanation. Indeed, the explosive expansion of the historical archive makes it virtually impossible to avoid a certain arbitrariness in the selection of which pieces of factual evidence to apply to which narratives.

2.2 The New Experientialism

If Popperian falsificationism failed to provide conclusive answers to the challenge of truth in history, some commentators, equally unhappy with the radical constructivist alternative encouraged by the "linguistic turn," have been tempted to bypass epistemological and rhetorical questions entirely and return instead to what may appear to be a more ontological version of historical truth. This is the stratagem apparently adopted by a group of theorists—sometimes called the "new romanticists,"[56] although "new experientialists" is more accurate—who focus on the question of "historical experience," but redefined in an unexpected way.[57]

Rejecting the empathetic "re-experiencing" of the original experience of the actors of previous generations, promoted in the nineteenth century by Wilhelm Dilthey as the most fruitful way of revealing the meaning of the past, the "new experientalists" have turned to a more direct communion with the past in the present, which their leading

---

56. Grethlein 2010.

57. See Ankersmit 2005; Runia 2014; and Carr 2014. See also the literary historian and critic Gumbrecht 2003. For an exploration of differences between Ankersmit and Runia, see Froeyman 2012. Ankersmit was first known as a narrativist akin in many ways to Hayden White, but became disenchanted with the linguistic turn. For a critique of his later position from an adherent of his earlier one, see Icke 2012.

exponents Eelco Runia and Frank Ankersmit respectively call "presence" and "sublime experience."[58] The epistemological objectivism of the positivists and the linguistic idealism of the constructivists are both based, they claim, on a dubious dualism between present subject and past object. Instead, they prefer the metaphor of proximate touch and immediate contact to that of distancing perspectival sight or rhetorical imposition to describe an experience of history prior to the very split between subject and object.

Rather than explaining events causally or offering a meaningful interpretation of the past through narrative emplotment, the "new experientialists" extol present experiences that seem to overcome temporal distance and make the past alive now, rather than merely empathetically duplicating the putative experience of past actors. Inspired by the great Dutch historian Johann Huizinga's notion of "historical sensation"[59]—an epiphany manifest in rare but life-altering encounters with the past, unfiltered by conceptual mediations or interpretative prefigurations—they celebrate fissures "in the temporal order so that the past and the present are momentarily united in a way that is familiar to all of us in the experience of déjà vu."[60] Jacob Burckhardt's account of his first visit to the church of Santa Croce in Florence, which magically brought the Renaissance to life, is one example.[61] Neither scientific history with its penchant for causal explanations of past events nor historical narration imbued with rhetorically inflected meaning drawing on implicit tropes can contain and normalize such disruptive and illuminating experiences.

Are the "new experientialists" returning from an epistemological to an ontological approach to the question of history and truth,

---

58. For an account of the role of experience in historical reasoning, including Ankersmit's notion of sublime historical experience, see Jay 2005: chapter 6.
59. For an account, see Ziegler 2006.
60. Ankersmit 2005: 132.
61. Ibid., 161–162.

one in which pre-predicative experience gets us in direct touch with the presence of the past? Ankersmit concedes that what he seeks is "closer to moods and feelings than to knowledge; like them it is ontological rather than epistemological; and sublime experience is to be defined in terms of what you *are* rather than in terms of what knowledge you *have*."[62] Runia, for his part, stresses the role of non-interpretative metonymy rather than metaphor as the master trope of historical experience, and contends that it "wants us to believe that it imparts one 'meaning'—the truth—that this 'meaning' lies right at the surface, and that this one 'meaning' is all that it conveys."[63] Such an anti-representational agenda may seem even reminiscent of the Christian doctrine of "real presence" in which the body and blood of Christ is substantially, not merely symbolically present in the Eucharist.[64]

But it would be wrong to draw too hasty a conclusion about the actual return of an emphatic, ontological concept of truth in history. For Ankersmit explicitly declares his radical indifference to the question of truth, understood ontologically as well as epistemologically. In a passage in *Sublime Historical Experience* set entirely in italics, he writes:

> *Sublime experience is sovereign master in its own territory and no longer subject to the epistemological legislation of truth (as experience is in its more trivial form that we know as the scientific experiment). It therefore makes no sense to ask for "the truth of (sublime) experience" or for what might or should (in)validate historical experience.*[65]

62. Ibid., 225; emphasis in original.
63. Runia 2014: 96.
64. Steiner 1991.
65. Ankersmit 2005: 233.

And while Runia may contend that the metonymic transfer of presence—in which parts stand for the whole—as opposed to the metaphoric transfer of meaning—in which analogous comparisons convey sense—is in the service of something called the truth, he nonetheless acknowledges that "metonymy is the trope of *dissimulation*."[66] That is, although metonymic representation may seek to give the impression of being prior to the split between subject and object, history as experienced and history as written, it in fact fails to achieve it. Whatever attraction we may feel for the presence of a sublime historical experience—and its defenders do make suggestive arguments for its virtues, which cannot be addressed now—it gives us little, if any, help with the issue of truth and history. Although situated in the contested territory between the positivist and constructivist extremes, it survives the turbulence by hunkering down and refusing to be drawn into the crossfire. But the relationship between truth and history remains a vexed issue, which, despite what may seem the disdain of Ankersmit and Runia, continues to exercise anyone who conducts research into and writes the story of the past.

2.3 *Institutional Justificationism*

Does the alternative that I've called "institutional justificationism" provide a more plausible solution? Traceable to the pragmatist C. S. Peirce's ideal notion of a credentialed scientific community of inquiry, which has come to be called a "community of the competent,"[67] it displaces the question of the truth about the past to that of the truthfulness of the historian in the present. More precisely, "institutional justificationism" replaces a concern with the truth of our accounts of the past with a focus on the integrity of historians, the

---

66. Runia 2014: 96; italics in original.
67. See Haskell 1977: 237–238, Novick 1988: 570–572. For Peirce's original argument, see Peirce 1997.

sincerity of their claims, openness to counter-arguments, and adherence to standards of evidentiary authenticity. Although acknowledging that truthfulness is normally accounted a virtue for individuals, "institutional justificationalism" emphasizes the pressures to produce it dialogically and institutionally. "Institutional justificationism" defines historians collectively as a loosely integrated, professionally credentialed community engaged in a collaborative, critically vetted enterprise with no final resting place, no unified "posterity" at the end of the day, no last judgment that ever comes. The community's members operate only with an "as if" concept of truth, which provides an underlying asymptotic telos for their endeavors, but which they know is always unreachable.

The importance of the intersubjective assessment of historical accounts was already clear to Collingwood, who contrasted fictional narratives with their historical counterparts, even though both were based on an active imagination. In addition to their explicitly bracketing truth claims, fictions were distinguished from historical narratives, Collingwood argued, by the possibility of repeating the intellectual labor that produced the latter. Although certainty can be elusive, we can at least form an educated opinion about the plausibility of an earlier historian's narrative "by doing his work over again for ourselves, that is, by reconsidering the evidence upon which his picture is based and, exercising upon this evidence our own historical imagination, finding that we are led to the same result."[68] No one, in other words, would think of judging the truth content of, say, *War and Peace*, by duplicating Tolstoy's authorship and rewriting his novel; but many historians have found cause to rewrite the account of many of the same events written by Armand-Augustin-Louis Caulaincourt in *With Napoleon in Russia*.[69] Although there is no definitive final

---

68. Collingwood 1999: 164.
69. Caulaincourt 1935. The original French version appeared in part in the 1820s.

account, the process of frequently revisiting earlier ones fuels the ongoing effort to reach some sort of rough consensus about which assertions are warranted and which not. While eschewing the ideal of an absolutely definitive history that makes further revision unnecessary, it understands the cumulative impact of multiple perspectives on the "same" historical events or developments.

The value of this distinction between fictional and historical narratives becomes even clearer if we reconsider the rhetorical moment in the construction of all narratives invoked by Hayden White. He stresses its importance to highlight the latent structural logic of our stories according to a finite number of conventional patterns or figural tropes. But rhetoric, *pace* White, can mean more than tropology or structural poetics; it can also signify the figures of speech through which intersubjective dialogue takes place.[70] That is, rhetoric understood as a normal part of everyday speech alerts us to the communicative function of language, which can involve persuasion rather than demagogic mystification or authoritarian imposition. Whereas White's focus on rhetoric meant recognizing formal structures latent within texts, its communicative counterpart alerts us to the dimension of manifest interactions between or among speakers.

As Jürgen Habermas argues in his defense of the public sphere, universal pragmatics, and communicative rationality, there is at least a potential for consensus based on the better argument and the most compelling evidence, following procedures which take seriously the resistance of that evidence to dubious interpretations.[71] The

---

70. Streuver 1980.
71. Habermas 1992. There is an immense literature on Habermas's notions of the public sphere, communicative rationality, universal pragmatics, and the ideal speech situation. For my own attempt to discuss its implications, which considers objections as well as arguments in its favor, see Jay 2016. What is important to note is that although he began with a theory of justification in which truth was an effect of reaching a consensus, Habermas came to appreciate the importance of practical action in the world to test the validity of such a consensus, action that allows for learning. For a succinct account of this issue, see Zuidervaart 2017: chapter 5.

justificatory exchange of reasons, including those couched in meta-phorical or metonymical terms, in a discursive community extend-ing over time characterizes the modern discipline of history, with its professional credentialing and vetting procedures enabling respon-sible evaluation. Rather than being reduced to the pseudo-reasoning damned by Plato as sophistic, rhetoric can be employed to persuade, not seduce. It can support what the analytic philosopher Michael Dummett calls a "justificationist," rather than verificationist or falsifi-cationist approach to the unending quest for truth, which maintains a realist attitude towards the object of inquiry, but knows that such an object is accessible, if at all, only through intersubjective argumenta-tion always open to future revision.[72] For Dummett propositions are not like "arrows" that we aim at a target called reality (which may well be so far away that we can never know if we actually hit it), but rather tools we use according to rules or moves in a language game. We can still talk of "truth" if we avoid understanding it in the terms of an arrow hitting its target, because there is no ultimate standard by which we can measure our efforts, no transcendent observer able to judge our success. Even Ankersmit, returning to the question of cognitive veracity after *Sublime Historical Experience*, acknowledges that "historical truth is firmly attached to the practice and rational-ity of historical discussion . . . . [D]isciplinary truth is not in need of philosophical explanation—unless the philosopher has the preten-sion to be better informed about historical writing than historians themselves."[73]

It would, of course, be easy to belittle the actual functioning of this community of justification, showing its departures from an ideal Habermasian model of undistorted communication. It can be mocked as another case of liberal delusion about the free market of

72. Dummett 2004.
73. Ankersmit 2010: 42–43.

ideas or of unwarranted faith in Peirce's meritocratic standard of recognized "competence."[74] The process of professionalization, it is often
charged, can exclude those who are deemed beyond the pale: uncre-
dentialed amateurs, autodidacts, and what have come to be called
"barefoot historians," whose unvetted work appears in unauthor-
ized venues, which have proliferated mightily with the growth of the
Internet. Rather than a single "community of competence," there
can be several, driven by incommensurable interests or values that
impede unbiased communication. In short, all the familiar arguments made by Michel Foucault about the inextricable entanglement
of knowledge and power in discrete "regimes of truth" can be mar-
shalled to cast doubt on the naïve conclusion that historians in the
collective are able to do any better than any single historian in avoiding the dangers of relativism and dogmatism.[75] Such reservations are,
it must be admitted, worth taking seriously.

But there may well also be a positive lesson in how these qualms
have been taken on board by historians, insofar as doing so has created an awareness on a meta-level of the ways institutions, including
the ones in which historians are more or less embedded, have histories of their own, which themselves are open to intersubjective critiques that can influence subsequent practices.[76] That is, historians
can take seriously voices from outside the guild, relentlessly weed out

74. Thus, for example, de Certeau writes, "This community is also a factory, its members distributed along assembly lines, subject to budgetary pressures, hence, dependent on political decisions and bound by the growing constraints of a sophisticated machinery (archival
infrastructures, computers, publishers' demands, etc.). Its operations are determined by a
rather narrow and homogeneous segment of society from which its members are recruited.
Its general orientation is governed by sociocultural assumptions and postulates imposed
through recruitment, through the existing and established fields of research, through the
demands stemming from the personal interests of a boss, through the modes and fashions
of the moment, etc." De Certeau 1986: 204.

75. Foucault 1980.

76. For a history of the professionalization of history, which unlike Novick's focuses on the
European rather than American examples, see Torstendahl 2015.

deliberate falsifiers of evidence, and become self-consciously aware of the rhetorical dimension of the narratives they write and the standards of competence they employ. Despite their differences, some productive discursive exchange can occur between communities that may appear to be grounded in utterly incommensurable assumptions. Historians, in short, can learn reflexively from the history of historiography with all of its vicissitudes. Putting it in terms that resonate with the new experientialism, we can say that historians' most valuable experiences may not be sublime quasi-ontological encounters with the "presence" of the past but rather their entrance into and engagement with the ongoing meta-community of historians, past, present and future, which is a regulative ideal of their craft.

Although such a community always falls short of its ideal norm, it can install in those who enter it the imperative to be vigilant about its limitations and shortcomings. This means acquiring a reflexive appreciation of the value of truthfulness, even if historians know they can never reach a final truth and embracing the process of pluralist argumentation about their always tentative conclusions, which will never reach a perfect consensus. Perhaps most telling of all, becoming sensitive to the importance of the collective obligation to be truthful, even in the face of doubts about reaching ultimate truth, forces them to realize that their enterprise is not only epistemological and rhetorical, but also inherently moral in character. This is not to suggest, I hasten to add, that historians should set themselves up as moral judges of past actors, measuring their deeds by contemporary standards of behavior. It means instead that they should feel duty-bound to do all they can to avoid imposing their own prejudices and interests on to the people who came before them, acknowledging the otherness of historical actors even as they try to empathize with their struggles and dilemmas. If it didn't sound so old-fashioned, we might call this a code of honor tacitly underlying membership in the guild, where the truthfulness of the telling is valued over the truth of the told.

Perhaps no less importantly, sensitivity to the importance of truthfulness without illusions about the truth of our accounts of the past also means historians are morally obliged to honor the protocols and master the practices of the professional community they join, however imperfectly those standards may be observed in reality. As Bernard Williams contends in *Truth and Truthfulness*, "While we must demand that interpretations of the past should tell us the truth, in the sense that they should not lie or mislead, what we need them for is not to tell us something called 'the truth about the past.' We need them to be truthful, and to make sense of the past—to us."[77] That is, in addition to their obligation to the people who have preceded us to tell their stories as honestly, fairly, and judiciously as possible, historians also owe to their present and future audiences the example of their vigilant efforts to do so. For they too, after all, will come to depend on later historians to tell their own stories with comparable integrity.

3. CONCLUSION

The truth of history, understood in either ontological or epistemological terms, may forever elude us. But I would argue in conclusion, it is crucial to maintain an abiding commitment to the truthfulness of historians—or, more precisely, to that of historians as an intersubjective community of fallible scholars who honor the imperative to justify their accounts. This means being truthful about our motives, truthful about the validity of the evidence as best we can judge it, and truthful in our willingness to accept the better counterargument and the force of new evidence. For without that commitment to truthfulness, we have no way of preventing the triumph of "fake news" and "alternative facts," or surviving the threat posed by Orwell's ominous

77. Williams 2002: 258.

warning in *1984*: "Who controls the past controls the future. Who controls the present controls the past."[78]

BIBLIOGRAPHY

Ahearne, Jeremy. *Michel de Certeau: Interpretation and its Other*. Stanford, CA: Stanford University Press, 1995.

Ankersmit, Frank. *Sublime Historical Experience*. Stanford, CA: Stanford University Press, 2005.

Ankersmit, Frank "Truth in History and Literature." *Narrative* 18:1 (2010): 29–50.

Appleby, Joyce, Lynn Hunt and Margaret Jacob. *Telling the Truth About History*. New York: Norton, 1994.

Barthes, Roland. "The Discourse of History." In *The Rustle of Language*, translated by Richard Howard. Berkeley: University of California Press, 1989.

Beiser, Frederick C. *The Fate of Reason: German Philosophy from Kant to Fichte*. Cambridge, MA: Harvard University Press, 1987.

Bernstein, Michael André. *Foregone Conclusions: Against Apocalyptic History*. Berkeley: University of California Press, 1994.

Bowersock, Glen Warren. *Fiction as History: Nero to Julian*. Berkeley: University of California Press, 1994.

Breisach, Ernst. *On the Future of History: The Postmodernist Challenge and its Aftermath*. Chicago: University of Chicago Press, 2003.

Burke, Peter. "Historical Facts and Historical Fictions." In *Filozofski Vesnik 2*, 169–186. Chicago: University of Chicago Press, 1994.

Carr, David. *Time, Narrative, and History*. Bloomington: Indiana University Press, 1986.

Carr, David. *Experience and History: Phenomenological Perspectives on the Historical World*. Oxford: Oxford University Press, 2014.

Caulaincourt, Armand-Augustin-Louis. *With Napoleon in Russia*. Translated by Jean Hanoteau. New York: Morrow, 1935.

Chartier, Roger. *On the Edge of the Cliff: History, Language and Practices*. Translated by Lydia G. Cochrane. Baltimore: Johns Hopkins University Press, 1997.

Collingwood, R. G. *The Idea of History*, edited by Jan van der Dussen. New York: Oxford University Press, 1994.

Collingwood, R. G. *The Principles of History and Other Writings in Philosophy of History*, edited by W. H. Dray and W. J. van der Dussen. Oxford: Oxford University Press, 1999.

78. Orwell 1963: 109.

Cousins, Mark. "The Practice of Historical Investigation." In *Post-structuralism and the Question of History*, edited by Derek Attridge, Geoff Bennington and Robert Young, 126–136. Cambridge, Cambridge University Press, 1989.

De Certeau, Michel. *Heterologies: Discourse on the Other*. Translated by Brian Massumi. Minneapolis: University of Minnesota Press, 1986.

Diamond, R. J. "Resolution of the Paradox of *Tristram Shandy*." *Philosophy of Science* 31:1 (January 1964): 55–58.

Dray, William. *History as Re-enactment: R. G. Collingwood's Idea of History*. Oxford: Oxford University Press, 1995.

Dummett, Michael. *Truth and the Past*. New York: Columbia University Press, 2004.

Foucault, Michel. *Power/Knowledge: Selected Interviews and Other Writings, 1972–1977*, edited by Colin Gordon, translated by Colin Gordon, Leo Marshall, John Mepham, Kate Soper. New York: Pantheon, 1980.

Friedlander, Saul. *Probing the Limits of Representation: Nazism and the "Final Solution."* Cambridge, MA: Harvard University Press, 1992.

Friedlander, Saul. *Nazi Germany and the Jews*, 2 vols. New York: Harper, 1998, 2008.

Froeyman, Anton. "Frank Ankersmit and Eelco Runia: The Presence and Otherness of the Past." *Rethinking History* 16:3 (2012): 393–415.

Gadamer, Hans-Georg. *Truth and Method*. New York: Crossroad, 1986.

Gallagher, Catherine. *Nobody's Story: The Vanishing Acts of Women Writers in the Marketplace, 1670–1820*. Berkeley: University of California Press, 1994.

Genette, Gérard. *Narrative Discourse: An Essay in Method*. Oxford: Blackwell, 1980.

Ginzburg, Carlo. *Clues, Myths and Historical Method*. Translated by John and Ann C. Tedeschi. Baltimore: Johns Hopkins University Press, 1989.

Gordon, Peter E. "Weimar Theology: From Historicism to Crisis." In *Weimar Thought: A Contested Legacy*, edited by Peter E. Gordon and John P. McCormick. Princeton, NJ: Princeton University Press, 2013.

Grethlein, Jonas. "Experientiality and 'Narrative Reference' with Thanks to Thucydides." *History and Theory* 49 (October 2010): 315–335.

Gross, David. *Lost Time: On Remembering and Forgetting in Late Modern Culture*. Amherst: University of Massachusetts Press, 2000.

Gumbrecht, Hans Ulrich. *Production of Presence: What Meaning Cannot Convey*. Stanford: Stanford University Press, 2003.

Habermas, Jürgen. *The Structural Transformation of the Public Sphere: An Inquiry into a Category of Bourgeois Society*. Translated by Thomas Burger. Cambridge, MA: MIT Press, 1992.

Hacohen, Malachi Haim. *Karl Popper: The Formative Years 1902–1945*. Cambridge, UK: Cambridge University Press, 2000.

Handlin, Oscar. *The Truth in History*. Cambridge, MA: Harvard University Press, 1979.

Hartog, François. "Herodotus and the Historiographical Operation." *Diacritics* 22:2 (1992): 83–93.

Haskell, Thomas. *The Emergence of Professional Social Science: The American Social Science Association and the Nineteenth-Century Crisis of Authority.* Champagne: University of Illinois Press, 1979.

Hempel, Carl. "The Function of General Laws in History." *The Journal of Philosophy* 39:2 (1042): 35–48.

Howell, Martha and Walter Prevenir. *From Reliable Sources: An Introduction to Historical Methods.* Ithaca, NY: Cornell University Press, 2001.

Hughes, H. Stuart. *History as Art and as Science: Twin Vistas on the Past.* New York: Harper, 1964.

Husserl, Edmund. *Experience and Judgment.* Translated by James Spencer Churchill. Evanston, IL: Northwestern University Press, 1975.

Icke, Peter. *Frank Ankersmit's Lost Historical Cause: From Language to Experience.* New York, NY: Routledge, 2012.

Iggers, Georg. "The Image of Ranke in American and German Historical Thought." *History and Theory* 2 (1962): 17–40.

Iggers, Georg. "A Search for a Post-Postmodern Theory of History." *History and Theory* 48 (2009): 122–128.

Jay, Martin. "Vico and Western Marxism." In *Vico: Past and Present*, Vol. 2, edited by Giorgio Tagliacozzo, 195–212. Atlantic Highlands, NJ: Humanities Press, 1981.

Jay, Martin. "Astronomical Hindsight: The Speed of Light and Virtual Reality." In *Refractions of Violence*, 119–132. New York, Routledge, 2003.

Jay, Martin. *Songs of Experience: Modern American and European Variations on a Universal Theme.* Berkeley: University of California Press, 2005.

Jay, Martin. "Historical Explanation and the Event: Reflections on the Limits of Contextualization." *New Literary History* 42 (2011): 557–591.

Jay, Martin. "Intention and Irony: The Missed Encounter Between Hayden White and Quentin Skinner." *History and Theory* 52 (February 2013): 32–48.

Jay, Martin. "Historicism and the Event." *Against the Grain: Jewish Intellectuals in Hard Times*, edited by Ezra Mendelsohn, Stefani Hoffman, and Richard I. Cohen. New York: Berghahn Books, 2014.

Jay, Martin. *Reason After its Eclipse: On Late Critical Theory.* Madison: University of Wisconsin Press, 2016.

Jenkins, Keith. *Re-thinking History.* London: Routledge, 1991.

Klein, Kerwin Lee. *From History to Theory.* Berkeley: University of California Press, 2011.

Koselleck, Reinhardt. *Futures Past: On the Semantics of Historical Time.* Translated by Keith Tribe. Cambridge, MA: MIT Press, 1985.

Kracauer, Siegfried. *History: The Last Things Before the Last.* New York: Oxford University Press, 1969.

LaCapra, Dominick. *History and Criticism.* Ithaca, NY: Cornell University Press, 1985.

Lorenz, Chris. "Drawing the Line: 'Scientific' History Between Myth-Making and Myth-Breaking." In *Narrating the Nation. Representations in History, Media and the Arts*, edited by Stefan Berger, Linas Eriksonas, and Andrew Mycock, 35–55. New York: Oxford University Press, 2008.

Lowenthal, David. "The Frailty of Historical Truth: Learning Why Historians Inevitably Err." *Perspectives on History* 51:3 (March 2013). https://www.historians.org/publications-and-directories/perspectives-on-history/march-2013/the-frailty-of-historical-truth.

Morson, Gary Saul. *Narrative and Freedom: The Shadows of Time*. New Haven, CT: Yale University Press, 1994.

Nicolas, Dean. "Zhou en lai's Famous Saying Debunked." *History Today*, June 15, 2011.

Novick, Peter. *That Noble Dream: The "Objectivity Question" and the American Historical Profession*. Cambridge, UK: Cambridge University Press, 1988.

Orwell, George. *1984: Text, Sources, Criticism*, edited by Irving Howe. New York, Harcourt, Brace, 1963.

Peirce, C. S. "The Fixation of Belief." In *Pragmatism: A Reader*, edited by Louis Menand, 7–25. New York: Vintage, 1997.

Pihlainen, Kalle. "The Eternal Return of Reality: On Constructivism and Current Historical Desires." *Storia della Storiografia* 69:1 (2014): 103–115.

Poovey, Mary. *A History of the Modern Fact: Problems of Knowledge in the Sciences of Wealth and Society*. Chicago: University of Chicago Press, 1998.

Popper, Karl. *The Poverty of Historicism*. London, Routledge and Kegan Paul, 1957.

Popper, Karl. *The Logic of Scientific Discovery*. Translated by Karl Popper. London: Hutchinson, 1959.

Popper, Karl. *Conjectures and Refutations*. New York: Basic Books, 1963.

Ranke, Leopold von. *The Theory and Practice of History*, edited by Georg G. Iggers and Konrad von Moltke. Indianapolis: Bobbs-Merrill, 1973.

Rasmussen, Joshua, *Defending the Correspondence Theory of Truth*. Cambridge, UK: Cambridge University Press, 2014.

Ricoeur, Paul. *History, Memory, Forgetting*. Translated by Kathleen Blamey and David Pellauer. Chicago: University of Chicago Press, 2004.

Ricoeur, Paul. *History and Truth*. Translated by Charles A. Kelbley. Evanston, IL: Northwestern University Press, 2007.

Roberts, David D. *Nothing But History: Reconstruction and Extremity After Metaphysics*. Berkeley: University of California Press, 1995a.

Roberts, David D. "Croce in America: Influence, Misunderstanding and Neglect." *Humanitas* 8:2 (1995b): 3–34.

Roberts, David D. "The Stakes of Misreading: Hayden White, Carlo Ginzburg and the Crocean Legacy." *Rivista di Studi Italiani* 20:2 (December 2002): 1–30.

Roth, Michael. "Ebb Tide." *History and Theory* 46 (2007): 66–73.

Runia, Eelco. *Moved by the Past: Discontinuity and Historical Mutation*. New York: Columbia University Press, 2014.

Scott, Joan Wallach. *Gender and the Politics of History*. New York: Columbia University Press, 1986.

Shapiro, Barbara. *A Culture of Fact: England, 1550–1720*. Ithaca, NY: Cornell University Press, 2003.

Skinner, Quentin. "A Reply to My Critics." In *Meaning and Context: Quentin Skinner and his Critics*, edited by James Tully, 231–288. Oxford: Polity, 1988.

Spitzer, Alan. B. *Historical Truth and Lies about the Past*. Chapel Hill: University of North Carolina Press, 1996.

Steiner, George. *Real Presences*. Chicago: University of Chicago Press, 1991.

Stepantsov, Pavel M. "The Significance of the Issue of Events' Identity under Different Descriptions for Social Theory and Social Philosophy." *International Journal of Social Science and Humanity* 3:3 (May 2013): 259–262.

Streuver, Nancy. "Topics in History." *Beiheft 19: Metahistory: Six Critiques, History and Theory* 19:4 (1980): 66–79.

Sidney, Sir Philip. *The Defense of Poesie*. Oxford: Oxford University Press, 1974.

Torstendahl, Rolf. *The Rise and Propagation of Historical Professionalism*. London: Routledge, 2015.

Vann, Richard. "Turning Linguistic: History and Theory and *History and Theory*, 1960–1975." In *A New Philosophy of History*, edited by Frank Ankersmit and Hans Kellner. Chicago: University of Chicago, 1995.

Weber, Samuel. "Objectivity Otherwise." In *Objectivity and its Other*, edited by Wolfgang Natter, Theodore R. Schatzki, and John Paul Jones, 33–47. New York: Guilford Press, 1995.

Weymans, Wim. "Michel de Certeau and the Limits of Historical Representation." *History and Theory* 43 (2004): 161–178.

White, Hayden. *Metahistory: The Historical Imagination in Nineteenth-Century Europe*. Baltimore: Johns Hopkins University Press, 1973.

White, Hayden. *Tropics of Discourse: Essays in Cultural Criticism*. Baltimore: Johns Hopkins University Press, 1978.

White, Hayden. "Historical Emplotment and the Problem of Truth." In *Probing the Limits of Representation: Nazism and the "Final Solution*," edited by Saul Friedlander. Cambridge, MA: Harvard University Press, 1992.

White, Hayden. *Figural Realism: Studies in the Mimesis Effect*. Baltimore: Johns Hopkins University Press, 1999.

Williams, Bernard. *Truth and Truthfulness: An Essay in Genealogy*. Princeton, NJ: Princeton University Press, 2002.

Ziegler, Joanna E. "Scholarship as/and Performance: The Case of Johan Huizinga and his Concept of 'Historical Sensation.'" In *Practicing Catholic: Ritual, Body and Contestation in Catholic Faith*, edited by Bruce T. Morrill, Joanna E. Ziegler, and Susan Rodgers, 247–255. New York: Palgrave Macmillan, 2006.

Zuidervaart, Lambert. *Truth in Husserl, Heidegger, and the Frankfurt School*. Cambridge, MA: MIT Press, 2017.

Chapter 10

Developing Truth Seekers

PHILIP E. DOW

If you want to build a ship, don't drum up people to collect wood and don't assign them tasks and work, but rather teach them to long for the endless immensity of the sea.

—*Antoine de Saint-Exupery, 1950*

The pursuit of truth has always been central to the human story. Across cultures and historical epochs, it has stimulated innovation, motivated growth, provided a foundation for human flourishing, and been inseparable from our quest for meaning. For all of these reasons, healthy societies have actively encouraged the quest for truth among the young. This has certainly been the case in many modern nations, where truth seeking has been the lifeblood of education—its raison d'être. Recently, however, this fundamental commitment to truth seeking has waned as an educational priority. The consequences of this shift toward a "post-truth" culture are sobering, but they need not be irreversible.[1]

This chapter will argue that the vision for developing truth seekers found in the intellectual virtue movement has the potential to revitalize

1. In 2016 the *Oxford Dictionaries* declared "post-truth" as its word of the year, calling it "one of the defining words of our time." https://www.bbc.com/news/uk-37995600

Philip E. Dow, *Developing Truth Seekers* In: *Integrity, Honesty, and Truth Seeking*. Edited by: Christian B. Miller and Ryan West. Oxford University Press (2020). © Oxford University Press.
DOI: 10.1093/oso/9780190920487.003.0010

contemporary education, and with it, the quest for human flourishing. We will begin by defining "truth seeker" before turning our attention to a number of practical ways we can develop truth seekers in a classroom context. We will conclude by looking at some of the ways that a renewed focus on truth seeking can revitalize the field of education.

1. AREN'T WE ALL "TRUTH SEEKERS"?

If our aim is to set out a helpful plan for developing truth seekers, it is necessary to start by asking who, in the context of educational theory and practice, is a truth seeker? Many contemporary educational theorists begin with the assumption that all children are natural truth seekers. If this is accurate, the task of developing truth seekers is relatively straightforward and involves equipping students with the skills necessary for expanding their understanding of the world, giving some guided inspiration, and then largely getting out of the way.[2]

But does this faithfully describe reality? Are children innately as intellectually virtuous as we wish them to be? What happens when truth seems to cut away at our self-esteem, fails to support our desires, or threatens our deeply held beliefs? What happens when truth doesn't appear to be what we want it to be? Whether it is in the form of "confirmation bias," "rationalization," or any number of similar and well-established human tendencies, multiple studies across disciplines and periods provide sobering evidence that our allegiance to truth tends to end where our self-interest begins.[3]

Indeed, a preponderance of evidence coming out of the social sciences suggests that intellectual expediency and self-serving

2. Reece 2001.

3. Nickerson 1998: 175–220, Haidt 2001: 814–834, Ten Elshof 2009: 54–74, and Leib and Shalvi (chapter 6 in this volume). To be clear, self-interest and truth seeking are not inherently incompatible. In fact, they can be mutually reinforcing.

justifications are far more "natural" to us than principled truth seeking. As the moral psychologist Jonathan Haidt has persuasively argued, our minds often function much more like press secretaries seeking post hoc rationalizations for our beliefs than scientists objectively pursuing truth for its own sake.[4] And this appears to be true no matter how smart, or how well educated, we are. In fact, David Perkins and others have shown that most of the time having a higher IQ or more education, simply means we are better at justifying ourselves.[5] On this view, a Harvard PhD is not necessarily an advantage in authentic truth seeking. It might even be a hindrance. Thus, despite widespread acknowledgment that truth seeking is critical to both individual and societal well-being, academic studies consistently suggest that seeking truth for its own sake doesn't come "naturally" for many of us.

Yet all is not lost. The often opportunistic relationship we have with truth, witnessed daily in boardrooms and classrooms around the world, need not completely eviscerate the contention that humans do have a tremendous capacity for truth seeking. It does, however, suggest that truth seeking, at least in a meaningful sense, is less common than we would like, and that developing truth seekers may require more than the offering of knowledge-acquisition skills and the freedom to implement them. In fact, even John Locke, whose optimistic views of human nature have made him an inspirational figure to some progressive educators, concluded,

> There is nobody in the commonwealth of learning who does not profess himself a lover of truth: and there is not a rational creature that would not take it amiss to be thought otherwise of. And yet, for all this, one may truly say, that there are very few lovers of

4. Haidt 2013: 106.
5. Perkins, Farady, and Bushey 1991: 95.

truth, for truth's sake, even amongst those who persuade themselves that they are so.[6]

In other words, if truth seekers are people whose allegiance to truth, for its own sake, is capable of superseding self-interest, something more than a "natural" affinity for truth seems to be needed. But what is it that we need?

Since the 1990s, a group of researchers at Harvard's Project Zero have argued that learning requires more than thinking skills and our sometimes capricious interest in understanding. "Passions, attitudes, values, and habits of mind," they argued, "all play key roles in thinking, and, in large part, it is these elements that determine whether learners use their thinking skills when it counts."[7] Almost simultaneously, what might now be described as the intellectual virtue movement was also beginning to take root. This movement, made up of philosophers, educators, and cultural critics, helped provide a conceptual framework for Project Zero's emphasis on "thinking dispositions," but employed the more philosophically rich language of virtue epistemology to argue that ultimately what lasts, and what is of greatest intrinsic value and practical worth in education, is the character of a student's mind—the deeply rooted thinking traits by which every person should seek, evaluate, and apply knowledge. Remembering the correct date for the signing of the Magna Carta, or correctly applying the quadratic formula matters. But of greater significance is whether, in the course of her education, a student is becoming the sort of person whose traits of thinking—for instance, curiosity, tenacity, carefulness, and fair-mindedness—habitually lead her to greater knowledge and understanding.[8] Underlying the intellectual

---

6. Locke 1998: 614.
7. Perkins and Tishman, http://www.pz.harvard.edu/projects/patterns-of-thinking.
8. Baehr 2016: 5–8.

virtue movement was the assumption that these traits are not universal or "natural." At least to some extent, they have to be developed.

Project Zero's Ron Ritchhart was among the first educators to give voice to these ideas, arguing that education, in its fixation on skills and test results, had lost sight of its deeper, and ultimately more compelling, mission. Writing in 2002, Ritchhart asked,

> So what ideals are worth setting our sights on when it comes to education? . . . When all is said and done, when the last test is taken, what will stay with a student from his or her education? Memories certainly. Treasured experiences, positive relationships, meaningful interactions, yes. But what about the knowledge and skills teachers have worked so hard to impart? Surprisingly, we don't have much evidence that these have a very long shelf life. So what sticks? What kind of learning lasts beyond a given year that we can grab hold of to guide our vision? I contend that what stays with us from our education are patterns: patterns of behavior, patterns of thinking, patterns of interaction. These patterns make up our character, specifically our intellectual character. . . . Schools can do much to shape and influence these patterns. This is the kind of long-term vision we need for education: to be shapers of students' intellectual character.[9]

Put differently, the intellectual virtue movement argues that because the intellectual habits that lead to understanding are not anything like consistent or universal human traits, the central task of education must be to nurture in students those intellectual virtues that will faithfully guide them to an ever-increasing understanding of truth and reality. To educate for intellectual virtue is to develop truth seekers.

9. Ritchhart 2002: 9

To summarize, while some level of attraction to truth seems to be a universally human impulse, not everyone with a passing interest in truth can rightfully be called a "truth seeker." A "truth seeker" is someone whose commitment to pursuing truth is so deeply rooted that it consistently supersedes self-interest. Indeed, as Confucius observed, a truth seeker's commitment to truth will often include a substantial element of self-sacrifice. "Love learning," he pleaded, and "be ready to die for the Good Way."[10] Thanks to this deep allegiance to truth, the "truth seeker" will develop the skills, abilities, inclinations, sensitivities, and thinking habits that are most likely to produce an ever-increasingly accurate understanding of truth and reality. Which is to say, truth seekers are people of increasing virtuous intellectual character.

And why does it matter, practically speaking, that we seek to develop truth seekers? Ultimately, people of virtuous intellectual character produce the sort of intellectual and practical goods that form the foundation for human flourishing—the advancement of knowledge, healthy economic and political systems, and interpersonal trust.[11] It is for this reason that Epictetus stated that someone who "seeks truth and loves it must be reckoned precious to any human society."[12] Therefore both for its intrinsic worth and for the many practical goods that it produces, developing truth seekers must be central to the mission of twenty-first-century education.

2. HOW DO WE DEVELOP TRUTH SEEKERS?

If a primary aim of education is to develop truth seekers, and if the intellectual virtues are the character traits of truth seekers, then it is

10. *Analects*, vii. 13 (as quoted in Lewis 1996a: 108).
11. Inglehart 2000: 91. This has also been demonstrated by Almond and Verba 1963, Coleman 1988, 1990, Putnam 1993, and Fukuyama 1995.
12. Popularly attributed to the stoic philosopher Epitectus, but not confirmed by the author.

hard to imagine a task more significant than that of discovering and applying effective ways to develop intellectual virtue in our students. The majority of this chapter will be devoted to helping us begin that journey. A comprehensive catalogue of strategies for educating for intellectual virtue is found in Jason Baehr's *Cultivating Good Minds*.[13] Instead of trying to summarize, or add to, the multitude of excellent suggestions found there, I will highlight several of the most important ideas related to the development of intellectual virtue that have come out of our experience at Rosslyn Academy and the experience of other like-minded schools.[14]

2.1 Culture

While individual teachers can and do effectively teach for intellectual virtue, we have found that it is within a truth-centered school culture, saturated with the ideas and practices of intellectual virtue, that truth seekers are most likely to develop and flourish. Strategies and virtue-related pedagogy do matter; but, as Peter Drucker famously said, "Culture eats strategy for breakfast."[15] Like most institutions that have healthy, mission-compatible cultures, a school focused on developing truth seekers needs at its core a compelling vision, cast in clear language, known and valued by its stakeholders, and then authentically and effectively put into practice. This means that

---

13. Baehr 2015. Downloadable from: http://intellectualvirtues.org/why-should-we-educate-for-intellectual-virtues-2/

14. Rosslyn Academy, where I have served as Superintendent since 2010, is a private, American-curriculum, international Christian day school in Nairobi, Kenya, that serves approximately 650 students from over 50 different nationalities. It has been educating for intellectual virtue for the last ten years. The Community of Intellectual Virtue Schools is an initiative begun by Rosslyn Academy and the Intellectual Virtue Academy, a public charter school in Los Angeles, which includes a small but growing number of schools who are committed to developing virtuous intellectual character in their students. http://rosslynacademy.org/community-of-intellectual-virtue-schools/.

15. Greer and Horst 2014: 149.

schools interested in developing truth seekers must make this aim explicit and enshrine it in the key documents that serve to provide vision and accountability to the institution. This is the case at Rosslyn Academy in Kenya, and at other schools like the Intellectual Virtues Academy in Los Angeles and the Black Forest Academy in Germany, where the core values, the learner profile, the graduate profile, and other guiding documents make explicit the school's commitment to intellectual character development.[16]

But guiding documents provide the vision for a learning community only to the extent that those documents are widely known and clearly influential in the day-to-day life of the school. Cultures are notoriously difficult to change. They have a life and power of their own. Therefore, even changes that are positive and have grassroots support will take hold only if there is intentional, consistent, and lasting leadership behind the change. For this reason, Rosslyn Academy made the choice to hire an Intellectual Virtue Coordinator, whose responsibility is to support the school's efforts in educating for intellectual virtue by leading teacher training, compiling and making available excellent resources, encouraging momentum among parents through intellectual virtue parent workshops, and otherwise keeping the ideas in front of the school community in attractive and practical ways.

One effective initiative has been the "IV Drip," a brief, weekly e-mail to elementary teachers on one of the virtues with several simple suggestions for integrating that virtue into the classroom. Another has been the substantial revision of the elementary school's report cards to better reflect the school's emphasis on thinking habits over traditional letter grades. While traditional letter grades are included on the report card to designate relative mastery of content, the first

---

16. An online sample of these documents is available at: http://rosslynacademy.org/community-of-intellectual-virtue-schools/.

page is dominated by a clear assessment of the student's growth in each of the school's seven intellectual virtues: curiosity, humility, carefulness, courage, honesty, fair-mindedness, and tenacity. Based on a combination of teacher observation and student self-evaluation, students earn a designation of "Beginning," "Growing," or "Maturing." These assessments are given further color and definition in the teacher comment section, which details specific, observed instances of a given virtue being demonstrated by the student in the course of the grading period. Significantly, the revised report card has slowly begun to shift parents' and students' perceptions of the purpose of education away from grades and towards truth seeking. In this way, the emphasis on intellectual character in the report card is helping to reshape the school culture.[17]

, When it comes to culture building, new schools enjoy a luxury that established schools do not. Since they have no preexisting culture that must be overhauled, new schools can foster a robust culture of truth seeking even before they open their doors, by developing every part of the school with an eye toward educating for intellectual virtue. The best example of this is the Intellectual Virtues Academy (IVA), whose emphasis on intellectual character development starts with its name and weaves its way through its marketing, its hiring and admissions processes, its curriculum development, and its assessment philosophy and practices. It is impossible to interact with IVA and not see that the pursuit of intellectual virtue permeates every part of the school's culture and has energized the classroom.

17. It should be stressed that Rosslyn Academy's emphasis on intellectual character development has not meant a complete rejection of traditional assessment—not at all. Instead, the emphasis on virtuous thinking habits has simply acted as a rich and healthy complement to more traditional assessment. Samples of intellectual-virtue-based report cards from both Rosslyn Academy and Intellectual Virtues Academy are available at: http://rosslynacademy.org/community-of-intellectual-virtue-schools/.

The results have begun to convince the sceptics. Despite having open enrollment, and despite explicitly teaching toward intellectual virtue and away from standardized tests, in the first two years, IVA students have outperformed their peers in the Long Beach United Public Schools by almost 26 percentile points.[18] Even more encouraging for IVA, however, have been the initial results of a study done on IVA by scholars at Boston University. In the first study of its kind, these researchers have verified significant growth among IVA students in those intellectual character traits that IVA believes will transform the way their students approach life and learning for the rest of their lives.[19] As the example of IVA attests, culture matters.

Yet to be truly effective in developing intellectually virtuous students, the truth seeking culture of a school must include specific and effective educational practices. With the aim of thinking clearly about intellectual character development, Rosslyn Academy has found it helpful to place many of these methods into four general categories: name it, model it, practice it, call it out.

2.2. Name It

The effective teaching of any concept rests, in part, on the language used to transmit the idea. This is especially true when an idea, such as intellectual virtue, is new or unfamiliar. Thanks to the work of virtue epistemologists, the language of intellectual virtue is simultaneously clear and "thick"—that is, it is accessible, highly descriptive, and normative. The thick language of intellectual virtue also provides added depth and practical value to already existing but otherwise vague or shallow educational concepts. Consider, for instance, the

18. http://www.ivalongbeach.org/academics/state-test-scores-sbac. At the time of writing only two years of standardized testing results had been made available by the state.
19. Seider, Porter, and Clark 2018. It should be noted that not every virtue showed significant improvement, although most did.

nearly ubiquitous educational mantra of developing "lifelong learners." Nearly every educator believes they are doing this, but almost no
one knows what it means—at least in a truly substantive, concrete,
or actionable sense. Jason Baehr suggests the reason for the chasm
between the promise of the phrase and its practical impotence is
that it lacks thickness. He contrasts describing Steve as a "good guy"
(a philosophically "thin" term) with describing Steve as an "open-
minded" person. In the first instance, we have a vaguely positive
impression of Steve, but we don't really know why. We don't have any
information that might helpfully guide our actions or thinking toward
Steve. Conversely, knowing Steve is open-minded gives us something
meaningful to work with. In contrast to the phrase "lifelong learners,"
the language and concepts of intellectual virtue are thick. They give
us a rich description of the traits of a lifelong learner, allowing us to
get past impotent sentimentalism and on to developing meaningful
goals and concrete methods for achieving this noble but otherwise
nebulous end.[20]

Schools like IVA and Rosslyn Academy have benefitted from the
powerful language of intellectual virtue, but have also sought to make
this language developmentally appropriate to the students they hope
will become partners in the pursuit of virtuous intellectual character. For instance, intellectual humility may be defined for adults as
"having a consciousness of the limits of one's knowledge, including
a sensitivity to circumstances in which one's native egocentrism is
likely to function self-deceptively; sensitivity to bias, prejudice and
limitations of one's viewpoint."[21] But for Rosslyn's elementary school
students, the virtue is summed up in the simple, memorable, and cognitively powerful principle: "There is always more to learn." Similarly,
in the language of Rosslyn's elementary school:

---

20. Baehr 2015: 26–28.
21. http://www.criticalthinking.org/pages/valuable-intellectual-traits/528.

- Intellectual curiosity is described as: "Wonder! Discover! Explore!"
- Intellectual carefulness is described as: "Think and learn with care."
- Intellectual courage is described as: "Take risks. Be brave with your brain!"
- Intellectual fair-mindedness is described as: "Listen to others' ideas."
- And intellectual tenacity is described as: "Chase the truth. Never give up."[22]

In short, our success in developing truth seekers will rest, at least in part, on the quality and intentionality of the language we use. Rosslyn Academy, IVA, and a growing number of like-minded schools have found the language of intellectual virtue to be a powerful ally in the pursuit of truth.

Visual culture is also indispensable in engaging students in key concepts and providing opportunities for enriching the learning community's understanding of those concepts. Walk into any class-room at IVA and you are confronted with images of heroes of intellec-tual virtue or graphics that help to explain and symbolize to students and teachers alike the school's driving purpose. At Rosslyn Academy this takes the form of engraved plaques highlighting a teacher-chosen virtue hanging over every classroom door in the Middle and High Schools, and student-created visual representations of the virtues in the Elementary School. The act of students translating their under-standings of a given intellectual virtue into a symbolic but accurate representation of that virtue is an opportunity for these young stu-dents to grapple with the concepts at a deeper level, while simul-taneously giving teachers a chance to guide students whose visual

22. http://rosslynacademy.org/elementarylower-school-resources/

representations might suggest an inaccurate or otherwise underdeveloped understanding of the virtue. In summary, the accessible and thick language of intellectual virtue, when coupled with the intentional use of engaging visual culture, have provided schools like these with a cognitively clear and common basis upon which teachers can inspire truth seeking and from which students can be meaningfully engaged in that aim.[23]

The latter point is not insignificant. Research strongly suggests that students learn best when they understand the framework within which they are learning.[24] If the language that drives educational theory and practice is both philosophically thin and inaccessible (even to many of the teachers expected to put the theory into practice), then what are the chances of that language being effectively used to create a partnership with students in learning? The failure to effectively explain much of the theory utilized in the contemporary classroom to the students who are the intended recipients of that theory (let alone to many of the teachers who are implementing it) is certainly a lost opportunity. The accessible and thick language of intellectual virtue, by contrast, facilitates effective teaching and supports student engagement.

2.3 Model It

Concepts become most powerful when they are given flesh and lived out in front of the students. In that way, the theme of "naming it" leads naturally to the second theme: "model it." The importance of modeling ideas is certainly not new, but it has particular power in the case of educating for truth seeking. For instance, my natural response

23. See Rosslyn Academy's website: http://rosslynacademy.org/community-of-intellectual-virtue-schools/. See also Intellectual Virtue Academy's website: http://www.ivalongbeach.org/.
24. Wiggins and McTighe 2005.

as a teacher when I make an error in thinking, or get some content wrong in the course of a lesson, is to ignore, distract from, or otherwise rationalize my error. I do this because, often, my allegiance to ego supersedes my allegiance to truth. By contrast, the teacher whose highest allegiance is to truth will respond to situations in ways that might surprise the rest of us. They might be quick to bring attention to their error in thinking (humility), and to enlist the students' help in analyzing both how the error was made (courage) and what thinking processes might have avoided it (curiosity). By putting truth above ego, this teacher has not only transformed an embarrassing moment into a dynamic and powerful learning opportunity, but also demonstrated to her students that learning is directly linked to intellectually virtuous thinking.

But the modeling of intellectual virtue is powerful for other reasons as well. For one, by prioritizing truth above ego, the teacher is also beginning to change the culture of the classroom into one where making mistakes in the pursuit of understanding is not shameful, and where moments of failure can be transformed into opportunities for learning. The teacher modeling intellectual virtue is simultaneously laying the groundwork for what psychologist Carol Dweck and others call a "growth mindset"—a mentality now seen by many as foundational to learning.[25] An entire cottage industry has grown up around Dweck's research, including long lists of axioms crafted to encourage a positive attitude towards intellectual risk-taking and development—phrases like, "I like a challenge" instead of "I'll stick with what I know," and "Have I done my best work?" instead of "I'm

25. Dweck 2007. Steve Porter's concept of intellectual therapy is also directly relevant here, in that by modeling the intellectual virtues (such as tenacity and courage), teachers help craft classroom cultures within which many of the real but invisible psychological obstacles that keep individual students from learning are combatted. Indeed, it is in practicing and modeling intellectual fairmindedness in particular that teachers listen to their students closely enough to uncover the psychological hurdles keeping each student from thriving. Porter 2016: 221–237.

all done."[26] Yet no matter how many perfectly manufactured phrases educators may employ, they are nowhere near as powerful as seeing your teacher live it out in front of you. In that sense, there is no greater asset to a truth-centered classroom than a teacher who is a living, breathing example of intellectual virtue.

While modeling is typically associated with the authentic display of a trait by a teacher, the power of modeling is also present as students relate to exemplars of intellectual virtue present in the curriculum. They might not be physically present, but these historical and contemporary exemplars represent unmistakably inspiring real-life examples—not only of the virtues being lived out, but also of their transformative influence on the course of history.[27] Whereas teachers provide personal and down-to-earth examples of truth seeking, the example of key historical or contemporary figures can provide a different sort of inspiration. Abraham Lincoln's potentially Civil-War-ending choice to listen fairly to the advice of an arrogant general despite the general's widely known disdain for the president, for instance, not only inspires in its own right; it also breathes greater significance and emotional force into the otherwise apparently mundane examples of fair-mindedness that students might see lived out in the classroom or on the playground.[28] In short, modeling helps students develop a richer understanding of what a virtue can look like in practice and can give them a more tangible and emotionally fulfilling ideal towards which they may aspire.

2.4 Practice It

As philosophers throughout the ages have noted, however, character development requires more than just the vision produced by

---

26. https://www.weareteachers.com/classroom-poster-8-phrases-that-nurture-growth-mindset/
27. Zagzebski 2017.
28. Dow 2013: 72–73.

clear definitions and attractive modeling. It requires regular practice over an extended period of time. As James K. A. Smith writes, "Dispositions are inscribed into our character through rhythms and routines and rituals, enacted over and over again.... [They are] a sort of learned, second-nature default orientation."[29] Just as the concert violinist's ability to fly effortlessly from note to note belies a lifetime of practice, so the person whose apparently "natural" disposition to think courageously belies countless decisions to seek the truth despite intellectual risks.

Like the court is for the aspiring basketball player, the classroom is a context tailor-made for the practice of intellectual virtue. Schools serious about learning will, as a matter of course, confront their students each day with instances in which they are pushed beyond what they currently know. Each of these moments is an opportunity to practice, or to fail to practice, intellectual tenacity—the trait of a thinker who is willing and able to fight through challenges to their learning. In much the same way, the typical school day naturally produces myriad opportunities to practice intellectual courage—the third grade math student scared to betray his ignorance by raising his hand to ask for help, for instance, or the high school student who speaks up in class even though she knows her opinion is at odds with those of her teacher and friends. And so it is with all of the traits of mind we call intellectual virtues. To grow, they require practice, and the academic context is ideally suited to provide opportunities for that practice.

To summarize to this point: Students are most likely to become people of intellectual virtue when they (1) understand what they are aspiring towards (Name it), (2) see the ideas lived out in appealing ways by people they trust (Model it), and (3) are given opportunities to exercise the virtues themselves (Practice it). However, a

29. Smith 2016: 18–19.

long-standing body of research suggests that something else is still crucial.[30] Unless students have learned how to recognize dynamic and real-life opportunities for truth seeking, they often miss the chance to grow. Our last theme, "call it out," is perhaps the most powerful way to develop this important ability to see and, thus, capitalize on opportunities for practicing intellectual virtue.

2.5 Call It Out

For our purposes, "call it out" simply means being intentional about identifying (and helping students recognize) opportunities for the authentic expression of a given intellectual virtue. Calling out intellectual virtue in a private and informal setting can be particularly powerful because it is highly personal and usually specific. Consider the following example. Ms. Johnson quietly takes Jill aside and warmly tells her, "You impressed me today with the way you carefully gathered and analyzed data during our experiment. It certainly would've been easier to rush things and do a sloppy job; but do you think that you learned a lot more by being so intellectually careful? My guess is that you did. Really well done, Jill. Keep it up!"

As a result of this short and simple interaction, Jill will likely take away a number of important lessons. In addition to becoming increasingly aware of the opportunities for practicing intellectual carefulness in the course of her studies, Jill will likely conclude that (1) the teacher cares enough about me to notice details like this, (2) being intellectually careful is a trait people admire, (3) intellectual carefulness has helped me become a better learner, and (4) for all these reasons, I want to continue to think in intellectually careful ways. There were no gold stars given, but, in a small way, the conversation has changed Jill. By becoming more aware of the practical

30. Perkins, Jay, and Tishman 1993: 1–21.

value of this particular virtue, she has taken an important step on the road to becoming a genuine truth seeker.

In order to further encourage students to reflect creatively on what the virtues are, and what they look like in practice, one teacher at Rosslyn Academy has developed the Secret Intellectual Virtues Spy strategy. She assigns each student a secret partner for a week. Each student is given a simple template and asked to secretly observe her partner and record any positive examples she sees of the intellectual virtues the class has been learning about. At the end of the week the student then shares her observations with her partner. Because the students not only were looking for authentic expressions of the virtues in others, but also were aware that a secret peer was doing the same for them, they begin to look for and recognize opportunities to practice the virtues that they almost certainly would not have seen otherwise.[31]

In similar ways, the informal but public identification of acts of intellectual virtue can also be valuable in helping the class both gain a richer understanding of a virtue, and grow in their ability to recognize situations in which it can be usefully practiced. Consider this fictional conversation between a teacher and his class:

> Great debate class! Whenever we debate controversial issues like this one, things can get pretty heated. When this happens, it's really hard to be fair-minded, isn't it? But the point of debating is not to win (although that is fun). It is to grow in our understanding of the truth. There were a number of very strong points brought up in the debate, but what impressed me most was Billy's approach. Any ideas why? . . . That's right. Billy was genuinely listening to the other side. Why do you think that was

31. This practice is a repurposed application of a "strengths-spotting" exercise, related to the strengths-finders program. http://www.viacharacter.org/blog/an-exercise-on-via-strength-spotting/.

so important? . . . Good, by listening fairly, Billy demonstrated respect for the other side and a commitment to truth, and that changed the entire tone of the debate. We went from a shouting match to an intense, but earnest, pursuit of the truth. We all learned more because of Billy's fair-mindedness. This is true whether we are arguing around the dinner table or out on the playground with our friends.

While care should be taken to ensure that a public comment does not bring unwanted or unhelpful attention to a given student, specific public praise in moderation can build confidence in students, enrich the class-wide understanding of a virtue, and enhance students' abilities to recognize real-life opportunities for practicing that virtue.

Another slightly more formal but still fairly private way to help students understand, recognize, and grow as truth seekers is found in Rosslyn's elementary program. At the beginning of the year, after having been introduced to the virtues, students in many classes take an age-appropriate intellectual virtue self-assessment, which they then discuss with their teacher. From this, the students are asked to identify relative strengths and weaknesses and to develop some simple and practical goals for the semester. For instance, a student might write, "I want to become more intellectually careful by double checking my math work and by making sure that I understand the assignment directions before I start work." To keep these goals in front of them, students keep a journal where they regularly reflect on progress (or lack thereof) in achieving their goal, consider obstacles they might be encountering, and note additional places in their day when they might have the chance to practice that virtue. Finally, as they approach the end of the first quarter, and then again near the end of the first semester, the students meet with their teacher in preparation for a student-led teacher-parent conference in which the students share their goals, their efforts towards achieving those goals, and what they have learned in the process.

Formal assessments of the virtues included on otherwise traditional report cards can build on the self-assessment at the beginning of the year. IVA, for instance, has created a section of their report cards exclusively dedicated to a thoughtful discussion of a student's intellectual character development, as it is lived out in the context of classroom learning. Significantly at IVA, the intellectual character assessment—and not the letter grades designating content mastery—often takes center stage in parent-teacher conferences. As has been noted, Rosslyn Academy has followed suit with regard to evaluating intellectual virtue, and is also adding scenario-based assessments geared to measuring the relative depth of a student's understanding of the virtues and their ability to recognize and appropriately apply a trait in a given situation.[32]

Formal assessments like these are important in developing truth seekers for a number of reasons. First, as the educational adage goes, you value what you assess, and you assess what you value. Formally assessing for intellectual virtue communicates to students, parents, and even teachers, that education at your school is not primarily about test results or practical skills. It is about pursuing truth and developing in students the traits of character that will lead to an increasing understanding of the truth throughout their lives. Assessing for intellectual virtue also forces everyone involved to gain a clearer and richer understanding of the traits being assessed, and therefore, increases their ability to recognize areas of relative strength and weakness and grow as truth seekers.

32. For an example of the scenario-based assessment look under "assessment" at: http://rosslynacademy.org/community-of-intellectual-virtue-schools/. More specifically, see: http://s13489.pcdn.co/wp-content/uploads/2018/04/5th-Grade-EOY-IV-Assessment-Part-2-Google-Forms.pdf.

However, informal praise and formal assessment both give rise to one significant potential criticism—namely, that any form of external reward might encourage students to pursue intellectual virtue for the wrong reasons. As T. S. Eliot put it, "The last temptation is the greatest treason: To do the right thing for the wrong reason."[33] This is a legitimate concern and one of which educators must be wary, for if a student is behaving in intellectually virtuous ways simply to achieve some transient and external end, what happens when that end is absent? At the same time, despite naïve optimism to the contrary, because no student begins school with an unblemished and completely internalized love of truth, the attempt to eliminate all external incentives seems to be, at the very least, misguided. So what is the solution?

In a different context, C. S. Lewis put forward what seems to be a reasonable middle road with his conception of "pretending" Lewis observed,

> [T]here are two kinds of pretending. There is the bad kind, where the pretense is there instead of the real thing. . . . But there is also the good kind, where the pretense leads up to the real thing. . . . That is why children's games are so important. They are always pretending to be grown-ups—playing soldiers, playing shop. But all the time, they are hardening their muscles and sharpening their wits so that the pretense of being grown-up helps them to grow up in earnest.[34]

The whole premise of intellectual virtue development is that we don't start out as finished products. We don't typically begin to practice intellectual tenacity primarily because it feels good or we see its

---

33. Eliot 1935: 44.
34. Lewis 1996b: 163.

inherent value. We usually begin to practice intellectual tenacity after watching someone we admire demonstrate it, or because some other more immediately appealing reward is waiting for us. But then, having practiced the virtue and tasted its goodness, we slowly begin to develop a taste for it ourselves, and we are off.

2.6 Motivation

As we have just seen, why we do what we do matters a great deal. We will conclude this portion of the chapter by digging a bit deeper into the critically important question of motivation. A school can do a wonderful job of developing in students the tools needed to get at truth. They may even have implemented effective strategies for developing truth seeking thinking habits and sensitivities. But unless they are able to nurture in their students a lasting hunger for truth—for its own sake—they will still fail in the aim of developing truth seekers.

The principal reason that education often fails to produce truth seekers is that prioritizing truth seeking above our egos is neither natural nor easy. There are important reasons why John Locke concluded that, "one may truly say, that there are very few lovers of truth."[35] For one, an authentic pursuit of the truth regularly pushes us up to and beyond what we thought was our cognitive ceiling. Like the person training for a marathon, seeking truth requires us to do the hard work to push past our previous limits. Similarly, truth seeking will inevitably challenge our current understanding of the world, and necessitate that we consider the destabilizing possibility that our previous assumptions were incomplete or misguided. Finally, and perhaps most significantly, becoming a truth seeker is hard because truth can often get in the way of our other loves—reputation, power, advancement, comfort, pleasure, and so on.

35. Locke 1998: 614.

In short, while its fruits are ultimately and profoundly life-giving, truth seeking requires a love capable of overcoming the significant obstacles that stand in its way. This sort of deep-seated love for truth rests on at least three things: a set of beliefs about truth that encourage truth seeking, the personal experience of finding truth, and a strong emotional connection to truth that can result from these truth-related beliefs and experiences. Let's begin by looking at the importance of our beliefs about truth.

It is difficult to imagine someone developing a deep love for truth without first believing that truth exists, that we are (at least in some meaningful sense) capable of possessing it, and that it is worth seeking. Unfortunately, popular culture meets each of these pre-conditions with some level of cynicism. Allan Bloom observed in 1987 that, "There is one thing that a professor can be absolutely certain of: almost every student entering the university believes, or says he believes, that truth is relative."[36] This observation is at least as relevant today, where a convergence of the modern (truth is only what can be proven scientifically) and postmodern (there is no such thing as objective truth) has produced uncertainty in the classroom regarding many kinds of truth claims.[37] Harry Frankfurt recently observed that one logical consequence of our relativism and skepticism is an increasing intellectual malaise in popular culture where one "does not reject the authority of the truth, and oppose himself to it. He pays no attention to it at all."[38] In short, a lack of confidence reigns in our culture and classrooms with regard to the existence of truth, and this has had the effect of creating confusion and apathy regarding its pursuit. If there is nothing there, why would students and teachers expend any effort at all in searching for it?

36. Bloom 1987: 25.
37. McBrayer 2015.
38. Frankfurt 2005: 61.

Yet all is not lost. As we see in effective classrooms around the world, truth remains inherently compelling. The deep human impulse to discover and learn, however weakened by the philosophical assumptions of our age, is not dead. Indeed, as it relates to the motivation to learn, there remains a world of difference between the tantalizing notion that truth is elusive but out there waiting to be discovered, and the prevailing and intellectually deadening assumption that it is nonexistent, unknowable, or socially constructed. We see first-hand the enduring appeal of truth whenever a teacher presents an intriguing historical mystery and the students sit up in their chairs just a little more, or when a class is confronted with an unsolved equation and the energy level in the room noticeably cranks up a notch or two. Relativism and skepticism may have dampened our enthusiasm for truth, but they haven't killed it.

Students are much more likely to pursue the truth when they believe it exists and is waiting to be found. But they also need to believe that it is valuable enough to make sacrifices in its pursuit. As we have already seen, there is no more powerful apology for the value of truth than the teacher whose thirst for learning is consistently, enthusiastically, and explicitly on display. But there are a host of other ways that students can come to more fully appreciate the value of truth. Intellectual exemplars, for instance, who have sacrificed in the pursuit of truth inspire the question: what is it about the truth that would cause admirable people to risk or sacrifice in its service? Is truth really that precious? By our lives, and in the lives of the examples we use, we need to be able to demonstrate to our students that the answer is an emphatic: Yes![39]

But of all these, there is still no greater way to nurture a deep appreciation for truth than when a student experiences the personal rewards that come from its discovery, especially when it did not

---

39. For plentiful historical instances of exemplars of intellectual virtue, see Dow 2013.

come easily. Take, for instance, that breakthrough moment when, after struggling with a challenging geometric proof, a student suddenly sees how it fits together, or when a young child's world opens up as they see for the first time how the shapes we call letters can be combined to meaningfully describe the world around them. These can be transformational experiences. We have all felt the joy and sense of satisfaction that comes from these moments of discovery. To the degree that education pushes children beyond what they already know and celebrates the goodness and value of that knowledge, those moments, and our students' love for truth, will grow exponentially.

It is here where beliefs and experience combine to produce the authentic and appropriate emotional response to truth that can transform truth seeking from a duty to a delight. It was this sort of emotional connection to truth that seems to have prompted Thoreau to write, "Rather than love, than money, than fame, give me truth."[40] And it was this sort of love that inspired Solomon to plead, as if referring to his beloved, "Though it cost all you have, get understanding. Cherish her, and she will exalt you; embrace her, and she will honor you."[41]

3. HOW A TRUTH-CENTERED CLASSROOM CAN REVITALIZE EDUCATION

The critical task of developing truth seekers falls on all of us— teachers, parents, mentors, and friends—whether we participate inside or outside of a formal classroom environment. Nevertheless, it seems clear that the greenhouse of the classroom, with its principal focus on thinking, is a particularly natural and effective context within which to develop truth seekers. For this reason, it is especially

40. Thoreau 2017: 294.
41. Proverbs 4:7–8, New International Version, 1984.

important that educators see the benefits of this project—not just to their students and their society, but to their own vocation. The final section of this chapter will consider a number of ways that a focus on developing truth seekers can revitalize the field of education.

3.1 Easing the Tension (Part 1): Child-Centered Versus Teacher-Centered Classrooms

One significant way a focus on developing truth seekers can revitalize education is its ability to ease two long-standing and counterproductive tensions within the field: the tension between child-centered and teacher-centered education, and the tension between academic and character education.[42] The former is, perhaps, the single greatest tension in modern education. In its simplest form, it is a debate over who should drive learning. Supporters of child-centered education argue that learning is most effective when it is driven by student questions and interests. Those who favor a teacher-centered approach argue, instead, that learning should be driven by what society (symbolized by the teacher) has decided is worth learning.

Both approaches have real strengths and weaknesses. The child-centered approach, with its emphasis on student interests and questions, for instance, is designed to effectively tap into our intrinsic motivations, unleashing the educational power of curiosity, collaboration, critical thinking, and ownership of learning. These are clearly invaluable educational goods, and there is ample evidence that some forms of child-centered education are effective in achieving them.[43] And yet, when rigidly attached to the philosophical constructivism that so often sits at its roots, child-centered learning, with its assumption that every student question is valid and helpful, can also lend

---

42. I am indebted for this line of thinking to Christopher Smith of Richard Johnson Anglican School in Sydney, Australia.
43. Bronson and Merryman 2009: 160–173.

itself to classrooms that are chaotic, distracted, and potentially morally relativistic; not to mention ones in which the teacher, by nature of being a person with finite limits in energy, intellect, and emotion, must inevitably fail to effectively guide the multifarious interests and capacities of thirty different students.[44]

By contrast, the teacher-centered classroom, with its emphasis on the intellectual and moral authority of the teacher and the values and traditions of society, can produce learning that is consistently societally valuable and substantial, all within a classroom that is orderly and intentional. But when pursued in ideological purity, this highly structured and hierarchical model can also produce bored and disengaged students, whose curiosity and creativity wither on the vine.

In short, both models represent valid, if incomplete, paths to valuable education goals; and both models, when practiced with ideological rigidity, contain fatal flaws. How do we harness the strengths of each without simultaneously taking on their weaknesses? The first step seems to be an acknowledgement that, despite our tendency to choose sides, the choice between the two camps is a false one based on the assumption that, because education must have an authority, the only two valid alternatives are the individual (symbolized by the child) and society (symbolized by the teacher) As G.K. Chesterton noted well before the camps were given their current names,

44. An overview of this form of constructivism, and a modest window into what a more purely constructivist educational model might look like in practice, can be found in Larochelle, Bednarz, and Garrison 1998: 3–20. For the philosophical roots of constructivism, see Jean Baudrillard, who began his influential essay, "The Precession of Simulacra," with the quote, "The simulacrum is never that which conceals the truth—it is the truth which conceals that there is none." Baudrillard 1983: 1. It should be noted that there is also a powerful minority voice in educational research that claims—with considerable evidence—that constructivist methods are generally not effective when set alongside more traditional methods. See, for instance, Kirschner 2006: 75–86.

> You cannot anyhow get rid of authority in education. . . . [T]he educator drawing out is just as arbitrary as the instructor pouring in: for he draws out what he chooses. . . . [T]he only result of this pompous and precise distinction between the educator and the instructor is that the instructor pokes where he likes, and the educator pulls where he likes.[45]

Educating for intellectual virtue provides a solution to this long-standing tension by replacing the teacher-centered and child-centered classrooms with a truth-centered classroom. In a truth-centered classroom, teacher and student are allies in the common pursuit of understanding.[46] Truth is the authority to which both teacher and student are subservient, and the aim of their partnership. In this sort of classroom, child-centered methods are freely utilized in ways that engage students, while the teacher's typically superior knowledge base, thinking skills, and life experience can be unapologetically harnessed in the common pursuit of truth.

3.2 Easing the Tension (Part 2): Academic Versus Character Education

Another long-standing tension in education has been that between the development of the intellect on the one hand and moral and civic character on the other. Character education has a rich pedigree that extends from the Greeks and the Confucians (among many others in the ancient world) to contemporary apologists like Thomas Lickona and William Bennett.[47] Its central premise is that thriving societies require both a well-educated population and one rooted in

---

45. Chesterton 1910: 97.
46. Parker Palmer refers to a similar idea in his call to a "subject-centered classroom." Palmer 1998: 115.
47. Lickona 2004, Bennett 1993.

moral and civic virtue. A morally virtuous society that isn't developing intellectually grows stagnant, while a highly educated population lacking in moral virtue is dangerous (e.g., Nazi Germany). For this reason, Martin Luther King Jr. famously concluded, "Intelligence plus character—that is the goal of true education."[48]

Yet, for all of its obvious importance and respected advocates, character education has often felt like an awkward add-on to the intellectual training that is at the heart of formal education. One reason for this is that we learn best in relevant contexts. Moral and civic character training, therefore, seems best suited to life outside the classroom, where we are regularly and authentically called upon to live out our moral choices. That is not to say that efforts by teachers and administrators to infuse extra-curricular and non-traditional learning with opportunities for moral character development are without effect. Still, it often feels as if the best that moral character education can do in a traditional academic setting is to teach moral principles in the relatively artificial classroom context and hope that students will appropriately apply them when confronted with authentic moral choices outside of the classroom.

Educating for intellectual virtue increases the effectiveness of "character education" by creating a bridge between the classroom and moral/civic character. It does this in at least two ways. First, intellectual, moral, and civic character, while distinct, are closely connected and mutually reinforcing. For instance, it is difficult to consistently act in morally or civically virtuous ways without also thinking in intellectually virtuous ways.[49] Conversely, if a student

---

48. King 1947: 10.
49. As Jason Baehr has pointed out, the intellectual virtues are distinct from other categories of virtues in that the intellectual virtues are "the character traits of a good thinker," while moral virtues are "the character traits of a good neighbor," and civic virtues are "the character traits of a good citizen." Baehr 2015: 17, 36–41.

has become an *intellectually* courageous person—someone who, in the pursuit of truth, consistently asks hard questions and is willing to stand up for truth against the ideological powers that be—she is also far more likely to have become the sort of person who will act in *morally* or *civically* courageous ways. So strong is this connection that it is often hard to determine where one set of virtues ends and the others begin.

Educating for intellectual virtue enriches moral and civic education in a second important way. The thinking of an intellectually virtuous person typically produces a number of important results. Chief among these is an ever-increasing understanding of the world and our relationship to it. By understanding reality more accurately, we are more likely to make wise decisions on matters that impact the lives of others (an essential component of moral and civic virtue). For instance, consider the difference between a population whose approach to voting is rooted in the intellectual habits of carefulness, fair-mindedness, and tenacity, and a population whose thinking is habitually careless, biased, and lazy. The former is likely to produce a healthy, thoughtful, and vibrant democracy. The latter is not. As John Adams remarked more than two centuries ago, "virtue is the only foundation of republics."[50] Civic virtue and intellectual virtue are intimately connected. For these reasons and more, it makes sense that the person of virtuous intellectual character is also more likely to be a person of moral and civic virtue. By effectively bridging the gulf between academic and character education, educating for intellectual virtue eases a significant and unhelpful tension in contemporary education.

50. Adams 1776. https://founders.archives.gov/documents/Adams/06-04-02-0044

3.3 Intellectual Virtue as a Unifying and Inspirational Vision for Education

Educating for intellectual virtue can also act as a unifying umbrella under which many effective current teaching theories and practices can flourish. We have already seen how an intellectual virtue framework (a truth-centered classroom) can strengthen the best in child-centered and teacher-centered learning without succumbing to their inherent flaws. Much the same can be said regarding key educational concepts such as critical thinking, meta-cognition, and understanding by design, for each is similarly enriched when applied within a truth-centered, intellectual virtue framework. Consider Scriven and Paul's definition of critical thinking,

> Critical thinking is the intellectually disciplined process of actively and skillfully conceptualizing, applying, analyzing, synthesizing, and/or evaluating information gathered from, or generated by, observation, experience, reflection, reasoning, or communication, as a guide to belief and action. . . . [I]t is based on universal intellectual values that transcend subject matter divisions: clarity, accuracy, precision, consistency, relevance, sound evidence, good reasons, depth, breadth, and fairness.[51]

As seen here, there is little question that critical thinking is a valuable educational aim. Yet this account presents critical thinking as a mere set of skills or outcomes. Complementing critical thinking's focus on skills and outcomes, the intellectual virtue approach looks at the thinkers themselves, their dispositions and habits related

51. http://www.criticalthinking.org/pages/defining-critical-thinking/766

to learning.[52] Instead of polishing the apple hanging from the tree, educating for intellectual virtue seeks to cultivate a healthy tree, convinced that a healthy tree will produce good fruit. Far from being a competing educational theory, critical thinking is enriched by an emphasis on the character of the thinker. Strong critical thinking is a natural byproduct of virtuous intellectual character, and intellectual virtue is honed by the adoption of logical reasoning and the skills of critical thinking.[53]

Finally, educating for intellectual virtue within a truth-centered classroom can help revitalize education by providing inspiration for both students and teachers. To the extent that they have reflected on it, it is safe to say that most educators did not pursue their relatively non-lucrative vocation just in order to provide students with the means of landing a good job, buying a nice house, and retiring comfortably. As legitimate as these material aims may be, educating for intellectual virtue reminds us that education should be about more. It should speak not only to our stomachs but also to our souls. As the great nineteenth- century civil rights leader Fredrick Douglass said, the purpose of education should be "the uplifting of the soul," or as Cornel West put it, "Soulcraft."[54] When placed next to the mechanized goals of maintaining state standards or meeting mandated benchmarks, the lofty and challenging aim of developing intellectually virtuous truth seekers is life giving. It is an aim worthy of the thousands of hours that we pour into our craft, and the sometimes literal "blood, toil, tears and sweat" we invest in our students.[55]

---

52. As Christian Miller has pointed out to me, a number of philosophers do see virtue as being primarily (or exclusively) a group of skills. See Stitcher 2013: 331–346.
53. Byerly 2017.
54. Douglass 1894; for West's language, see his recent speech at Yale University: https://news.yale.edu/2018/02/05/keynote-address-cornel-west-urges-integrity-action-and-soulcraft.
55. Churchill 1940.

4. CONCLUSION

In this chapter I have argued that the development of truth seekers within the context of formal K–12 education should be a principal aim of a healthy society. I further argued that while the fruits of truth are profoundly satisfying, truth seeking is neither easy, nor natural, nor widespread. To develop the sort of truth seekers capable of producing the intellectual and moral goods that lead to long-term human flourishing, we need a truth-centered vision for education—a vision that aims to develop in students the deeply rooted and virtuous traits of intellectual character that flow from a love of truth.[56]

BIBLIOGRAPHY

Adams, John. "Letter to Mercy Otis Warren." April 16, 1976. Available at: https://founders.archives.gov/documents/Adams/06-04-02-0044.

Almond, Gabriel, and Sidney Verba. *The Civic Culture*. Princeton: Princeton University Press, 1963.

Baehr, Jason. *Cultivating Good Minds: A Philosophical and Practical Guide to Educating for Intellectual Virtue*. Self-published, 2015. Available at https://intellectualvirtues.org/cultivating-good-minds/.

Baehr, Jason. "Introduction: Applying Virtue Epistemology to Education." In *Intellectual Virtue and Education*, edited by Jason Baehr, 1–17. New York: Routledge, 2016.

Baudrillard, Jean. "The Precession of Simulacra." In *Simulations*, 1–79. Semiotext (e): New York, 1983.

56. This chapter could not have been written without the innovative thinking and work being done by the teachers, students, and administrators at Rosslyn Academy and Intellectual Virtue Academy. In particular, I am indebted to Jennifer Watson, Melanie McKee, Kim Gilmer, Rileigh Schunk, and Jacquie Bryant. I am also grateful for the insights and practical suggestions of Christian Miller and Ryan West, whose thorough and insightful feedback has made this a far stronger chapter than it otherwise would have been. Finally, I am grateful for the feedback from the other contributors to this volume. In particular, thanks to Jason Baehr and Steven Porter, whose trailblazing work at IVA continues to inspire other schools around the world.

Bennett, William. *The Book of Virtues*. New York: Simon and Schuster, 1993.

Bloom, Allan. *The Closing of the American Mind*. New York: Touchstone, 1987.

Bronson, Po, and Ashley Merryman. *Nurture Shock: New Thinking About Children*. New York: Twelve, 2009.

Byerly, T. Ryan. *Introducing Logic and Critical Thinking*. Ada, MI: Baker Academic, 2017.

Chesterton, G. K. *What's Wrong with the World?* Pantianos Classics, 1910.

Churchill, Winston. "Blood, Toil, Tears and Sweat." Speech delivered on May 13, 1940. Available at https://winstonchurchill.org/resources/speeches/1940-the-finest-hour/blood-toil-tears-and-sweat-2/.

Coleman, James S. "Social Capital in the Creation of Human Capital." *American Journal of Sociology* 94 (1988): 95–121.

Coleman, James S. *Foundations of Social Theory*. Cambridge: Harvard University Press, 1990.

Douglass, Frederick. "Blessing of Liberty and Education." September 3, 1894. Available at http://www.academia.edu/19171229/_The_Pathway_from_Slavery_to_Freedom_Education_Emancipation_and_Political_Activism_in_Douglass_s_Narrative.

Dow, Philip E. *Virtuous Minds*. Downers Grove, IL: IVP Academic, 2013.

Duckworth, Angela. *Grit: The Power of Passion and Perseverance*. New York: Scribner, 2016.

Dweck, C. S. *Mindset: The New Psychology of Success*. New York: Ballantine Books, 2007.

Eliot, T. S. *Murder in the Cathedral*. New York: Harcourt Brace, 1935.

Frankfurt, Harry G. *On Bullshit*. Princeton, NJ: Princeton University Press, 2005.

Fukuyama, Francis. *Trust: The Social Virtues and the Creation of Prosperity*. New York: The Free Press, 1995.

Gardner, Howard. *The Disciplined Mind*. New York: Penguin Books, 2000.

Greer, Peter, and Chris Horst. *Mission Drift*. Bloomington, MN: Bethany House, 2014.

Haidt, Jonathan. "The Emotional Dog and Its Rational Tail: A Social Intuitionist Approach to Moral Judgment." *Psychological Review* 108 (2001): 814–834.

Haidt, Jonathan. *The Righteous Mind: Why Good People Are Divided by Politics and Religion*. New York: Penguin Group, 2013.

Inglehart, Ronald. "Culture and Democracy." In *Culture Matters: How Values Shape Human Progress*, edited by Lawrence E. Harrison and Samuel P. Huntington, 80–96. New York: Basic Books, 2000.

King, Martin Luther Jr. "The Purpose of Education." *Maroon Tiger* (January–February 1947): 10.

Kirschner, Paul A., John Sweller, and Richard E. Clark. "Why Minimal Guidance During Instruction Does Not Work: An Analysis of the Failure of Constructivist, Discovery, Problem-Based, Experiential, and Inquiry-Based Teaching." *Educational Psychologist* 41:2 (2006): 75–86.

Larochelle, Marie, Nadine Bednarz, and Jim Garrison, eds. *Constructivism and Education: Beyond Epistemological Correctness*. New York: Cambridge University Press, 1998.

Lewis, C. S. *The Abolition of Man*. New York: Touchstone, 1996a.

Lewis, C. S. *Mere Christianity*. New York: Touchstone, 1996b.

Lickona, Thomas. *Character Matters*. New York: Touchstone, 2004.

Locke, John. *Essay Concerning Human Understanding*. New York: Penguin, 1998.

McBrayer, Justin P. "Why Our Children Don't Think There Are Moral Facts." *New York Times*, March 2, 2015.

Nickerson, Raymond S. "Confirmation Bias: A Ubiquitous Phenomenon in Many Guises." *Review of General Psychology* 2:2 (1998): 175–220.

Palmer, Parker J. *The Courage to Teach*. San Francisco: Jossey-Bass, 1998.

Perkins, D. N., Eileen Jay, and Shari Tishman. "Beyond Abilities: A Dispositional Theory of Thinking." *Merrill-Palmer Quarterly* 39:1 (January 1993): 1–21.

Perkins, D. N., M. Faraday, and B. Bushey. "Everyday Reasoning and the Roots of Intelligence." In *Informal Reasoning and Education*, edited by J. F. Voss, D. N. Perkins, and J. W. Segal. Hillsdale, NJ: Lawrence Erlbaum, 1991.

Porter, Mark, ed. *John Baudrillard: Selected Writings*. Palo Alto: Stanford University Press, 1988.

Porter, Steven L. "A Therapeutic Approach to Intellectual Virtue Formation in the Classroom." In *Intellectual Virtue and Education*, edited by Jason Baehr, 221–237. New York: Routledge, 2016.

Putnam, Robert. *Making Democracy Work: Civic Traditions in Modern Italy*. Princeton: Princeton University Press, 1993.

Reece, William J. "The Origins of Progressive Education." *History of Education Quarterly* 41:1 (Spring 2001): 1–24.

Ritchhart, Ron. *Intellectual Character: What It Is, Why It Matters, and How to Get It*. San Francisco: Jossey-Bass, 2002.

Ritchhart, Ron, Mark Church, and Karin Morrison. *Making Thinking Visible*. San Francisco: Jossey-Bass, 2011.

Roberts, Robert C., and W. Jay Wood. *Intellectual Virtues: An Essay in Regulative Epistemology*. Oxford: Oxford University Press, 2007.

Saint-Exupery, Antoine de. *The Wisdom of the Sands*. New York: Harcourt Brace, 1950.

Scherer, Michael. "Blue Truth, Red Truth." *Time*, October 15, 2012.

Seider, Scott, Tenelle Porter, and Shelby Clark. "The Development of Intellectual Character Virtues in Adolescents on Adolescents' Intellectual Character Development." Unpublished manuscript. Boston University School of Education, 2018.

Smith, James K. A. *You Are What You Love*. Grand Rapids, MI: Brazos, 2016.

Stitcher, Matt. "Virtues as Skills in Virtue Epistemology." *Journal of Philosophical Research* 38 (2013): 331–346.

Ten Elshof, Gregg A. *I Told Me So: Self-Deception and the Christian Life*. Grand Rapids, MI: Eerdmans, 2009.

The Holy Bible, New International Version. Grand Rapids, MI: Zondervan, 1984.

Thoreau, Henry David. *Walden (Life in the Woods)*. New York: Amazon Classics: 2017.

Whitbeck, Caroline. "Truth and Trustworthiness in Research." *Science and Engineering Ethics* 1 (December 1995): 403–416.

Wiggins, Grant, and Jay McTighe. *Understanding by Design*. 2nd exp. ed. Alexandria, VA: ASCD Books, 2005.

Williams, Bernard. *Truth and Truthfulness: An Essay in Genealogy*. Princeton, NJ: Princeton University Press, 2002.

Zagzebski, Linda. "Exemplarist Virtue Theory." Gifford Lectures, delivered October 1–9, 2015 at the University of Edinburgh. Available at https://www.giffordlectures.org/lectures/exemplarist-virtue-theory.

Zagzebski, Linda. *Exemplarist Moral Theory*. New York: Oxford University Press, 2017.

Additional Online Sources

http://rosslynacademy.org/community-of-intellectual-virtue-schools/

http://rosslynacademy.org/elementarylower-school-resources/

https://www.bbc.com/news/uk-37995600

http://www.gallup.com/poll/5392/trust-government.aspx

http://www.ivalongbeach.org/

http://www.ivalongbeach.org/academics/state-test-scores-sbac.

http://www.pz.harvard.edu/projects/patterns-of-thinking

http://www.viacharacter.org/blog/an-exercise-on-via-strength-spotting/

INDEX

For the benefit of digital users, indexed terms that span two pages (e.g., 52–53) may, on occasion, appear on only one of those pages.

Figures are indicated by *f* following the page number